THE WORLD'S GREATEST RIP-OFFS

THE WORLD'S GREATEST RIP-OFFS

THE EXTRAORDINARY INSIDE STORY OF THE BIGGEST, MOST INVENTIVE CONFIDENCE TRICKS OF RECENT TIMES

BY TOP INVESTIGATIVE JOURNALISTS

EDITED BY COLIN ROSE

STERLING PUBLISHING CO., INC. NEW YORK

© 1978 by Sterling Publishing Co., Inc.
Two Park Avenue, New York, New York 10016
© 1977 by Topaz Publications Ltd

Manufactured in the United States of America

All rights reserved

Library of Congress Catalog Card No.: 78-57888
Sterling ISBN 0-8069-0140-3 Trade
0141-1 Library

CONTENTS

TO SUSAN AND HELEN
(who were not quite sure whether
they wanted a dedication in a book
on this theme)

INTRODUCTION

This book is the product of a powerful team of top investigative journalists. It does not pull any punches or change any names. On the other hand, it is NOT a crusade against any of the individuals in it. Their stories have been included because this book is not only an enjoyable mixture of near comedy and fascinating detective work but is in a real sense 'a timely warning'.

A recent Police statement claimed that: 'The dividing line between legitimate business and fraud is becoming very blurred.' If you learn anything from this book, it will be never to take anything at face value (no-one with a legitimate offer will object to you checking it out) and never to be greedy. The victims of nearly every confidence trick *want* to believe. Most get-rich-quick schemes that are too good to be true – are just that!

There is nothing small time about the modern day buccaneers in this book – and to be fair some of them cut a distinctly stylish dash as they peddled their dreams with a fine disregard for legal niceties. However, the reader who may harbor a sneaky regard for today's con-man will also learn that he has a price to pay for his life style. Not necessarily the (often short) jail sentence but the continuous fear of the 'knock on the door', and the need to live out of a suitcase.

One thing is for sure–the Confidence Trick or Rip-Off is becoming ever more sophisticated and many are on a mind-boggling scale. Even as this is being written a 'situation' is developing in Namibia – South West Africa – where one company is allegedly laying claim to mining rights over 25,000,000 acres of some of the richest mineral land in the world. . . .

Every event in this book is strictly factual and the material has been meticulously researched by the following individual investigative writers:—

Fred Lawrence Guiles	American journalist and author (books include *Norma Jean*, the biography of Monroe)
Michael Gillard	A leading UK TV and newspaper investigative journalist
William Hastings	Crime Reporter
Elliott J. Mason	Freelance Writer
Richard Milner	Chief Feature Writer, *Sunday Times* Business News
Tom Tullett	Crime Editor, *Daily Mirror*
Maggie Ward	Freelance Writer

My very sincere thanks to each of the contributors and in a sense to the subjects of their investigations. Their past mistakes, for which they have now paid their dues, can make us all a little wiser.

COLIN ROSE

N.B. Currency comparisons and equivalents are relevant to date of individual chapters.

COLIN ROSE

The Editor of this book completed his formal education at the London School of Economics, where he reports the most formative influence as being a talk by the then Chairman of Unilever. During his speech the Chairman concluded that 'In life there are two sets of people, the doers and the talkers. The talkers inevitably get paid more.' He presumed the faster the talker the higher the pay.

Colin Rose obtained his first commercial experience with a hairspray manufacturer and then an advertising agency. He developed an academic interest in confidence tricks. His first practical experience with fraud, however, was nearly his last. It has come to be known as 'The Cold Tea Job' and is still apparently revived on occasions.

He was approached by a certain gentleman who (wink) claimed to have a consignment of whisky going cheap. Colin gathered that his potential business partner had not so much an occular problem as a 'good thing going'. The asking price for the well-known brand of whisky was very moderate and the lure of a fast buck overcame his common-sense.

Contracts were drawn up and the money was about to be paid over when an older and wiser colleague suggested a sampling session would be prudent.

The result of the tasting session was predictable – he had almost borrowed and paid £18,000 for 0 degree proof bottled cold tea.

The experience has left Colin Rose with an inquisitive attitude towards our acquisitive society.

THE BOGUS BANKS BONANZA

or

The paper hangers* who didn't need glue

by Richard Milner

Everyone should have a bank of their own. It confers instant financial status, provides a marvellous conversation gambit and generally tones up the sagging ego. It can even make your fortune. I have just such a bank. It is called the International Currency Bank, which is a pretty good name. It's a handy-sized bank, too. Every now and then, I take it out of my filing cabinet to admire its blue plastic spine and semi-stiff orange cover. And I'm not selling. In fact, I'm really only looking after the bank while a couple of other chaps have a legal hassle to decide which of them actually owns these pieces of paper.

What I have, for the time being at least, is a 'funny bank'. International Currency Bank is registered in the West Indian island of Anguilla and has a nominal (very nominal) capital of $9,600. It would normally cost £1,000 to buy but I might get it slightly cheaper shop-soiled. And there would be nothing except a twinge of conscience to prevent me from renting an office in the City of London, screwing a brass plate to the door and opening up for business. Chances are that I could take in £100,000 plus, probably by selling some tastefully engraved bank drafts or bearer bonds overseas, before the Secretary of State for Trade even realized what was happening.

* A 'Paper Hanger' in the jargon of the free wheeling but twilight world we review here, is a con-man who manages to 'hang' (i.e. deposit) bad 'paper' (forged or worthless securities and shares) in banks and other financial institutions in return for overdrafts or loans.

Everybody knows, of course, that banks normally make their basic profits by taking in money from private individuals and corporations (the depositors) and lending it out at a higher rate of interest to other private individuals or corporations (the borrowers). It is also well-known that even quite honest banks can come unstuck if their depositors become nervous and/or their borrowers go bust. But this does not happen very often and, as a result, people have come to trust not only the banks themselves but also the paper 'instruments' they use in their business – bills, certificates, drafts, guarantees and so forth.

If a customer goes to General Motors Corp. with a $1 million 'letter of credit' from Barclays Bank International of London, for example, GM will happily sell him $1 million worth of Cadillacs. Because it knows that, even if the buyer goes bankrupt the day after delivery, BBI will cough up. The bank has, in effect, guaranteed the buyer and therefore the seller. It is this basic trust that has been exploited by the 'funny banks', whose promissory notes are frequently not worth the paper they are printed on. Which can create major international problems when banks, companies and individuals accept them at face value.

Funny bankers come in all shapes and psyches. Bruce Parkyn Jackson of Eurobank, Intercontinental Banking Corp., and Island Bank is a fresh-faced 36-year-old American who admits to being a reformed 'scoundrel' but insists that he is now devoted to the relief of world poverty. Intercontinental Banking, which helped to divert the cash flow of meat firms and travel agencies, was appropriately located over an Indian restaurant in Belgravia. After assisting the FBI in their enquiries in 1976, he made a fresh mark as a painter and poet this year at the Galerie Saint-Antoine in Geneva and thoughtfully invited me to the private showing.

Dr William Kurt Samuel Wallersteiner of Rothschild Trust of Liechtenstein, Barclays Bank of Panama etc., on the other hand, is a rather distinguished 58-year-old bon viveur and (in the UK) bankrupt who qualified as a chemist before turning to unorthodox finance. His latest vehicle is General Bank of the Middle East, registered in Anguilla, loosely headquartered in Frankfurt and interested in multi-million propositions everywhere from California to Tanzania. Two of my favorites now face fraud charges here and are thus sub judice. But two others illustrate the diversity of the breed, Phil Wilson of the Bank of Sark and Allen Lefferdink of Atlantic Trust Bank.

Philip Morrel Wilson may not have been the greatest bank robber of all time but he was certainly the most fun. His Bank of Sark, which was actually located in Guernsey, is the classic 'funny bank'. To Britons, of course, even the name might sound oddly suspicious. Sark is the smallest of the main Channel Islands, a tranquil bird sanctuary best known (at the time) for the absence of motorized vehicles and the presence of the redoubtable late Dame Sybil Hathaway. It is an inherently bizarre spot from which to launch an active offshore banking operation. What mattered, though, was that *Americans* could not tell the difference.

Bank of Sark did not put on an impressive front. It occupied a couple of small offices, two floors up over an optician's shop in Smith Street, St Peter Port. For most of its short but active life, it was managed by a chap known simply and erroneously as B. Green. And yet this unobtrusive outfit issued approximately $50 million of worthless securities, ran rings round umpteen serious American bankers and got away with more than $5 million before the whistle blew. When the police finally cased the joint in the summer of 1970, the only person on the premises was a rather bewildered 17-year-old ex-barmaid.

Philip Wilson, who was just 33 when the Bank of Sark folded, does not look like a typical con-man. Nobody does, of course, but he is truly unusual. He is a short fellow with soulful eyes, a weak chin and a strong sense of humor. Born in St Louis, Missouri, he originally planned to become a schoolteacher but dropped out of the University College of Washington University and took up selling auto insurance instead. Within a year, he was running his own Bel Air Agency. And two years later in 1964, he diversified into offshore fraud with something called the Buckingham Insurance Company registered in Nassau.

It was here that Wilson ran across a character who was to provide a valuable service for several offshore finaglers. Dr Samuel J. Wilkinson, who worked for the Bahamas Electricity Corporation, was not exactly well-qualified. He failed to complete even his first lesson with the UK Chartered Institute of Secretaries, for example, and had to make do with a diploma bought from the so-called Metropolitan College. Wilkinson decorated himself almost as liberally as Uganda's president Amin, however, and listed a remarkable string of letters after his name – A.A.I.A., A.C.P.A., F.C.A.A., A.M.B.I.M., F.C.B.I. etc. etc. As an accountant, his chief merit was that he would certify absolutely *anything*.

For Buckingham Insurance to operate effectively in its chosen field of endeavor (e.g. selling phoney insurance, participating in fringe re-insurance or securing 'advance fees' by making worthless loan 'commitments'), one thing was essential. Buckingham had to have assets or, at least, *apparent* assets. Sam Wilkinson obligingly certified and approved an impressive balance sheet. And went on to certify later Wilson companies, whose 'paper' assets came increasingly to feature cross-holdings in his other concerns such as the Bank of Sark and the flamboyantly-named First Liberty Fund. Most of them had no *real* assets but their balance sheets looked simply terrific.

Even the most exciting paper-chase ends somewhere however. Wilson was finally nailed by the US postal inspectors in January 1972 over the wonderful Transcontinental Casualty Insurance, which claimed assets of more than $290 million but basically consisted of a post office box and a name-plate attached to a Nassau garage. It had ripped off an estimated $150 million in advance fees. Wilson and 21 associates faced a grand jury in Miami. Later that year, he and the Bank of Sark were named in a stock extortion indictment in New York. He pleaded guilty to mail fraud in Miami, was sentenced to eight years imprisonment and began to sing like a canary.

Like most dedicated self-dramatists, he loved playing to the gallery. 'From 1964 to 1972, I was involved in at least 150 paper frauds using offshore insurance companies, offshore banks, offshore mortgage companies . . .', Wilson declared at his command performance before the US McClellan Committee on Organized Crime in 1973. 'My practices in the field of fraud have extended from St Louis, Missouri, to the capital of Mongolia, to the reaches of Moscow, to Buenos Aires, Argentina, Panama, Australia and even to the far reaches of East Africa', he added. 'My dealings have led me to do business with first-class banks, merchant banks and government banks in many corners of the world.'

Indications are that Phil Wilson started hustling auto insurance around St Louis in relatively honest fashion, discovered that he could make a faster buck 'offshore' by more questionable methods and was soon carried away by the exuberance of his own imagination into outright fraud on a global scale. Back in 1965, he had taken a quite genuine pride in being 'the largest writer of substandard auto insurance in the eastern part of Missouri'. By 1972 he had taken part in half the offshore swindles in the world, had acquired heavyweight partners not unadjacent to the Mafia and had decided to tell everything (if not more) to the Department of Justice for one last deal.

Oddly enough, Wilson did not actually set up the Bank of Sark. It was officially 'founded' in 1966 by John Christian Konig, a 22-year-old inheritor who rather fancied himself as a banking and insurance tycoon. Unfortunately, Konig dropped £80,000 on his first venture, Southern Counties Insurance, and found himself strapped for cash. Bank of Sark wasn't doing anything, its £1 million nominal capital had cost him £1,700 in stamp duty and the name had to be worth *something*. So he advertised in the *Financial Times*, assured the Dame of Sark that he would only sell to a Channel Islander and waited.

Nobody was willing to go above £2,000 for the Bank of Sark in December, 1968. Until a solicitor's letter offered £3,000 on behalf of Jersey farmer Charles Howeson. It was accepted. More than $2\frac{1}{2}$ years later, farmer Howeson denied that he had ever 'bought' the bank but had merely signed a paper for an insurance broker friend, John Risely-Pritchard, in a five-minute meeting at Jersey Airport. 'I did it under the Old Pal's Act', he commented. 'I gathered he was buying the bank on behalf of (American) clients and they needed someone with Channel Islands residential status to be a director'.

Naturally, former owner John Konig had no idea that Bank of Sark had been sold to Americans. Nor apparently did go-between John Risely-Pritchard, though he was aware that the purchasers were not British. Helpful nominee Charles Howeson didn't know what was going on except that it hadn't cost him a penny. And the London solicitor maintained a discreet professional silence about his mysterious clients. But thousands of miles away in St Louis, Missouri, master-swindler Philip Wilson was in conference with his friends and associates, including Charles 'Carl' Brown, Jack Axelrod and Bernard Greenberg (alias B. Green).

Having secretly bought control of an offshore bank with a capital of £1 million (albeit very nominal) for an outlay of £3,000, the Wilson Group planned to hit North America with a positive blizzard of bogus worthless securities. Personal checks, bank drafts and certificates of deposit would be cashed, injected, pledged, substituted, transferred and used every which way to relieve banks, corporations or individuals of their actual cash. It would be paper hanging like nobody had ever hung paper before, not just on a grand scale but on several levels from retail check-writing to wholesale asset-removal.

Bank of Sark could hardly be made to look like a regular commercial bank to any passer-by in Smith Street. With some ingenuity, however, it could easily seem authentic to anyone 3,000-odd miles away. And the St Louis quartet, though not exactly authentic, were certainly ingenious. International banking, stripped to essentials, revolves around credibility, figures, paper and trust. Phil Wilson managed the credibility, Dr Samuel Wilkinson certified the figures, one Ralph Sonneschein arranged the printing and the bank's luckless customers provided the trust. It was appearances that counted.

The bank operated a Telex, which impressed smaller American banks that did not. It had sneaked itself into the bankers 'Bible', Polk's banking directory, thus reassuring skeptics who wanted to check things out. It had a helpful manager in 'Bernard Green', ever ready (given the nod from Wilson or Axelrod) to confirm to an inquiring American Banker that Client X had $2 million or whatever on deposit. It even had a bankers' code book, which a friendly Treasurer from West Side Bank in St Louis County allowed them to copy. 'He was having his own problems and we were trying to help him out', Wilson commented. 'It was one of the most valuable tools that we acquired'.

Bank of Sark paper started fluttering about in the second half of 1969. It proved remarkably popular. Partly because the bank did not promote itself with any particular hoopla. Its brochure was a fairly modest un-American affair, although the letter-conscious Dr Wilkinson struck a somewhat discordant note. It notionally offered a full range of conventional banking services from consumer loans to travellers checks. Its heraldic device featuring knights in armor with drawn swords might be considered quaintly British. Its slogan was arrogantly vague: 'In the Highest Tradition of Merchant Banking'.

In the context of unorthodox financial escapades by Bernard Cornfeld of Investors Overseas Services and his rival offshore fundsters, Jonathan Kwitny of *The Wall Street Journal* pinpoints what may have prompted Philip Wilson to activate the Bank of Sark. 'If Cornfeld and the others could get away with exaggerating the value of their fund shares and siphoning the customers' money by dribs and drabs', Kwitny writes, 'why not set up an offshore operation that would be *totally* dishonest, that would just steal every dime as it came in?' It was not quite as crude as that, of course, but very nearly. No other bank gave so little and took so much.

Dozens of American swindlers and quite a few desperate businessmen were ready, willing and able to deal in the Bank of Sark's natty pink drafts. Houston tycoon William Donald Shepherd, whose conglomerate interests in electronics, paint and insurance were already borrowed up to the eyeballs, bought a swatch of Sark drafts for $100,000 from Robert Ostrander in Chicago. With a little bit of help from a chap called Wesley Alexander, he hit the Mercantile Bank of Dallas for $320,000 and private bankers W. L. Moody & Co. of Galveston for $185,000. By the time he had finished, Shepherd had converted this bargain bundle of bogus paper into $1,290,000 of genuine cash by using the 'bad paper' as security for genuine bank borrowings.

Harold Audsley and Byron Prugh of Fort Lauderdale got into the Bank of Sark caper. So did Dominic Mantell and Neil Maloney of the same parish, so did Michael Strauss (alias Michael Stevens) and his friends over in Birmingham, Alabama. 'Bird dogs' were contacted throughout the United States and beyond to flush out hard-pressed borrowers and short-sighted bankers. 'Street men' were despatched to take down these marks for whatever they were worth and maybe a bit more with Bank of Sark certificates of deposit, international bankers' drafts, letters of commitment or just plain old-fashioned worthless checks . . .

Louis Pasquale Mastriana, a 51-year-old hustler from upstate New York, told the McClellan Committee how it worked. 'On yet another Bank of Sark transaction, I met Ron Kotler at the Fairmont Hotel in Dallas, Texas . . . He had the grey and pink Bank of Sark checks . . . Kotler asked me if I had a bank lined up. I said: 'Yes, I am going in and open up an account at this particular bank'. He said: 'Good, I have to know because I will have to call Phil Wilson tonight. Phil Wilson will call Bernard Green'. Green would verify what he had already been told by Phil Wilson, that, for example, Mr Mastriana had a trust account of maybe $3 million, a very good customer.

'That was to give me credibility', Mastriana added, in case Senator Jackson hadn't noticed. 'Of course, this was the door-opener with the victim we were going to beat. On this occasion in Dallas, I walked into the Dallas Bank & Trust Co., and opened up an account. I believe I put in a Bank of Sark check in the amount of $250,000, a quarter of a million dollar check. At that time, Kotler had given me about $175,000 of First Liberty Fund stock . . . I deposited the First Liberty shares as 'props' to make the account look good. I beat the Dallas Bank & Trust for $10,000 on the same day . . . by making a withdrawal on the account'.

In this case, Mastriana's $250,000 dollar check bounced clean out of sight. 'Later, when the bank knew it had been taken for the $10,000, it instituted a civil action against me', Mastriana continued. 'I, in turn, countersued them for $1 million for the loss of the Bank of Sark check. They lost the check.' Or at least the check was lost. 'When the original check was mailed by the Dallas Bank & Trust directly to the Bank of Sark, B. Green of the Bank of Sark would then take the check and then put it in another envelope and send it to Nassau. When the check reached a post office box in Nassau, someone would then mail it back to Phil Wilson'. In this way the original 'target' bank lost its documentary proof.

To avoid a premature collapse of the Bank of Sark, Wilson and his college chum Bernie Greenberg not only attempted to ensure that such 'take-downs' were spread throughout North America but also devised several ingenious methods to stall indignant bankers. The 'vanished check' procedure was one option. Another was the 'irregular signature' gambit, which Mercantile National Bank experienced. ('The drafts in question are signed by a depositor, not an officer of the bank, and we feel we definitely do not have liability in this matter'.) And then there was the 'Sark stand-off' where the draft was merely returned with the enigmatic message 'We thank you for your continued co-operation' . . .

Louis 'The Doctor' Mastriana, who dressed quietly in Boston, loud in Las Vegas and occasionally wore an Elks pin to match his victims', did not restrict himself to penny-ante stuff like lifting $10,000 and leaving $425,000 of apparent security behind. With practiced versatility, he could handle anything from a complex advance fee deal to simple check kiting. On one memorable occasion, he transformed two Bank of Sark checks totalling $75,000 into three Lincoln Continentals and $15,000 cash. In more relaxed mood, he beat a Vegas casino for a $40,000 check and sportingly lost it back again. 'The Italians have a wonderful saying', he remarked philosophically. 'Money makes the blind see and the lame walk'.

Swindler-in-chief Philip Wilson was apparently having the time of his life. In the autumn of 1969 his St Louis group teamed up with Michael Strauss and several others in the mighty Cumberland Insurance Investment Corporation. Such an important event, naturally, required some hectic asset shuffling. Cumberland emerged with notional assets of $53.8 million, consisting largely of paper from Trans-Continental Casualty and other largely fictional corporations. And in November these imaginative fraudsters dreamed up the super-colossal Tangible Risk Insurance Co.

To spell out the full cross-linked ramifications of the Bank of Sark, Cumberland Insurance, Trans-Continental Casualty (plus others too numerous or nefarious to mention) and the aptly-named Tangible Risk would be bewildering and a waste of time. Which is exactly what Philip Wilson, his partners and his associates had in mind.

'To complicate matters when you commit a fraud is one of the pre-requisites', Wilson comments. 'It gets so confusing that you even get confused when you are doing it'. He did his best to keep it all together, though. When he

moved to a new $50,000 flat in Fort Lauderdale, one bed-
room was cleared for a filing area, the dining table was
shifted round to make room for the Telex and three-line
telephones were installed everywhere including the two
bathrooms. In reporter Kwitny's words, he converted the
place into 'a residential swindling parlor'.

Though Wilson was collecting an untaxed income of
'several hundred thousand a year', his personal life-style
was relatively modest. He dressed casually, drove a Pontiac
GTO and his only concession to rich international swinging
was an elderly 135 ton yacht (c. 1923) owned by First
Liberty Fund. (It didn't make sense to alert the tax
inspectors.) And he apparently got his kicks from little
tricks, like kissing off a Polish air insurance claim with
a Bank of Sark draft. Or cheekily informing UK immigration control that he would be staying at the Sherlock
Holmes Hotel – and going someplace else. But he *did*
have demanding 'partners'.

In particular Lou 'The Doctor' Mastriana wasn't just
an ordinary confidence trickster. Earlier in his varied
career, he had worked as a heist man, numbers runner,
enforcer and shylock for (among others) such well-
connected businessmen as Vincent 'Jimmy Blue Eyes' Alo,
Charles 'The Blade' Tourine and Owney 'Killer' Madden.
He had been jailed at Lorton in Virginia, Atlanta State
Penitentiary and New Jersey State Prison. As a sideline
from swindling banks, he had invented the Amalgamated
Service Employees Union of North America to back up
some vigorous labor consultancy: 'A lot of people want to
go home at night', he observed, 'but they don't want to go
home all busted up'.

Mastriana was a laugh a line but he was also a fairly
tough cookie. And his prime function in the Wilson operations was to look after the interests of Dom Mantell, who
himself was acting as a kind of regional manager in Florida
for the 'family' interests of three Mafia bosses – Stefano
Magaddino of Buffalo, Angelo Bruno of Philadelphia and
Carlo Gambino of New York. 'They had Trans-

Continental, there was various other situations', he commented vaguely. 'I was never directly involved. I was sort of an overseer to make sure that nobody got away with anything. They turned in their piece of the action to Mr Mantell . . . Everybody cut up the pie equally'.

How much Phil Wilson got away with under Mastriana's supervision is a moot point. He must have had a nasty shock in February, 1970 when my colleague Charles Raw, who had been ferreting around in the dark corners of world insurance, published a major article in the *Sunday Times* entitled 'Hunt for the big fish in the crowded offshore seas.' It started off with the news that Lloyds of London had privately circulated what amounted to a black list of 50 names the previous summer. And he went on to name some names including Philip Morrel Wilson, the Bank of Sark, Frank Blosser. Trans-Continental Casualty, Dr Samuel Wilkinson . . .

'The 50 names (on the Lloyds list), plus others that keep cropping up – some say there are 100 companies and 250 people involved – form a massive, mysterious syndicate', Charles Raw wrote. 'The links between the firms are often tenuous, if they exist at all, but a common factor is that many keep turning up in the weakest, most exploitable financial markets around the world: reinsurance in London, mortgage business in America, direct insurance in Israel and Belgium and mutual fund selling in Germany and the international markets'. He went on to warn that there were 'strange and exotic fish beginning to swim in the offshore sea'.

Quietly minding his own business in Guernsey, the man who had 'bought' the Bank of Sark was caught on the hop. 'I know this sounds awfully stupid', said John Risely-Pritchard, 'but I really don't know who owns the bank. Anyway, I'm resigning'. Risely-Pritchard resigned. And was replaced by Herbert Lion Singer of Quebec, whose qualifications to act as a bank director were even less obvious. He had been employed in 1968 as an Encyclopaedia Britannica salesman.

Considerably embarrassed, the Guernsey authorities decided that they would have to *do* something about their problem banks – not just the mysterious Bank of Sark but also Allen Lefferdink's so-called Atlantic Trust Bank. They had passed a Prevention of Fraud Act in 1969, which forbade any company to call itself a 'bank' unless it actually was. They struck the Bank of Sark off the Guernsey register in March, 1970. And in May they announced that all 'banks' would have to satisfy the Finance Committee. But rumors of a closure were denied. 'The bank is still right here', announced B. Green. It kept going for some time.

Nobody realized at the time quite how exotic some of those offshore fish were. Even in his testimony to the McClellan Committee, Philip Wilson played down his connection with Dominic Mantell. White-collar fraudsters dealing in stolen securities, he admitted, *were* liable to be taken over. 'The end result is that the white-collar fraud individual ends up being dominated and owned by the Mafia-type criminal', he commented. 'This necessarily happens because the normal white-collar fraud individual, in essence, is a non-violent type of person'. But *he* (Wilson) always preferred to roll his own securities.

Mantell wanted to become a partner in the St. Louis group in 1970 but what could he contribute? 'We didn't need any muscle. We had money. We had cash flow. We had assets. What was he going to do? What could he supply?' commented Wilson, with a fine show of independence. 'He did know a lot of people round the country, so this is one thing he could supply – additional swindlers and possibly victims'. It was not an altogether convincing explanation of their relationship. Messrs. Magaddino, Bruno and Gambino, for example, were not the likeliest bunch of entrepreneurs to provide an auxiliary service without helping themselves to a large slice of the pie.

Moreover, Wilson was embrangled in another bank fraud in 1970 featuring Dominic Mantell and some $6 million worth of 'hot' securities tucked away in a Swiss trust account to cool off. And he momentarily dropped his guard to his inquisitor Senator Percy over a bid by one Dave Garowitz of Los Angeles to team up with the lads from St Louis. 'He attempted to move in at one time, not knowing who I was, *or who my friends were*', Wilson remarked. 'He wanted to become my partner. I advised him that . . . he had better check with people in Florida before he moved in'. Garowitz checked and stayed out.

Talking himself out of trouble, Wilson had named five other banking operations similar to the Bank of Sark 'but not as sophisticated' that were in business at about the same time. Two rate special mention, one to conclude the saga of Phil the Flam and the other to highlight a different approach to funny banking.

By 1971 both Philip Wilson and Michael Strauss had moved to Fort Lauderdale, swindle center of the western world, and for a while concentrated their attentions on Canada. (Every marksman knows that it is more difficult to hit a moving target.) An operation called Anglo-Canadian Group, which seemed to have taken over the mighty Tangible Risk, opened a small office in Montreal. It was fronted by Herbert Lion Singer, lately of the Bank of Sark. And its business was to induce would-be borrowers to part with brokerage fees (advance commission) for loans that they would never receive. It was shut down by the police. But a new vehicle was already on the road.

Normandie Trust of Panama was even more super-colossal than Anglo-Canadian or Tangible Risk. It boasted assets of $170 million, including $63 million of Tennessee real estate (i.e. worthless land grants) and $40 million of 'platinum certificates'. (Auditor Philip Gottesman wanted to disclaim this balance sheet but says a thug came up from Florida and intimidated him.) Normandie's managing director was one L. Michael Stewart, an alias for Michael Strauss. It also specialized in the advance fee racket but said the loans were coming from (well, well) London & Cambridge Insurance.

For a man accustomed to earning upwards of $200,000

a year (or as he put it 'enough money to live on'), Philip Wilson was ostensibly in a very poor financial condition when he faced the McClellan Committee in September 1973. 'No, I don't have any money in a safe deposit box', he told Senator Gurney. 'Do you have money stashed away somewhere else?' the senator pressed. Wilson conferred with his counsel. 'I have no money personally', he replied carefully. 'In my discussions with the Fraud Section of the Department of Justice we have had no discussion over my money and that is the way it was left'.

Wilson had pulled off his greatest deal. What he had to offer the US Justice Department was not restitution but records, neatly stored in a Fort Lauderdale warehouse. And what he lacked in cash, he made up for in chat about everything and everyone. His sentence was reduced from eight years hard to a few comfortable months, the Internal Revenue Service forgot about his back taxes and he was provided with a brand new (Italianate) identity. But in 1976 he was back at the Justice Department asking for *another* name. Someone had issued a 'contract' against him. 'For Christ's sake, you've got to do something', he pleaded. 'My mother will never forgive me if I die an Italian'.

Allen Jonas Lefferdink, a tall handsome American who could charm *both* hind legs off a donkey, is perhaps the world's unluckiest financier. He was 43 when his first $30 million business empire fell apart in 1971. Some Americans still believe that it was the fault of those damn busybodies at the Securities & Exchange Commission. The SEC insisted that his brokerage firm's debt-to-asset ratio had got out of line. And so it had, to the tune of $1,845. But this minor slip was enough to unsettle the entire structure of his inter-locked conglomerate. He evened the score later, though, with Atlantic Trust Bank.

After commanding a US Navy subchaser in World War II, Lefferdink started his business career in 1945 by setting up an agency for Northwestern Mutual Life Insurance Co. in Boulder, Colorado. Within a year, this had broadened its base and become Allen Enterprises. He majored on consumer credit and founded Colorado Credit Life Insurance. It was a low-risk high-profit operation, guaranteeing department stores, car dealers and banks that payment on instalment credit contracts would be completed if the customers died before paying up. And it showed dynamic growth. By 1955, Colorado Credit had more than $100 million worth of insurance outstanding.

Even in the early days, though, he displayed a characteristic that both escalated his fortune and accelerated his downfall. Lefferdink preferred to do business with himself. If someone bought a car with finance from Allen Enterprises Loans, for example, then Allen Enterprises would handle the motor insurance and his Northwestern Mutual agency would tackle the driver about life insurance. Now, there is nothing the matter with that. Many keen insurance salesmen would do the same. Two commissions are better than one, after all, and three commissions are better still. The trouble was that Allen J. simply didn't know where to draw the line – or didn't care.

Lefferdink bought control of a bank or two, some insurance companies and built himself a $2 million headquarters at Boulder. He then decided to sell himself or rather Boulder Acceptance Corporation, incorporating a bank, a hotel, several loan companies and an insurance firm. Allen Investment Co., underwrote the issue, selling $18 million worth of stock – on the instalment plan. It worked so well that he did it again with Allied Colorado Enterprises or ACE. Money rolled in at the rate of more than $150,000 a month. Allen Advertising handled all the promotions, his Equity General Life Insurance bought the stocks – and so did his employee pension fund . . .

What bugged the Securities & Exchange Commission was not so much press comment suggesting that Allen Lefferdink was a genius who had licked the problem of perpetual motion. It was that this self-generating corporate machine could go even faster in reverse and that there was nothing they could do to check it. To be able to mind his own business, the shrewd businessman had restricted his hefty stock offerings to Colorado citizens – and the SEC had no authority over internal-state securities business. By the autumn of 1958, though, the SEC figured that at least one investor *must* have crossed the state line and notified him to this effect.

Lefferdink promptly agreed to stop selling ACE and Boulder Acceptance shares, pending formal registration with the SEC. And almost as promptly sold (intra-state) $3.3 million worth of shares in an amusement park on the outskirts of Denver and $5 million worth in an office block in the city center. Which might have seemed a pretty smart move. Except that both projects were being carried out by the same construction company, which stood to collect funds from these public flotations and just happened to be owned by Allied Colorado Enterprises. It got clean up the official nose of the Securities & Exchange Commission.

In October, 1959 the SEC jumped on the one company in Lefferdink's group that they *were* entitled to investigate, the brokerage firm Allen Investments Co. They suspected an 'excess debt' of close on $80,000, discovered on further investigation that the excess was less than $2,000 but contrived to make something of a federal case out of the affair. Then the amusement park ran out of funds, Colorado Credit lost its credit, the Boulder bank called in a receiver, Boulder Acceptance Corp., and Allen Enterprises Loans settled for bankruptcy and ACE followed suit. Shareholders sued for $292,000, the pension fund for $239,000.

To cap it all, a federal grand jury indicted Lefferdink and five associates for fraud in September, 1961. It asserted that they had misused $2.4 million collected in a public stock offer by Denver Acceptance Corporation, spending $1 million on shares in Colorado Credit, lending $350,000 to an officer of the company and diverting $350,000 elsewhere. Trading blow for blow, the state accused Lefferdink of trying to bribe the SEC and Lefferdink accused the SEC of extortion. Twelve months later, the case went to trial. It lasted four weeks and the jury acquitted each defendant on every count. Allen Lefferdink was free to go.

Lawrence Armour of *Barron's* magazine was absolutely livid about the SEC's actions. Lefferdink was a living legend, a regular Horatio Alger. 'A big company like General Motors or US Steel can fight back if it's attacked by the SEC', he protested. 'A little guy just doesn't have the funds to do it'. His sympathy may have been somewhat misplaced. This particular little guy still had enough funds to acquire a rather splendid ocean-going yacht, install a reported $1 million worth of telecommunications equipment on board and head for the wide blue offshore to become a living legend in more places than Boulder, Colorado.

Lefferdink's yacht was called the Sea Wolf and he lived up to the name. His principal vehicle was the Atlantic Trust Bank in Guernsey, but there were many Lefferdink corporations throughout the western world including World Insurance in Bermuda. He had salesmen dotted round the globe from South America to the Far East. Millions of dollars rolled in. Though now very mobile indeed (he was truly offshore in his floating Head Office, the Sea Wolf), the Arkansas traveller stuck to his established principles – maximum secrecy and circular trading. Take this extract, for example, from a typical brochure:

'Not only do we offer mutual funds as an opportunity for participation in the American economy, but we also have insurance companies that guarantee the fund investment plans will be completed and that there will be no loss of invested capital. In addition, we have our own bank to provide confidential accounts as well as a good interest return on liquid funds . . . No government has the authority to examine our record of mutual fund shareholders or bank depositors. We assign a confidential account number to each investor and all correspondence is mailed to the investor in a plain envelope showing only a post office box in the return address'.

Like most offshore operators, Lefferdink did not care where the funds came from so long as they arrived. 'Black', white or khaki, it was all money. Secrecy was attractive to offshore investors. Highly paid American expatriates keen to share in the US economic miracle, European businessmen intent on evading their tax inspectors, South American land-owners desperate to get their money out of the country and into hard currency were all eager to buy dollar funds and often without too many questions asked. It was only later that they realized that a PO Box number did have one potential snag. It could protect the seller as well as the buyer.

As his brochure implied, Atlantic Trust Bank was an integral part of a well co-ordinated money machine. It offered 6% interest on current (checking) accounts, which was not bad for starters. But nobody got more mileage out of the investment dollar than Allen J. Lefferdink. His World Investments (first located in Bermuda) advised customers to invest a planned amount each month in his fund shares. His World Insurance would then, for a 2% fee, guarantee them against loss after they had held the shares for ten years. 'Some (other) funds are too speculative for our underwriters to accept', the brochure explained with apparent caution, 'but many we will cover'.

Lefferdink had one additional quirk. Whereas Phil Wilson had relied on complaisant accountants such as Dr Samuel Wilkinson to give financial credibility to their fanciful corporate accounts, he relied on himself. In other words, he preferred not to use auditors at all. Stuffy conventional financiers, of course, would regard some 'outside' audit (however sketchy) as essential to reassure investors that the figures were correct. But he had an answer to that. 'The appeal of offshore funds', he once remarked, 'is confidentiality'. This aversion to outside interference with his accounts, however, did not prevent him from becoming a highly respected figure in offshore fraud.

From time to time, Lefferdink got together with Wilson and other offshore buccaneers in particular deals. But though he was a member of that 'massive mysterious syndicate', the syndicate itself was a rather catch-as-catch-can affair and he seems to have preserved some independence from the rest of the Fort Lauderdale circus. He provided bank references, insured and reinsured. But whereas the others swapped their 'securities' around with gay abandon, melding one company into another so fast that it was almost impossible for any outsider to keep up, Lefferdink had enough weight to 'rent' his securities out for a cash return.

Phil Wilson gave the McClellan Committee a quick lesson in how to use 'created' securities. 'We used them in our balance sheet so that we could get statements, item one. Item two, we used them as collaterals to guarantee other purchases. We used them as securities for other purposes. We used them as trading devices with other people in the business', he told Senator Gurney. 'Maybe they had a group of securities – *it was like Monopoly.* You would lay them out on the table and say 'I need one, two, three of those and I will trade you some of this'. I did that on several occasions with Harold Audsley in Florida'.

'Renting' stocks to plug a hole in some hard-pressed (and previously straight) company's balance sheet was one area in which the mercurial Wilson and the more methodical Lefferdink collaborated.* It was highly deceptive, of course, because everyone normally assumes that such securities are actually owned and not merely hired for the duration. But optimistic corporate executives, hoping that their financial embarrassment would be purely temporary, were prepared to bend the rules to stay in business. And Wilson was prepared to move the stock halfway round the world and back to cover up.

---

* 'Renting' forged and made up securities was a stroke of (evil) genius. Thus a trading company with a sick looking balance sheet could by injecting, say, $1 million of such shares into its 'assets' transform its apparent liquidity and company worth.

'If you take . . . the Reliance Mutual of America Insurance Company of Oklahoma City, which went into receivership in July of this year (1973)', he specified. 'In 1969 I arranged for this company to rent $1 million worth of securities from Allen Lefferdink . . . We took the Canadian mutual funds to Bermuda and from Bermuda organized a London-based holding company, transferred the London-based holding company to a Delaware corporation, transferred the ownership of the Delaware corporation to E. Ray Price and Reliance Mutual of America in Oklahoma City, put it in a statement and Mr Price signed the statement and it passed inspection for 1968, 1969, 1970, 1971, 1972 and part of 1973'.

This was just the kind of bewildering roundabout deal that Phil Wilson revelled in. If it was not totally honest, it was not totally fraudulent either. Mutual Funds of America seemed to have genuine substance, its share prices were certainly quoted in the *International Herald Tribune* and (above all) this complicated arrangement had *worked*. Allen Lefferdink, for his part, might have viewed the operation as low-risk high-reward corporate credit insurance. What the Reliance Mutual episode really highlights, though, is the way in which financial desperation can lead to calculated finagling – and spell profits for the con man.

Major fraudsmen always concentrate on the weakest point in any financial system and they often work as a team. Lefferdink's brief *public* encounter with the UK Board of Trade was a real classic. Ten years ago, the action was in car insurance. Sharp operators had discovered that it was child's play to set up an auto insurance company, collect a handsome revenue by offering cut-price premium rates and (hopefully) pay last year's claims out of this year's premium income. Several outfits mushroomed into business and the Board of Trade, realizing that its regulations were as loose as a baby's bowels, was naturally concerned.

Irish-American Insurance had been set up in 1964 and

two years later had some 70,000 motorists on its books. It was run by a man calling himself Michael Knowles and the Board of Trade, discovering to its dismay that this gentleman had a rather hairy record in the building industry as Robert Jacobs, decided to investigate. But by the time it got there, the cupboard was bare. 'Knowles' had reinsured 75% of Irish-American's business with another outfit known as Essex Insurance, based in Nassau and controlled by one Smith Brandom. He had contracted to pay a total of $504,000 to Essex, which had reinsured business yet again with World Insurance of Bermuda.

World Insurance of Bermuda, you may recall, belonged to Allen Lefferdink. Whose Mutual Funds of America had, by an odd coincidence, simultaneously bought Irish-American Insurance from Michael Knowles and his partner – for exactly $504,000. And a new adviser was despatched to 'reorganize' Irish-American in the shape of Harold D. Audsley, professional swindler from Fort Lauderdale. To say that the Board of Trade was disturbed by this turn of events would be an understatement. It was positively amazed by the money-go-round and powerfully suspicious. So it summoned the skipper of the Sea Wolf to explain what he was up to.

Lefferdink had enough chutzpah to choke a horse. He would be prepared to inject up to $500,000 into Irish-American, he said, consisting partly of cash and partly of real estate in Denver, Colorado. *Provided* the Board of Trade (a) accepted Mutual Funds of America as the owner, (b) declared the company solvent and (c) called off the investigation. Perhaps suspecting that the cash element might be more UK premium payments taking a circular tour, the B.o.T. decided that this was an offer it could afford to refuse. Irish-American crashed with a deficit of around £700,000, several associated outfits folded and 150,000 motorists were left without insurance cover.

Undeterred by this official rebuff, the lads carried on insuring and reinsuring each other. In October, 1968 an executive of Hunt Foods & Industries Inc., was surprised to learn that a chunk of its $15 million insurance had been placed with Farmers & Merchants Mutual Fire Insurance Co. (a Phil Wilson company), which had reinsured 90% with World Insurance of Bermuda. Lefferdink's W.I. also assumed liability, among other things, for an 80-boat fishing fleet in Seattle. Eventually, in November, 1968 the Washington state insurance commissioner Karl Herrmann got so mad that he suggested a total ban by American companies against *all* Bermudan insurers.

'By hitting legitimate Bermuda companies in the pocketbook', Herrmann declared, 'we would get them on our side in efforts to clean up a situation that now pollutes the US insurance and reinsurance markets'. Bermuda's prime minister Sir Henry Tucker seems to have got the message and the following month Lefferdink was kicked off the island or rather, in a smoothly diplomatic phrase, 'left by agreement'. This does not appear to have inconvenienced him too greatly. His local headquarters was closed down, World Insurance was re-registered in the Bahamas and he embarked in the Sea Wolf for Europe to set up shop again in downtown Brussels.

Lefferdink had already made a start in the boldest caper of his banking career. He had fixed up a deal to buy a 15% stake in Capital National Bank of Miami from an unorthodox Texan financier, Mort Zimmerman, with an option to buy the latter's remaining 80% stake for a total of $4.5 million. He deposited the $25,000 down payment in the name of a Zimmerman company at his own Atlantic Trust Bank in Guernsey, joined the board of Capital National and was elected chairman. And for some time the affairs of Capital National and Atlantic Trust Bank were intertwined in a highly irregular fashion.

For a start, Lefferdink added Capital National's $43 million assets into Atlantic Trust Bank's balance sheet (even though he only owned 15% of it) and then used the Miami bank to cash his Guernsey checks – 'TO ANY BANK OR BANKER – Mail this check direct to Capital

National Bank of Miami . . . for collection', he printed on the back. 'This check is payable at par in the currency indicated by the maker'. And he was chockful of fresh circular ideas. 'Let's assume that (an) investor borrows $5,000 from Capital National Bank', he wrote. 'He can then use that $5,000 to buy shares in one of our four funds. Atlantic Trust Bank will then loan him 75% of the amount he had invested in our funds. This will provide a real leverage situation for the sophisticated investor'. He was right back on the old money-go-round.

As an expert in sophistication (in the strict dictionary sense of fallacious or misleading argument), Allen Lefferdink had recognized that his connection with Capital National Bank could not have come at a better time and decided to make the most of it. Not least because investors in Atlantic Trust Bank had recently found that it was easier to put cash in than to get it out again. Towards the end of 1969, in fact, he had been obliged by circumstances apparently within his control to bounce a few of their ATB checks.

Expatriate employees of the Asiapac-Fargo civil engineering group, for example, had deposited around $80,000 in Atlantic Trust Bank from Vietnam. They had run across a Lefferdink agent, Fred Fredericks, who emphasized that the bank paid 10% on one-year deposits, and it seemed like a good idea at the time. 'Fredericks must have promoted upwards of $1 million of deposits for Atlantic Trust Bank', reported Asiapac-Fargo chairman Frank A. Hopkins. 'There were Atlantic checks floating all over Saigon. As far as he was concerned, it was like shooting fish in a barrel because everyone was loaded with money'. So there was quite a ruckus when their checks came bouncing back.

It seemed there was a quite simple explanation – they had the wrong kind of check-books. Atlantic Trust Bank had been split in two. Atlantic Trust Bank Limited of Guernsey would continue to handle sterling accounts but Atlantic Trust Bank SA of Panama had been set up to deal with dollar accounts. (This amoebic subdivision may have been prompted by Guernsey legislation, already mentioned, attempting to regulate the island's 'banking'.) Come November 1969, these dollar depositors received their new Atlantic Trust Bank SA check books, plus news of extra banking services. 'You will note on the back of your new checks that they are to be sent to the Capital National Bank of Miami for processing', ATB wrote emolliently. 'In this way, we hope to give you a faster service'.

Lefferdink seemed cock-a-hoop over this new deal. 'Our organization now owns the controlling interest of Capital National Bank', the ATB letter continued. (This was not true unless, by some chance, S. Mort Zimmerman was included in the 'organization'.) It added that deposits could also be made via the Foreign Commerce Bank of Zurich. (This was apparently not true either. 'They have used our address for publicity purposes without our consent', a Foreign Commerce spokesman commented later. 'We have nothing to do with them.' It is perhaps worth noting that FOCO did have something to do with Ed Markus of Agri-Fund, the 'food situation' swindler.)

Two months later, Atlantic Trust Bank changed its system yet again. Depositors wanting to cash their new checks got 'drafts' instead. 'We have had to overcome a number of obstacles in instituting our new draft system', the bank reported bafflingly. 'Enclosed are three drafts for your use in making further withdrawals. These replace the Atlantic Trust Bank SA checks which are no longer valid'. What was going on? 'Our organization has grown so rapidly that we have found it necessary to establish additional offices to handle the increasing volume of business', it explained offhandedly. 'We will, from time to time, notify you as to which service office will be handling your account'.

If anyone felt he was being given the run-around, he was absolutely right. In April, 1970 Lefferdink failed to keep up the payments on Capital National and Capital National stopped chasing ATB's checks. The 'organization', such as it was, appears to have been shrinking. What *was* constantly increasing was the blood pressure of disgruntled investors trying to get their money back.

In August that year, they received a polite letter from Allen Lefferdink. 'First, let me give you my personal apology as I am the person responsible for the administration of the bank', he began. 'Unfortunately, in March of this year, we were hit by substantial withdrawals at the bank which absorbed our liquidity and made it necessary for us to call loans of some of our customers'. Many could not pay up straight away. 'We now have one large loan in the amount of $616,000 that should be paid to us within the next 60 days which will more than absorb all current depositors' requests', he continued more hopefully. 'We would appreciate it a great deal if you would continue to suffer with us for a little longer'.

Asiapac-Fargo staffers continued to suffer with Lefferdink and their suffering became all the more acute when they received a cable from Brussels in October. It said: 'OUR MESSAGE YESTERDAY SHOULD READ LEFFERDINK ADVISES NECESSARY TO EXTEND $616,000 ATB LOAN ADDITIONAL 90 DAYS STOP REGRET PAYMENT YOUR ACCOUNT DELAYED ACCORDINGLY'. Ninety days came and went. And in July the following year, another letter arrived. 'Due to the continued expansion of our operations and our desire to give our clients a good administrative service . . .' this blathered, 'we have found it necessary to open a new service office'. In the West Indies, for a change.

Atlantic Trust Bank Limited had already been obliged by the Guernsey authorities to change its name to Sterling Investments Ltd., which was a less misleading (if hardly perfect) description. What was rather alarming about this latest communication from offshore was not so much that Lefferdink transferred his mobile service office from PO Box 229 at Philipsburg on St Maarten in the Netherlands Antilles to PO Box 853 on Grand Cayman in the Cayman Islands. It was that what had left St Maarten as Atlantic

Trust Bank SA had arrived at Grand Cayman as Atlantic Trust *Company* SA. Somewhere between the Dutch Antilles and the West Indies, the actual 'bank' seemed to have sunk without trace.

My own interest in Allen Lefferdink had been roused by a high-living salesman of his International Cash Card money dispenser business called Paul Beynon, who was recruiting his own 'sales executives' for a European management consultancy operation in mid-1971. (He claimed to have been a McKinsey consultant but was, in fact, nothing of the kind). The result was a *Sunday Times* article 'Why won't banker Lefferdink pay up?'

How much he got away with, Lefferdink only knows. In 1969 and 1970 alone, he passed $3.5 million in foreign currencies through Deak National Bank in New York. One Swedish investor claimed losses of $1 million, a South American monastery in Bogota dropped $4,146 and 47 cents. It was enough to keep him going for quite a while, though he abandoned the Sea Wolf in a dry-dock rather than pay the repair bills. But the Feds eventually caught up. In March, 1976, he was found guilty in Miami on 17 counts of wire fraud, mail fraud and conspiracy involving upwards of $5 million, three foreign banks (I must have missed one) and 26 other companies. He was sentenced to eight years imprisonment the following month but stayed out on $100,000 bail pending appeal.

With the apparent retirement of Philip Wilson and Allen Lefferdink from active banking, and reluctantly ignoring the careers of others who are (at the time of writing) legally unmentionable, Dr William Kurt Samuel Waller-steiner must now rate as the world's leading unorthodox banker. Like all virtuoso financiers, Wallersteiner has (or rather had) a highly individual style. To have founded the Rothschild Trust of Liechtenstein and to have retained the name despite vigorous protest from the actual Roths-childs would have been enough for most men. Only the imperturbable Kurt would have had the nerve to follow this up with a Barclays Bank of Panama.

For some years, Dr Wallersteiner looked in danger of becoming the retired elder statesman of funny banking. He acquired control of a publicly-quoted UK engineering group, Hartley Baird, back in 1962 with a typical master-stroke. (His Investment Finance Trust paid off £285,000 owed by its parent company Camp Bird to Hartley Baird, which promptly lent the money back to Investment Finance Trust. 'When I took control . . . it was hopelessly insolvent', he commented later, 'so the circular check arrangement seemed reasonable'.) He then devoted £50,000 of HB's money to buying his own Watford Chemical Co., and lost it and another £246,000 in his Anglo-Canadian Cement.

Wallersteiner's drawn-out feud with shareholders' friend Martin Moir did his reputation no good. Though relieved by moments of sheer farce, (like the spectacle of two lawyers fighting for the microphone at the 1967 annual general shambles), this campaign threatened to make him the bore of the decade by the time he was booted off the Hartley Baird board in mid-1974. It also obscured the conceptual brilliance of a Third World coup some two years earlier when he strengthened the balance sheet of the Central African Republic with $100 million of paper from his Barclays Bank of Panama and stood to collect $100 million of Banque Nationale de Developpement notes guaranteed by the French government. (Even the Bank of England, it was reported, wound up with one such $1 million bill.)

With a judgment of £602,239 (including interest) against him in the United Kingdom, he emigrated to Frankfurt. Where in October, 1976, downing a couple of bottles of champagne with Barry Phelps of the *Daily Mail*, he complained about the astounding unfairness of HM Inspectors acting for the Department of Trade. 'IFT always intended to repay the money as the instalments fell due', he insisted. 'Indeed it did so until in 1968 I lost $20 million in Togoland. The plane in which I was carrying the cash had to land and the authorities refused to believe that the money was mine – especially as there were 25 guns and the mercenary Major Mike Hoare on board'.

Wallersteiner also claimed to be the first German in World War II to have served with the Brigade of Guards, having previously enlisted with the Chinese army to fight Hitler, and to have risen to the rank of acting colonel. (It must have been very good champagne.) Why did he not come back to England to defend himself? 'I have to be in Germany and able to travel and run my businesses', he explained, 'and to pursue some legal matters'. (These legal matters are believed to involve bail of DM 700,000 and, though travelling from Los Angeles to Dar-es-Salaam, he was unable to attend his UK bankruptcy hearing.)

Though Barclays Bank of Panama was exorcised in a local purge on 'phantom banks' in 1972, Wallersteiner (or 'Dr Kurt' as he occasionally prefers to be known) is back in the banking business. Efforts to discount a $10 million (£5.7 million) bill of exchange guaranteed by the General Bank of the Middle East in London last autumn were greeted with skepticism. (It was, of course, dismissed as a forgery.) But the bank which claims assets of $82 million certified by National Accountants and Auditors Limited of Nassau, is dickering all over the world for fees in advance of loan commitments.

Kurt Wallersteiner bought his latest banks ready-made from an affable Yorkshireman called Tony Wilkinson, who has (quite legally) registered everything from American Banking Corporation to United Arab Bank in Anguilla and sells them off at £1,000 apiece or £800 to the trade. 'He asked me if I could register Barclays Bank', Wilkinson recalls. 'I said I could but in no way was I going to'. So the retiring 'Dr Kurt' of Jalex Trust in Frankfurt had to content himself with Bank of Europe, General Bank of the Middle East and hand-me-down United Banking Corporation.

Bank manufacturer Wilkinson, who runs his own Vanguard Bank along more conventional lines, was slightly

miffed to discover that Wallersteiner had also acquired five
of his ready-made insurance companies by a trick. These
had been ordered by one Dr Moishe Baharov, who couldn't
pay, and the diverse Dr Kurt offered to take them off his
hands cut-price. It turned out that Baharov was Kurt's
partner. 'I've been done', Tony remarked.

Which brings me back to my own (almost) International
Currency Bank, another Wilkinson creation with a somewhat checkered non-trading history. The original American
buyer had some trouble over a forged bank draft. His UK
agent was shortly afterwards charged in connection with
a long firm fraud. I like to think that I have frustrated the
latest endeavors of Philip Wilson, now re-named under
the US Witness Relocation Program. I expect he's picked
up another bank by now, though.

Editorial Note

There is an organization in the USA called the Securities
Validation Commission. It keeps records of all genuine
stocks and shares – serial numbers etc. – and can inform
an enquirer within 60 seconds whether a stock is on the
'hot' list of stolen or counterfeit securities. Despite this
service, an official of the organization, Henry Dupont,
guesstimates that the value of bogus shares 'lost' and
probably deposited as 'security' against bank loans exceeds
$10,000,000,000. We can only conclude that some actual
banks once they discover they have been the recipients of
such unwelcome security, are joining in the paper chase
by passing the dud securities among themselves. After
all, it's not too different from a government printing money
to finance grandiose political schemes and it could be
argued that the paper hangers have had a stimulating, if
inflationary, effect on our Economies!

THE PIG IN A POKE SCANDAL

1958 was before the real impact of the fast moving, fast talking, jet setting, funny money, offshore sharks. Nevertheless, even then the average man was dubious about his ability to follow the intricacies of the share market.

Consequently, when a certain Livestock company began to advertise in the newspapers of their (literally) down to earth scheme to 'invest in a pig' it caught the imagination and check books of a large number of smaller investors. Instead of mentally wrestling with 'bulls' and 'bears', the advertisements and brochures offered a simple concept. Invest your money in a sow, they suggested persuasively. The sow will have litters (two a year were promised so they were only the most fertile and enthusiastic sows). The piglets will grow up and most will go to market. Some will themselves become breeding stock to fuel this pig population explosion. Living compound interest.

And – a nice touch of reality this – your sow will have a name tag clipped on its ear, so, as it is snuffling around 'the most modern pig farm in Europe', you would know which was yours.

The money rolled in – over £1,200,000 of it – and all over England armchair farmers settled down to imagine their piglets, hoping no doubt that theirs was an oversexed sow, and viewing their bacon and egg breakfasts with extra relish.

After eighteen months, however, some of the pig gamblers were becoming somewhat nervous. They may not have been expert breeders but their investment should surely by now be bringing home the bacon.

Letters to the company brought the reply that 'Some returns on investments have not been received on the dates expected, and we must be frank,our administrative procedure required overhaul and speeding up'.

Eventually, a reporter from one of the newspapers which specialize in investigating dubious investment situations involving public money, was despatched to check out one of the 'most modern pig farms in Europe'. The company had admittedly exaggerated the extent and up-to-dateness of their 'farms'. To be tediously accurate it actually turned out to be someone's back-yard. However, they had followed through with their promise to tag the ears of their investor's pig. But this is unfortunately exactly what they had done – tagged the ears of ONE pig. The compound contained a solitary sow with hundreds of metal tags affixed to its ears – causing it to hang its head with more weight than shame. They had sold the same pig over and over again.

The results for the investors – most of whom were small savers – was disastrous. Of £1,200,000 flowing in, some £800,000 plus was declared as loss when the final figures were added up. The architect of the plausible scheme went to jail but due to recent legislation we are not able to name him, as after ten years, restitution is assumed to have been made and even the recounting of facts is considered to be potentially libellous.

VICTOR LUSTIG – THE MAN WHO SOLD THE EIFFEL TOWER

by Elliott J. Mason

Many men evolve a confidence trick or a fraud as extension of a legitimate business. Victor Lustig, or Count Lustig as he styled himself, was a professional confidence trickster. A con-artist, the like of whom there has not been this century. Other men may well have 'ripped off' larger sums of money but no-one has been so imaginative or so stylish as the man born in Hestinne, Czechoslovakia, in 1890 and who died, uncharacteristically, in prison in Springfield, Missouri on March 9th, 1947.

When confidence tricks are discussed, the man who sold the Eiffel Tower is often cited as the prime example of the bizarre confidence trick. Comparatively few people know precisely how it was done. The 'con' for which Victor Lustig, (or Robert Miller or any one of ten aliases that he assumed), has gone down in history, was by no means his only nor necessarily even his most imaginative fraud. It does illustrate perfectly his method of working, however.

It was a beautiful May in Paris in 1925. Paris in Spring has a certain charm which may drop the guard of even the most skeptical of men. Certainly that month Victor Lustig and his confederate from New York 'shook down' a hardheaded French scrap-metal dealer for a great deal of money. Victor Lustig had met his confederate, 'Dapper' Dan Collins, in New York. 'Dapper' Dan had certain qualifications which appealed to Victor for this particular trip. Firstly, he himself was a con-man, although of a much cruder variety than Lustig. 'Dapper' Dan's introduction into the gentle art of separating people from their money was in the off-Broadway hotels where rooms may be rented by the hour rather than the day. Dan Collins, some years before, had approached a hotel clerk of one of these less than curious hotels to ask whether it was possible that some of the couples now occupying the rooms may have overlooked the formality of holy wedlock. The clerk, initially, had intimated that it was none of his business and he was quite uninterested until 'Dapper' Dan explained the advantages of the business proposition he had in mind. In fact, the plan was extremely simple. Once a night 'Dapper' Dan would visit the hotel and go through with the clerk a list of those couples who were suspected of a modicum of extra-marital activities. 'Dapper' Dan would then visit the couples in their rooms posing as a house detective and threaten them with arrest. He would allow himself to be 'bought-off' with all the cash that the couple could muster, whereupon the proceeds would be split with the desk clerk. In fact, this extremely simple and crude confidence trick had kept 'Dapper' Dan in considerable luxury for the last two or three years although he was not necessarily one of the more popular men on the New York circuit!

Victor Lustig had met Dan Collins while they were both 'playing the boats' between New York and Europe and was particularly attracted (professionally) to his good looks, his striking air of innocence and especially his perfect French. Although Lustig, himself, was an extremely good linguist, (he had mastered five languages in his early years in Czechoslovakia), he needed, for this particular swindle, an accomplice.

So it was that the two con-men, that Spring morning in Paris, checked into perhaps the best hotel of its time – the Hotel Crillon. Victor Lustig created his normal impression. He appeared every inch an aristocrat, with his formal, precise yet polite bearing and immaculate tailoring. The man who stood a couple of feet behind him, 'Dapper' Dan – now in the role of Monsieur Dante – appeared to be his secretary or personal assistant.

The two men were escorted to one of the best suites of rooms in the hotel and could have been seen leaving the hotel some hour later to take a stroll among the sidewalk cafes of the Champs Elysées. Indeed, over the next few days which stretched into weeks, the two would sit among the fashionable and idle rich of Paris taking the air and viewing the passers-by. Dan Collins, however, was not the self-possessed artist that Victor Lustig was and after some days he began to get restless and queried where was the 'mark'? Lustig turned to him with a somewhat quizzical smile and explained that he did not yet know. Perhaps fortunately for the patience of the simpler Collins the 'mark' and the opportunity were to present themselves shortly. For in the afternoon paper of May 8th appeared a short news story that reported that the Eiffel Tower was in need of repairs, estimated to cost many thousands of Francs. So much so that the government was investigating the possibility that it might be cheaper to dismantle the Tower rather than maintain it.

Dan Collins protested, however, that the possibility of the French Government actually tearing down the edifice which had become the national symbol was remote. It was, after all, part of Paris, perhaps THE part of Paris.

In the cultured tones that had already taken many people for many thousands of dollars, Victor Lustig patiently explained the background of the Tower to his confederate. Contrary to popular foreign opinion, the Eiffel Tower was only ever intended to be a temporary symbol created for the Paris Exposition of 1889. Even at the time of its construction there were many people who raised a great cry of indignation at the crude structure that had 'desecrated' the skyline of Paris. Alexandre Dumas called it a 'loathsome construction', Guy de Maupassant had asked 'what will be thought of our generation if we do not smash this lanky pyramid'? It was, explained Victor, by no means so beloved of the Parisians as cartoonists and foreigners would have thought. To prove his point, he rightly indicated that the newspaper report had provoked no cries of protest.

Whether the average Parisian liked the Eiffel Tower or not, however, the report in the paper was precisely the trigger that Victor Lustig was waiting for. From that afternoon on, he worked busily and quickly. He visited a contact in Paris who forged for him some letterheads of the Ministère des Postes et Telegraphes, the official authority responsible for the Eiffel Tower.

He researched carefully the principal iron and steel stockholders and scrap-metal dealers in the vicinity of Paris and found one who fitted his bill perfectly. Nonetheless, five invitations to a 'confidential meeting' were despatched including one addressed to the planned 'mark', a man whom the papers called Andre Poisson (we shall not reveal his real name either and those readers with a little knowledge of French will get the joke). Each invitee was a man in the scrap-metal business, each was extremely wealthy and each was invited to a meeting with the Deputy Director General of the Ministère des Postes et Telegraphes at the Hotel Crillon. As the five men sat down, they could hardly help but be impressed with the man that sat at the head of the table. Lustig, in his role as assistant to the Director General, with his handsome square face and his clipped moustache, looked every bit a successful government official. Drinks were served by Dan Collins who then made considerable play of closing the door of the hotel suite and ensuring that there was no-one around.

Victor Lustig began by telling them that they had been invited on a matter of extreme secrecy and national prestige. The invitations had been sent to them alone and they had been chosen because they were thought to be discreet as well as successful businessmen. The interest of the five men must have heightened considerably with these opening words. The 'come on' was perfect. Lustig became even more conspiratorial and confided that the secret he was about to impart was known only to his immediate superior, the Director General of the Ministry of Posts and Telegraphs, to the Prime Minister and of course to the President, President Doumergue. When the information becomes public, it will, he assured them, cause a furore – but by that time their business arrangements will have been consummated. There was complete silence in the room as the five businessmen awaited the next words. 'Gentlemen', said Victor Lustig, looking up, pausing and savouring the moment, 'the Government is going to have to scrap the Eiffel Tower'. Stunned silence. Lustig now had them eating out of his hand and continued rapidly to outline the plan. He referred to the report in the newspapers of the extremely high cost, not only of upkeep but of repair to the Eiffel Tower. The men nodded their heads – yes, there had been such a report in the papers. He continued ruefully that the state of the nation's finances was not at that moment at its highest, and that the governmen had decided that the structure which, in any case, was only intended as a temporary symbol for the exposition, would have to be scrapped. The costs of repair were completely disproportionate and the Government believed that after the first complaints of the effect on tourism had died down, nothing but good would come from the project. In fact it would remove what many people considered to be an eyesore from the skyline of Paris.

Lustig then moved to the 'set up'.

'Gentlemen, you are invited to make a tender for the scrap metal involved.' All the details were summarized on an 'official' Government specification – the main points of which were the height of the tower (984 feet), the base (142 yards in each direction) and the fact that the interlaced iron girders were made of 12,000 sections joined together by over $2\frac{1}{2}$ million rivets. The total salvageable high grade iron ore was calculated to come to 7,000 tons.

Victor then proposed to the spellbound scrap dealers that they take one of the official cars that had been put at their disposal that afternoon to view the Eiffel Tower. He further proposed that they return to their businesses, consider the value of 7,000 tons of high grade iron ore, deduct the considerable cost of dismantling the edifice and then put their bids in a sealed envelope addressed to him at the hotel.

Victor Lustig finally explained that the reason that they were conducting the meeting, and indeed, the whole negotiations from the hotel was that in a matter of this extreme delicacy, the Ministry could not be officially involved. Their bids, therefore, would be addressed to him and the name that they were to use in addressing those bids was Monsieur Dante (Fortunately none of the scrap dealers had had a classical education.) With that, Count Lustig and 'Dapper' Dan Collins swept majestically from the room with the five dazed businessmen following them. On arriving at the Eiffel Tower, Victor Lustig flashed an official-looking set of credentials at the guards, done brusquely enough to avoid close inspection, and stated that the party were guests of the Government – the Ministry of Posts and Telegraphs – and were to be admitted to the Tower. After some refreshments at the top of the Tower and a short sight-seeing tour, the businessmen were dismissed and asked to have their bids in within four days.

Victor Lustig had chosen his 'mark' perfectly. Andre Poisson was indeed successful – but he was a self-made millionaire from the country and despite his wealth, had never managed to establish himself with the society to which his money, but not his background, qualified him. He therefore looked on the project not just as a means of increasing his wealth but as a means of achieving the recognition that he thought his abilities and his success should have achieved. He could see himself go down in history as the man entrusted with the demolition of the Eiffel Tower. Well, he did go down in history but not quite in the way he had intended!

Poisson's bid was submitted on time, but it is the mark of the professional con-man not to rush things and Victor Lustig let him dangle for a few days. Eventually, there was a knock on the door of Andre Poisson's apartment and outside stood Monsieur Dante. He explained that Poisson's bid had been successful and he was required to bring, within two days, to the same suite of rooms at the Hotel Crillon, a certified check representing a quarter of his bid price. Upon receipt of this he would receive the necessary documents confirming his ownership of the Eiffel Tower and the terms on which he would be demolishing it. Monsieur Dante then took his leave and returned to his rooms at the Hotel Crillon.

Andre Poisson was overjoyed and for the first time broke his vow of secrecy and told his wife. His wife possibly had more natural suspicion than her husband and queried why it was necessary for the negotiations to be taking place in a hotel rather than at the Ministry. Although Poisson repeated the reasons given by Count Victor Lustig, it did sow a certain doubt at the back of his mind and therefore, while he arrived on the Thursday of May 20th with the certified check, he was in no immediate hurry to turn it over to the sophisticated-looking Deputy Director General.

Lustig sensed at once the hesitation and on the spur of the moment developed the sort of embellishment that had marked him as such an artist in his 'profession'. He turned to his 'assistant' – Monsieur Dante – and said 'I think at this supreme moment that it would be better if the negotiations were finalized between myself and Monsieur Poisson'. Dante bowed his way out and when he had gone, Lustig's attitude, which until then had been slightly supercilious, changed subtly. The Count looked at his watch and noted that the time was ten minutes past two o'clock. The time was important because the banks in Paris closed at half past two, and it was essential for his plans that the certified check which he was about to receive should be cashed and the two con-men would be on their way that afternoon. He, therefore, leaned forward to Monsieur Poisson and began somewhat nervously to explain that one of the problems of being an official in a ministry such as the Posts and Telegraphs was that one must conduct large scale negotiations with influential and important men (such as Monsieur Poisson) but unfortunately the salary of an official hardly matched the style which one's job demanded. Lustig hesitated and feigned embarrassment. It was, he continued diffidently, customary for an official, in this case, himself, to receive . . . a commission.

'A bribe you mean?' replied Monsieur Poisson.

Now he relaxed visibly and assumed the dominant role for the first time during their negotiations. Poisson's nervousness and suspicions instantly disappeared and were replaced by a feeling of superiority. A bribe! This was a situation he really did understand. This was how the majority of his business transactions had been accomplished. At last he knew the deal was genuine! Poisson was at pains to emphasize *he* was not unsophisticated in the ways of business and had Lustig only intimated such a thing before, days could have been saved on the project. With a studiedly careless gesture, Poisson removed a wallet stuffed with bank notes from the inside of his pocket and tossed it over to Lustig. Victor smiled at him, removed what must have totalled several thousands worth of Francs and with a short bow returned the wallet to the 'mark' – and stretched his hand out for the certified check.

The 'sting' that was to go down in history as, perhaps, the definitive con-trick had been completed. By the end of the afternoon Lustig and Dan Collins had boarded the train for Vienna and for the next week or more bought and studied every French paper from the sanctuary of their Vienna Hotel. Not a word of the hoax ever came out in the newspapers. Clearly they had selected their 'mark' with perfection for Andre Poisson had decided that his dignity and his pride were worth more than the several hundred thousand francs that the extraordinary caper had cost him. Within 2 weeks Lustig decided that he could breathe freely and that the operation would never be reported to the police. So it was that within three weeks of his arrival in Vienna, he had smiled at 'Dapper' Dan Colllins, his accomplice, and informed him that it was time for them to leave Vienna and return to Paris.

'We are selling the Eiffel Tower again', he grinned.

It is a matter of record that Victor Lustig and his accomplice did indeed return to Paris and they did indeed sell the Eiffel Tower again. This time however when the 'mark' discovered the deception he created so much fuss that the two were forced to return rather more rapidly than planned to America.

The Eiffel Tower Touch had significantly boosted Victor Lustig's resources and ready cash is one of the primary requisites of a really good confidence trickster. A con-man must put up a front and ideally he must appear to be totally without need of money himself. Only in this way can he gain the confidence of the people who represent the easiest pickings – the rich and especially the 'nouveaux riches'. It is the latter's greed for status as well as money that makes them such attractive 'marks'.

Victor Lustig's next caper continued his role (which by that time had become a natural part of him), as the European Count, dispossessed of his family fortune, castles and feudal rights but nevertheless with considerable residual wealth and above all family background.

The following incident is well documented from newspaper reports and from firsthand accounts. If it reads like high farce you are reminded that it is strictly factual and that a hard-headed businessman was actually taken for $25,000 for a piece of equipment that the average 8 year old at a Christmas party would have giggled over. Such is the magic of the true con-man, however, that he can imbue even the most far-fetched scheme with credibility, providing only that he had one important ingredient to work with – the greed of his victim.

Victor Lustig sailed from France to New York in the summer of 1925 and by the winter had made his way down to Palm Beach, Florida. At that time, Palm Beach was the playground of the very wealthy and to create an impression in Palm Beach, which was necessary to Lustig's plan, required out-of-the-ordinary style. He achieved it because he had the gift of the true showman. On a December afternoon at precisely the time at which the majority of the inhabitants of the best hotel in town would be sipping pre-dinner drinks on the verandah and gazing out along the beach, a stately and discreet Rolls-Royce drew up outside the hotel. It was not the car however but the chauffeur that was the classic touch, for he was neither white nor was he black. Victor Lustig had chosen a Japanese chauffeur. It added a talking point – something different. From the car stepped an extremely elegantly dressed, handsome man with a cane in one hand and brief-case in the other. He checked into the hotel and made his way to one of the best suites near the top floor. Then, to the considerable disappointment of many of the matrons with eligible daughters , disappeared from public view for some days. His first appearance in public was some mornings later on the beach where he sat in solitary splendor, reading a book. After some moments the Japanese chauf-feur arrived in a considerable state of agitation with a telegram. This the Count read without sign of emotion and stuffed in his pocket. Some short time later a further tele-gram arrived. It too was read and discarded. This pro-cedure was followed throughout the day and indeed into the next day. By the end of the second day the telegrams were arriving at frequent intervals and the Count was no longer even bothering to read them but idly thrust them in his pocket. This extraordinary sequence of events naturally caused considerable discussion among the monied visitors at the hotel. They were not to know, of course, that the telegrams were completely blank and contained no in-formation whatsoever. Over the next week the Count allowed himself to relax a bit and was seen swimming and playing a little tennis but no-one was able to obtain more than a few words of polite conversation from him. He was reserved and discouraging to any obvious opening con-versational gambits. In practice he was spying out the visitors to decide on his target. At the end of the first week, he found precisely the right 'mark'. A man who was very much 'nouveau riche' and although Victor did not know it at the time, a man who made his money by starting from the very bottom as an engineer on a lathe and who had built up a sizeable engineering company. The man's name was Herman Loller and though he had all the trappings of wealth, he was bored and in particular aggrieved that he could not enter the 'true' monied aristocracy of America. Loller was staying at the hotel with his wife and rather ineligible daughter, and his whole bearing, particularly the way in which he over-tipped, told Lustig that he was indeed a member of the newly rich.

One afternoon of the second week, Lustig contrived to meet Loller at a newsvendor's kiosk and to be drawn into conversation by him. Loller was completely captivated by the politeness of the man who spoke with only the merest trace of a foreign accent. When he got round to asking Lustig's profession, Victor was able to smile, nod politely and explain that as a Count, although dispossessed of his real family wealth and fortunes, he had sufficient funds to live in a reasonable style and did, in fact, have no work as such. Now, European aristocracy, even today, carries weight in America. In those days, to meet a 'true-life' Count was a social coup.

Loller could not help betraying his excitement. It was, therefore, doubly pleasurable to him to find that when he extended an invitation to Lustig to dinner, the Count accepted. Their relationship blossomed with Lustig maintaining just the right amount of distance but nevertheless encouraging a fairly frequent set of meetings at dinner and drinks time. Loller was flattered and his increased status among the other guests in the hotel as the only man to capture the attention of Lustig, was proof enough to him of Count Lustig's worth as a friend. And so it was one evening when the two men were alone and taking a drink together, Loller felt sufficiently bold to tell Lustig of his current problems.

His engineering business, apparently, which had been extremely successful was currently in difficulties as the market for the products which were the basis of his business was fast disappearing. He had been supplying parts to the automotive industry, when there had been many brands on the market. Now however the concentration of production in Detroit in the hands of large manufacturers who had no need for outside contractors, had begun to diminish the volume of his factory and Loller could see his wealth was potentially threatened. Lustig nodded sympathetically and he outlined his problems. When Loller mentioned that, of course, Count Lustig was hardly likely to truly appreciate this type of financial problem, Lustig was quick to rejoin that his own life had by no means been totally without its problems. He had already mentioned his family background and the fact that his country estate had been confiscated back in Europe and Lustig apparently chose this moment to confide in his new friend that his own money problems had been solved by what could only be called a 'money-making machine'.

Loller looked at Lustig, incredulously. 'You mean you actually counterfeit notes?' he asked in amazement.

Count Lustig explained patiently and quietly, that it was nothing so crude. He 'merely' had a secret chemical process which would duplicate any paper currency, of any denomination, with complete accuracy. It was a machine which was built for him by a fellow exile in New York. A dollar bill was inserted into the machine and after a period of time the machine automatically processed blank paper of precisely the right size and specification to produce two identical bills. In other words, he was duplicating genuine dollar bills not counterfeit dollar bills because it was quite impossible to tell the new bill apart from the original. The banks accepted them and nobody got hurt. Indeed said Lustig, warming to his theme, he could almost claim to be doing his bit to prime the country's economy. The semantic difference between counterfeit and self-reproducing bank notes and the novel view of Keynesian economics were lost on Loller. He could only gaze in bewilderment at the Count and protest that it was impossible.

'Perhaps', said Lustig patiently, 'but nevertheless that's the source of my wealth'.

Loller by this time was hooked – and nothing would satisfy him but to see such an incredible machine. Lustig professed himself to be reluctant but eventually allowed himself to be persuaded and he promised to show his confidante that afternoon. Before Victor Lustig demonstrated his money producing machine he 'romanced' it with some background detail . . . how the box was produced, how a Rumanian friend of his in New York (also a Nobleman) who had been left penniless by the Revolution, had perfected the process but had died within weeks of its development.leaving the prototype to him. Victor explained to Loller that his friend was not the originator of the duplicator; that honor belonged to the inventor, a certain Emile Dubre who had been captured by the central powers in Yugoslavia after the Sarajevo assassination of the Arch Duke Ferdinand. Dubre was known to be working on a top secret duplicating process, and as such was installed by the Germans in a modern laboratory with the most up-to-date equipment. He was given the brief to continue and perfect his work. The result was a foolproof method of duplicating foreign currency which the Germans had originally planned to use to undermine the currency of the enemy powers. (This story, which was of course a complete fabrication, does interestingly predate an actual project which the Nazis virtually carried out to success at the end of the 1939–45 war.) The duplicator, Lustig explained, was the only one of its kind in the world. With such a machine, he said, underlining the obvious, why would anyone want more than one?

And so came the demonstration. Victor Lustig brought out the dollar duplicator, which was a beautifully crafted mahogany box studded with sophisticated looking dials and with a pillar-box slot at one end and a crank which, when a dollar bill was inserted into it, sucked the bill into the interior. Into this slot, Lustig inserted a piece of bank note specification paper cut to precisely the size of the dollar bill he was duplicating. In fact, it was a $100 bill. He explained that the bill and the blank paper were now pressed together within the machine and immersed in a chemical bath which transferred all the images from the dollar bill to the blank paper without losing any definition of the original dollar bill. The process, he further explained, would take some six hours after which they would return to examine the results. At the end of the six hour period Lustig returned with his 'mark'. With great showmanship, Lustig delicately adjusted all the knobs and then turned the ejector lever. Out came two wet and limp $100 bills! The bills were identical to the last detail. They should have been, because they were both, in fact, completely genuine bills. Victor Lustig had, prior to the whole performance, concealed the second bill in the machine.

By carefully selecting bills of similar numbers and by altering the 'threes' and the 'eights', he was able to ensure that even the serial number of the bills matched. At this point, Lustig again demonstrated his complete mastery of the art of 'conmanship'. He extended both notes. 'Look', he said, 'when they are both dry why don't you take them to the bank and ask them for their opinion'. Somewhat diffidently, Loller accepted both notes and as Lustig had instructed, took them the next day to a nearby bank and explained that he had won the money in a poker game and was anxious to validate the bills. The bank official examined one of the bills and gave his technical assurance that they were indeed, genuine. Loller went to another bank to validate the second bill which was, of course, the same serial number and therefore could not have been authenticated at the same bank, and received an identical reassurance. The 'mark' was hooked. Lustig received Loller into his room in a state of great excitement. Loller bubbled with the 'news' that the bills checked out – the machine was fantastic, he said.

Lustig nodded calmly (he could now afford to underplay his duplicator's magical properties) and admitted that it had served him well for some considerable years and had meant that he had never had any money problems. Loller rushed headlong into his own trap. He demanded to know whether there was another machine, could it be copied, did Victor know the specification. . . ? Lustig pondered the questions – then with a show of reluctance he said slowly that he thought it would be unwise to have more than one machine in existence. Despite their friendship, said Victor, Loller might be tempted to sell the second machine to somebody else and it was, after all, worth literally a fortune.

Loller protested vehemently that he would guarantee that never ever would its existence be revealed to anybody. He then offered to pay Victor $25,000 for a copy of the machine. Victor Lustig considered the offer. This is the point that all flimflam artists savour – when the 'mark' is trying to persuade *them*!

'Well', he said, 'I suppose it matters little what you pay me. $25,000 . . . $50,000 . . . you are, after all, going to recover the amount within a few days by duplicating your own dollar bills'. Then he came to an apparent decision. He said that in view of their very pleasant relationship he felt he would like to help Loller. So he extracted the eager victim's solemn word that he would not pass the money duplicator on to anybody nor reveal its existence to a soul. The fish was landed!

Loller was quick to make the promise and such was the Count's magic that even when the money had changed hands, even when Victor had checked out of the hotel (which he did within 4 hours), and even when the machine patently failed to work, Loller for months and months was convinced not of Lustig's duplicity but that somehow he had the chemical balance wrong or that he had failed to dial the knobs in the correct sequence. Indeed it was almost a year before the whole story was told to the police, to become eventually public knowledge and part of the incredible legend of Victor Lustig.

To those readers who feel that the whole story is too fantastic to have fooled anybody but the most gullible, let us only repeat that is a matter of history-of-fact – that Victor Lustig not only devised yet more exotic confidence tricks but actually pulled this identical hoax, the Rumanian Box Caper, on a Sheriff Richards of Remsen County, Oklahoma some few years later. He not only used the same story on Sheriff Richards but he actually sold him the machine for $10,000 and the chance to walk unhindered out of jail!

The follow-up to this incident however reveals a less buccaneering side to Victor Lustig's nature. It showed he had also a cold and remorseless streak.

Sheriff Richards whom he had conned out of $10,000 and into releasing him (quite illegally) from jail in return for the Rumanian Box, eventually tracked Victor Lustig down to a hotel room in Chicago. The meeting by all accounts was dramatic. There was a knock on the door early one morning and Victor Lustig opened it to be faced with the barrel of a gun and an extremely irate Sheriff on the end of it – promising there and then to kill him. Lustig was equal to the crisis.

'What seems to be the problem?' he queried.

'You son-of-a-bitch!' replied the Sheriff, 'I'm going to kill you. You conned me . . . you completely fooled me with that damn box of yours!'

Lustig feigned puzzlement.

'You mean it's not working?'

'You know it's not working', replied the Sheriff.

'But that's impossible', said Lustig, 'there's no way that it couldn't be working. It's perfect, did you operate it properly?'

'I did exactly what you told me to', said the Sheriff.

Lustig then launched into a highly technical stream of gobbledegook totally confusing the Sheriff who began to waver in his conviction. 'Look', said Lustig, who sensed victory. 'Look, I will give you your money back, right now. I'll also give you written instructions on how to work the machine and I'll come out to Oklahoma, make sure it's working properly and then I'll take the money back again. Is that O.K.? There's no way in which you can lose on that.' The Sheriff considered the proposal for a moment and nodded slowly.

'Well . . . that does seem fair,' he said, hesitantly.

Lustig took his wallet from his coat and pulled out 100 $100 bills and handed them to the Sheriff with the parting advice, 'You have had enough problems – you've obviously been upset over the last few months – why don't you take a couple of days off in Chicago and have yourself a really good time'.

The Sheriff hardly needed any encouragement. For the next few days Victor Lustig, rather as he had done some years before in Vienna, bought every paper in Chicago. At the end of the week he found what he was looking for – a small report that a Sheriff Richards from Oklahoma had been arrested for passing counterfeit notes in a nightclub in Chicago. The Sheriff was charged, tried, convicted and transported to the Federal Penitentiary in Pennsylvania. He didn't trouble Victor Lustig again and we can safely surmise that Victor Lustig's conscious was also not troubled.

One particular escapade of the Cavalier Count, perhaps more than any, although simpler than many of his other bizarre con-tricks, does illustrate perfectly the way that the 'sting' can be set up given the necessary ingredients of human greed. The venue was Texas where, by reputation, everything is bigger, bolder, brassier and richer. Victor Lustig decided to chance his arm in 'God's Own State'. His set-up was meticulous as was his researching of the 'mark'. For the con he recruited a smart young clerk in a stock-broking house in New York which specialized in selling stocks and shares by mail. His other confederate was a counterfeiter. With the confederates well briefed, he headed south for Texas and to the house of a certain Mr Ray Murdoch. This time Victor Lustig dropped the Count title and became for the purposes of the Texas 'take' – Mr George Simon. He telephoned Ray Murdoch who was a customer of the particular stock-broker and offered to see him personally to offer advice and to see whether the stockbroker company services could be further extended to the wealthy Texan. Mr Murdoch entertained him well and over dinner the conversation was gradually brought around by Victor to the question of 'inside dealing' and 'inside information'. He had hit the Texan on a particularly vulnerable spot. It was apparently precisely what the Texan resented about the stock-broking houses in New York. He felt, quite rightly, that at his distance from New York he never got to know the really hot inside tips. Lustig, he supposed, looking at Victor in his role of stock-broker adviser, *did* have the hot inside information.

Victor was in his familiar role – the 'innocent' being pursued by his victim! Reluctantly he admitted that he did get to know things but – and he hesitated. The Texan encouraged him to continue. Victor explained that the problem was that he didn't have the capital to make the real killing. And without the capital, he couldn't really exploit the information. The Texan was hooked. He exclaimed that he had the capital and the problem was solved. But Lustig refused to let his mark become suspicious by agreeing too easily. He explained that he did not wish to enter any business relationship where he did not put up at least half of the capital. This, of course, was precisely the sort of deal the Texan wanted to hear. It established Lustig immediately as a man of integrity and reliability. Conversation was general for some time and the Texan then asked quietly, whether there was any particular deal that Mr Simon had in mind at the moment.

Again Lustig let himself be drawn. There was a particular goldmining company whose shares had long since been languishing on the stockmarket. Such shares are called 'shell companies'. The particular shares were considered worthless because the mines had been well worked out but he happened to know that very recently a new gold vein had been discovered and that the stocks were due for a very rapid take-off in the next few weeks.

The opportunity was to persuade some existing holders of the stock to sell on the basis that the stocks are currently worthless. They could then reap the benefits of the appreciation when it came.

That was *precisely* what the Texan called inside information! – and he was eager to hear the plan. Lustig again allowed himself to be pumped. At last he admitted that his visit to Texas was not purely to see his client but because the biggest single holder of the stock in the goldmine company lived within fairly easy reach of the town in which they were. In fact, he confided, his plan was to see the man and pursuade him to sell – although he was afraid that he didn't have the capital to buy the whole block. Murdoch was immediately anxious to join him as a partner and Lustig agreed it was better to join forces than risk losing the deal. Nonetheless Victor was at pains to point out that he was by no means without funds – he had some Government Bonds which were of significant value – worth as much as $20,000, but, of course, he was not anxious to realize them for cash (which was not surprising considering the fact they were forged!). The Texan saw no problem. He would be happy to take these Bonds as security and in that way they could go into a true partnership. He suggested he would put up $20,000 in cash, Victor would put up his Bonds. Lustig nodded his agreement and suggested that they lose no time in visiting the stockholder who controlled the biggest single block in the goldmining shares to see if they could persuade him to sell. The next day, Murdoch and Lustig drove down to Brownsville, Texas, to visit the 'stockholder'. The 'stockholder', of course, was a confederate hired by Lustig (in fact, he was the New York counterfeiter). He had prepared not only the Government Bonds that Lustig was using as security but also the shares in the Goldmining Company – a company that was quoted on the New York Stock Exchange at the time – but not daily.

The set-up was perfect. As they arrived at Brownsville, they found that the supposed owner of the shares was in a hotel room and clearly on his deathbed. It was a very sick stockholder that Lustig and Murdoch were interviewing, but after an hour it was agreed that Lustig and Murdoch would buy the Goldmining shares from the weak and dying owner. They promised to return the next day when the 'owner' had obtained the share certificates from his local bank. That evening Victor Lustig agreed with the Texan to send a cable to the stock-broking company (addressed to the Sales Clerk in the conspiracy) to ask what price the mining shares were selling. Back came the cable – 'your stock selling $78 and rising'.

Lustig turned to the Texan and put on the pressure. He suggested they get back to the hotel quickly in the morning because if the old man found out that the shares are going up he was hardly likely to sell. They just had to hope that he hadn't access to the same share information. The set-up was perfect. When they returned to the hotel the next day, it was to find that the old man was considerably better and in an aggressive mood.

'I've been thinking it over,' he said, 'I am not so sure if your original offer yesterday was at all fair. I am not going to part with this block of shares for under $40,000.'

Lustig and Murdoch exchanged glances. They knew that at the prices quoted on the telegram the block of shares was worth at least $90,000. After a further hour's haggling, the price of $40,000 was agreed – $20,000 in Lustig's negotiable bonds and $20,000 in the rancher's cash. The goldmining stock was handed over and the deal completed. As soon as they were outside the hotel and in the street, Victor Lustig gave the whole of the stock to the rancher and told him to take it to New York and cash it whereupon they would split the proceeds. The rancher could only admire the fact that Victor Lustig was trusting him with the stock and to return to split the proceeds. So the venue for the share-out meeting was set and the two men parted – for good!

Not all con-men get their just desserts but, if we wish to be moral we can say that retribution did come to Victor Lustig eventually. Throughout his career, as is almost inevitable in the case of a man dedicated to making his living through fraud, Lustig had been arrested many times – in fact a total of 47 times but never ever convicted. His downfall came perhaps through pride – ironically the identical weakness which had enabled him to con so much from so many people.

He became involved, as one of the principal characters, in a fraud so large that a special department of the Secret Service was formed in 1934 to deal with it. The fraud was for him a little untypical – it was counterfeiting money – but in this case the counterfeit notes were so good that they were thought to represent a genuine threat to the nation's economy. A special squad was therefore set up to track down and apprehend the forger behind the notes.

By this time, Victor Lustig's exploits had become well known in police reports throughout America and, via the newspapers, rather well known to the public. Yet for some 2-3 years, little or nothing had been heard of the Count, and indeed initially the flow of counterfeit notes circulating in New York was in no way connected with Victor. In a book of this size it is quite impossible to go through the details of the police operation which eventually tracked down the counterfeiter. Suffice it to say that Count Victor Lustig was the principle distributor of the counterfeit notes. He had at last overreached himself – and broken a cardinal rule. The con-man's biggest single advantage is that the 'mark' is normally reluctant to press charges for fear of looking stupid. This is true whether the 'con' is a large-scale one directed at one person or where a large number of people are taken for comparatively small amounts of money. Moreover the tedious police work involved in pinning down the average confidence trick breeds official inertia.

This time, however, the rules did not apply for the sums of money were immense and the threat to national security was substantial and Victor Lustig brought down upon himself the full weight of the American Secret Service. He was not equal to it. He was arrested in early 1935 and eventually jailed on December 10th of that year.

Even in what must have been his most dangerous hour –
the West St. Detention Center was one of the maximum
security centers in the United States – Lustig managed to
react with characteristic style. Although the details have
never been made clear he broke out of the jail in spectacular fashion. An onlooker who saw the whole thing, subsequently reports that 'I first saw a man appear in an
upstairs window of the detention center. He clambered onto the windowsill and began cleaning the window with
what appeared to be a white rag. I was about to look away
when suddenly he dropped the white rag over the windowsill and to my surprise it didn't fall to the ground but began
to slip down the side of the building. Even from some distance I could see that it was several sheets knotted together. By the time the makeshift rope had reached within
five feet of the ground the man stopped paying it out and
began to clamber down the rope of sheets. It never even
occurred to me that this was an escaping criminal and I
just watched the whole performance in amazement, as
did several other passersby! Lustig, apparently, reached
the ground, bowed politely to the 4 or 5 onlookers and
walked rapidly down the road to disappear from the eyes
of the policemen – for the next six months.

It was only sheer ill-luck that he was apprehended some
half year later in Cleveland but this time his luck had run
out for good.

On December 10th he was found guilty and sentenced
to 15 years plus another 5 years for his escape from the
Federal prison. After 10 years in Alcatraz where he,
incidentally, must have come into contact with Al Capone,
whom he had the nerve to con for $5,000 in Chicago –
Lustig became sick, contracted pneumonia and died in
Springfield jail on March 9th, 1947.

It is reported that on his Death Certificate, a clerk had
written, under the heading 'Usual Occupation' the laconic
entry 'Apprentice Salesman'.

JAIL BAIT

'Love laughs at locksmiths' is one of the more cryptic of English sayings. Certainly there were rather more laughs than love involved in a bizarre con-trick uncovered in May, 1977, in Salerno, Italy.

It all started when advertisements began to appear in foreign magazines. They were actually placed by five men who were already inside the Salerno jail pending trial for various offenses ranging from alleged murder, robbery, theft and attempted murder. Not that you would know it, for in the advertisements the men described themselves as Italian girls looking for the 'right man' to love and ready and eager to travel abroad to meet him.

Once the correspondence started the letters grew increasingly enticing and the men were given the distinct impression that here was a hot-blooded Latin lady who wanted nothing better than to join them to deepen the intimacy of their relationship. Only one small obstacle stood between them and fulfilled passion – the girl needed cash for the trip.

Scores of men and millions of lira were taken and the fraud only came to light when an Italian working in West Germany, Calogero Contrino, came to the seaside city near Naples to find out personally what had prevented his pen-pal reaching him after so many love letters and over £200 for travelling expenses.

Signor Contrino was somewhat amazed to find that the address to which he had been writing was the local jail and the whistle blew on the lonely hearts club. For once the police did not have far to go to apprehend the fraudsters.

The newspaper report that first revealed the saucy swindle stated laconically 'Under a law that went into effect a couple of years ago the correspondence of prisoners is guaranteed privacy.'

CLIFFORD IRVING –
THE HOWARD HUGHES HOAXERS

by Maggie Ward

In his own lifetime Howard Hughes created intentionally, and otherwise, many legends. However, his latter-day obsession with secrecy and avoidance of publicity gave one audacious writer the chance to perpetrate the biggest publishing fraud of the century. Hughes had not been interviewed by a journalist or photographed since 1958, but each year regularly brought fresh claims that the real story of Howard Hughes was about to be published. Few though managed to survive the legal manoeuvrings of his personal protection company, Rosemont Enterprises Inc.

However, such was the interest in the 'real' Hughes story that during 1971 the giant publishing company of McGraw-Hill Inc. of New York paid out a total of $750,000 for the 'authorized' biography of Howard Hughes by a man who in fact had never met him, never spoken to him and whose closest contact was his father who had met Hughes once over twenty years earlier! The lucky recipient – Clifford Irving.

McGraw-Hill like to keep their 'house' authors happy with advances and Clifford Irving, having had some modest success with them during the sixties, had already received half of an advance of $150,000 from them on his next three books. With this background of mutual dealings between the publisher and the author it was not really out-of-place for them to pay him a large advance on one of the greatest 'exclusives'. Watergate had yet to take the American public by the ears.

In keeping with the Hughes reputation for secrecy, Irving

insisted that only top executives of the book company should know about the story and that he should be the only go-between with the subject of the book – whose code name was to be 'Senor Octavio'.

Delighted with such a sensational scoop, McGraw-Hill fell in with Irving's suggested plans and also sold the condensation rights to *Life* magazine for a quarter of a million dollars. The book was clearly an enormous potential money spinner for the publishers and the first draft chapters were eagerly awaited.

The last authenticated Hughes interview had in fact been with a *Time* magazine journalist, Frank McCulloch. Although *Life* and *Time* were sister publications, sharing the same building in New York and although McCulloch was one of the few experts on Howard Hughes and had plenty of his own material on the former aviator/film producer, he was not told of the forthcoming publication. Irving's request for a total blackout of news was respected between the co-operating publishers.

Perhaps it was this very demand for tight security, which was totally in keeping with Hughes' mania for privacy, that helped further convince McGraw-Hill that Irving was genuine and made them less cautious on double-checking the validity of his claims. Certainly no-one appeared to investigate how Clifford Irving had managed to by-pass Rosemont Enterprises Inc. the company that the Hughes' organization set up to make illegal the use or reproduction by anyone but Rosemont of the name 'Howard Hughes'. Equally no-one probed deeply enough as to how Irving had managed to become sufficiently close to Howard Hughes to gain his confidence and to be appointed his 'official biographer'. Besides, there were so many rumors about the state of Hughes' physical and mental health that no-one could afford to ignore the chance of obtaining the truth about him.

The big sell to the McGraw-Hill organization was the culmination of an ingenious plan that was hatched on the popular holiday island of Ibiza where Irving had been living since 1962. At Christmas 1970 Irving was with his fourth wife, Swiss-born, blonde Edith Sommer, a talented artist, and their two sons, Edward 3, and Barnaby 2, on the island. A pleasant existence if not altogether stimulating.

It was in his self-imposed exile that the author read of the problems within the Hughes Tool Co. over the dismissal of Robert Maheu, an ex-F.B.I. man who had looked after the Hughes gambling interests in Las Vegas, and the hassle Hughes was having with the Nevada authorities. The magazine *Newsweek* ran an article including an extract from a letter hand-written by Hughes (complete with signature) to two of his senior executives, Chester Davis and Bill Gay. The publicity of the conflict first gave Irving the germ of an idea to write a book about Hughes. He reasoned, not illogically, that Hughes could not be completely in control of his empire – otherwise why were there so many problems to be sorted out in Nevada which could be simply resolved by a personal appearance by the eccentric billionaire. Why so much secrecy and why did his aides do all the fronting at the Las Vegas licensing appeals. Could Hughes be so ill that he was unable to face enquiries concerning his business world, so weak he could not be seen in public, so senile his power had been forfeited to his bodyguards and employees?

If so, with the help of the existing published background material on the billionaire – plus the unlimited inventions suggested by Irving's imagination – a biography could be produced with little risk that Hughes could or would appear to denounce it!

Irving began practicing the handwritten specimen in *Newsweek* and mapped out a series of letters between Mr Clifford Michael Irving and Mr Howard Robard Hughes. Two sets of letters invented and written by one man. 'A thoroughly exhilarating experience,' he later admitted.

He also claimed later that his original idea was to do a fictionalized biography of Hughes and approach the publishers with the idea. His friend, Richard Suskind, said 'You're out of your mind, no publisher will take part in what amounts to a hoax,' to which Irving's fatal reply was 'Then why don't we do it and *not* tell the publisher!' Irving subsequently maintained, however, he was prepared to tell McGraw-Hill the book was a hoax should the story break and to return any money that had been received by them. However, he became so overwhelmed by the hullabaloo when that time came, that he hung on to his original claim of authenticity.

He certainly worked hard at the letter-writing to himself including one later in 1971 of nine pages!! The letters to him were written on yellow, lined paper and this was one of the details that helped to have the Hughes' letters accepted as genuine. In fact, when Irving showed his collection of letters to the New York editors of McGraw-Hill, and asked them how they knew they were from Hughes, he was astonished to be told that there was a reproduction of an almost full-sized letter by Hughes in *Life* and the letters Irving had produced looked exactly like the one in the magazine. He dashed off to buy a copy of *Life* but when he compared the facsimile to his own efforts he personally could see little similarity. He therefore made two more versions of his letters. If McGraw-Hill had had a copy of *Life* in the office that day and made their own direct comparison a lot of money would have stayed safely in New York rather than taking the long flight to the Swiss Credit Bank in Zurich. But the Fates *and* the Muses were on Irving's side because no-one thought to check Irving's first 'original' letters from Hughes with the copy letter in *Life* and Irving had the chance to substitute his second drafts. Irving had the tide running with him right until the very end. Seemingly no-one at McGraw-Hill even jokingly suggested that the author who had written a book published by them called 'Fake' (about one of this century's most prolific art forgers) might possibly be compiling a fake biography himself. Nor did anyone – until too late – think to check on Irving's claimed clandestine meetings with the recluse at numerous exotic locations around the States.

So on December 7th, 1971, the book company announced

their intention to publish the exclusive story of Howard Hughes, due for publication on March 27th, 1972. The press release claimed that Hughes' reason for breaking his long silence was to set straight the record. Biographies and lies had been printed in the past but here at last was the truth.

When news-hungry journalists tried to check at the Britannia Beach Hotel, Nassau, where Hughes and his entourage had lived on the ninth floor for the past year, they were informed that no Mr Hughes was registered there.

Initial reaction from the Hughes' public relations firm, Carl Byoir and Associates, was one of confusion. Later they merely declared 'The Hughes Tool Company denies the existence of a Hughes autobiography.'

The Nevada authorities were none too delighted that Hughes could apparently skip around the country confiding his life history to Irving, but not manage a trip to Nevada where the law requires applications for gaming licenses to be supported in person by the owner of the gambling interests. Howard Hughes had managed to avoid this appearance before the authorities by claiming that a personal confrontation would be 'traumatic'. A letter hand-written by him, with his finger-prints duly authenticated had been accepted in the circumstances. To have this claim of trauma then flaunted by meetings with a little known author was not easy to swallow. Telephone lines buzzed.

Irving had a pre-planned and simple reaction to the denials by Hughes representatives. Hughes had explained to him that he had not informed his organization about their joint venture so it was not surprising that they should deny the existence of a book they had never been told about! Therefore the more denials that were issued by the Hughes organization, the more convinced the publishers were that they had the genuine article. In fact, the confusion had the typical stamp of a Hughes operation – secrecy and lack of detail were his trade-mark. If Howard Hughes had made up his mind to have his life story written he would not expose all the details of its composition right away.

In particular, he would not have revealed the finer details of the payment arrangements.

Clifford Irving had the financial deal beautifully organized. His planning of the arrangements was clever, calculated and cool.

In 1971 he already had his idea for his new book clear in his mind and had written to McGraw-Hill Executive Editor, Beverley Loo, asking if she knew of any proposed work due to be published on Howard Hughes. On receiving a negative reply he wrote again telling her that Hughes was interested in Irving becoming his official biographer. Irving had already written the official account of his fellow Ibizan, Elmyr de Hory, and his famous art forgeries. Indeed, Irving's story was that he had sent a copy of 'Fake' – the book about de Hory – to Hughes and this had subsequently resulted in an exchange of letters.

When Irving was in New York in February, 1971, he met his publishers and showed them the letters from Hughes. McGraw-Hill's only doubt was that Howard Hughes would change his mind and decide to cancel the arrangement. The anticipation of such a golden opportunity to have Hughes' story, plus the air of secrecy, made the meeting an exciting one.

Irving announced he had to pick up a plane ticket prior to seeing Hughes and Beverley Loo went with him. There, sure enough, was a pre-arranged ticket waiting for him, destinations Mexico City and Oaxaca. His first meeting with Hughes was apparently imminent.

After his return he regaled the publishers with the story of his encounters with the elusive billionaire. Two meetings had taken place and details of a proposed agreement had been discussed. The contract they proposed was $100,000 in advance, $100,000 on completion of research and $100,000 for the delivered manuscript.

After a further trip to San Juan, Puerto Rico in March, 1971, Irving returned to New York with an agreement between himself and Hughes. As well as the expected request for privacy there was also a stipulation that whatever monies

McGraw-Hill were to pay to Hughes it was to be via Irving, and the checks had to be made out to H. R. Hughes for deposit at any bank account of H. R. Hughes.

Irving certainly appeared to have gained the ear of 'Senor Octavio'. Not only was the 'Senor' confiding previously unrevealed particulars of his life to the good-looking author, he was also entrusting him with the negotiations for his money. The relationship looked solid. Irving was personally handling all the details that were normally dealt with by a host of lawyers and executives on Hughes' payroll.

Originally, Irving had asked that *all* the money should go to him and he would pass on Hughes' share. He did receive the first $100,000 but later McGraw-Hill made out the checks specifically to H. R. Hughes. It was also stipulated in the agreement that Hughes should receive his funds within 15 days of the publishers issuing the check.

During April, Beverley Loo approached *Life* magazine's Managing Editor, Ralph Graves, and gave him details of McGraw-Hill's great scoop. In May *Life* and McGraw-Hill had agreed on a sum of $250,000 for world magazine and newspaper rights. This covered half of the publishers' outlay to Hughes and Irving and more contracts could be expected from other publishing rights. On July 29th *Life* signed an agreement which included the proviso that if Hughes ultimately refused to authorize this story of his life McGraw-Hill would have to refund *Life*'s payments to them.

In April, 1971, Dick Suskind, an old friend of Clifford Irving arrived in New York to help research the book. He had once lived in Ibiza but had then moved to Majorca. In December, 1970, Irving and Suskind started exchanging frequent visits to each other's island homes. Suskind was a non-fiction writer whereas Irving was known as a novelist and their friends were more than curious about their intensified association and were especially intrigued to learn what the project entailed – a biography of Howard Hughes. But then they knew something that Mr Hughes did not!

The research began with Suskind ferreting out material from libraries, newspaper cuttings, etc., and Irving 'meeting'

Hughes for interviews in Nassau. Their biggest stroke of luck – without which the hoax might never have lasted so long – was to meet an old acquaintance, Stanley Meyer, in Palm Springs. Meyer was having a hard time financially and he asked Irving if he might be interested in re-writing a book on Hughes that had been started by James Phelan, an ace reporter who was collaborating with Noah Dietrich, *the* top former employee of Hughes and Hughes' only real confidante over many years.

It was coincidence but it gave Irving a golden opportunity. He played it cool though and professed himself too busy – but said he would appreciate a quick look at the material. Meyer handed over the semi-finished manuscript and the photocopier worked overtime!

Reading the Dietrich/Phelan material at leisure, Irving and Suskind realized with mounting excitement they had struck gold. Here was page after page of authentic unpublished details and anecdotes about Hughes the recluse. They had returned to the Mediterranean in July and all through August they read and digested everything they had laid their hands on regarding Hughes. They then returned to the States, this time to Florida.

From here Irving informed the publishers that the interviews were continuing productively but Hughes was after more money. This was not well received back at West 42nd Street but, sensing their reluctance, their diligent writer wrote back saying he had managed to drop the new Hughes' asking price from $1 million to $850,000 and – more good news – the story was developing into an *auto*biography. More money could therefore be justified if it could be said to be Hughes' own story.

In September the publishers were keen to include a new paragraph in the contract stipulating that H. R. Hughes had the sole proprietary rights to the book and would indemnify the publishers against any claim by Rosemont Enterprises Inc. or any other Hughes organization.

Perhaps again the success of having acquired the authentic story from Hughes suppressed any doubts that might have arisen at the unique omission by Rosemont of control over the use of Hughes' name and story. Anyway, argued McGraw-Hill, who was in charge, Hughes or the attorneys at Rosemont? No-one dreamed that the string-puller was Irving, supported by Suskind, manipulating not only Hughes' demands for McGraw-Hill's agreement but inventing them as well!

On the eve of the completion of the Book of the Year, if not the decade, McGraw-Hill were alarmed at the news Irving brought back from yet another trip to Nassau, via Miami. Hughes was holding out for the full $850,000 and was quite prepared to sell out to any other publisher who would be willing to pay the right money. Hughes had, however, signed a letter agreeing to the extra paragraph about the rights. Then, with a real stroke of bravado, Irving produced a check made out to McGraw-Hill, drawn on the Swiss Credit Bank and signed by H. R. Hughes for $100,000. This was the same amount Irving had received previously, $2,500 in March and $97,500 in April, 1971, and meant Hughes was apparently no longer indebted to McGraw-Hill and could negotiate with other publishers.

To soften the bad news Irving also had with him the draft material so keenly anticipated by the publishers, the *Life* representatives and the paperback publishers. After two days Irving had their reaction – Great! It was full of lively anecdotes of Hughes' boyhood and his business methods not forgetting detailed descriptions of his best love – aircraft!

The tasty bait of the partly-written manuscript was taken; the new offer to Hughes was then fixed at $750,000 and subsequently Irving returned with the big man's agreement.

More money changed hands – $25,000 to Irving and $275,000 to Howard Hughes. On receiving the check Irving pointed out a mistake. It had been agreed that Hughes' money should be made out to 'H. R. Hughes'. The check was duly changed, after all, what harm in agreeing to one of an extraordinary person's many eccentricities?

Money, however, was also being pulled in by McGraw-Hill. The profit forecast on the book ranged between $2 to

3 million. A possible blight on their projected harvest was the rumor of another 'authentic' autobiography of Howard Hughes edited by Robert Eaton, a Hollywood scriptwriter and novelist. It was due to be published in January, 1972, and extracts were promised in *Ladies' Home Journal*. McGraw-Hill contacted Irving, now back in Ibiza finishing off his story, and told him of the Eaton book. Irving was soothing to his anxious publishers and volunteered to ask Hughes to write to them. Irving's imagination and writing arm worked overtime and Harold McGraw, the Chairman of the Book Division, received a nine-page letter. It disclaimed the other book and at the same time granted permission to McGraw-Hill and *Life* to publicly announce that they were publishing the authentic Howard Hughes autobiography *provided* the final payment was made to Clifford Irving simultaneously to the announcement and Hughes was sent a copy of the announcement.

All this further convinced Harold McGraw of the validity of the project and the announcement was prepared.

Ralph Graves, Managing Editor of *Life* suggested that perhaps this latest letter from Hughes might be analyzed by a handwriting expert, Alfred Kanfer, who had studied the letter addressed to Bill Gay and Chester Davis the previous year. With the publisher's agreement the Hughes/McGraw letter was scrutinized by Kanfer. On December 2nd came his answer, ending 'the chances that another person could copy this handwriting even in a similar way are less than one in a million'. The letter was cleared.

Irving helped compose the press release ready to take to Florida for Hughes' approval. He wanted added to the draft the fact that 'meetings had taken place in various motels and parked cars throughout the Western Hemisphere'. It was included and on December 2nd, the date Irving was due to 'see' Hughes with the press release, he was given two more checks – $25,000 for himself and $325,000 correctly made out to H. R. Hughes. Irving left, ostensibly to meet Hughes' representative, George Gordon Holmes. He had now received all of the promised advances and had the prospect of a lot more money to follow from the royalties. Indeed, *Life* magazine had additionally proposed that Irving write a further story of his background dealings with Hughes so the year 1971 ended with a golden glow to it. There were no signs that he did not intend to carry on with his giant hoodwink of the publishing world and no sign of him returning money once he had achieved his object of having the manuscript accepted as genuine and the book scheduled for publication.

One person, however, was especially interested to hear of the announcement and that was James Phelan, the double-decade Hughes newshound who had his own five-foot-thick file on Hughesabilia. Phelan had invested a lot of time working with Noah Dietrich who had been writing his memoirs of the time he had worked for Hughes as chief accountant and general trouble-shooter over 30 years.

By now, however, Phelan and Dietrich had parted company as Phelan felt he was being outmanoeuvred. He was! Irving's friend from the early 60's, Stanley Meyer, was acting as 'referral agent' for Phelan and his early reactions had been favorable as had those of literary agent Paul Gitlin. Gitlin's job was to negotiate publishing rights for the Phelan/Dietrich team. By Spring, 1971, however, the feedback from Meyer and Gitlin to Phelan's work became more critical despite the fact that 18 chapters had been completed. In May Phelan decided to finish his association with the others. He had no idea that his 'referral agent', Meyer, had been referring the draft manuscript to Gregson Bautzer, a Los Angeles lawyer who worked for Hughes as his personal attorney. One of Bautzer's main jobs was to stop anyone publishing books about his best client! Phelan certainly had no idea at all that Meyer had shown Irving a copy of his work nor that Irving had taken a copy.

Although he could not know that he had been unwittingly used, when Phelan heard of the McGraw-Hill announcement he wanted to check it out. After all, had his collaboration with Dietrich been completed, it could have been their book creating the interest instead of Irving's. So Phelan telephoned his contacts within the Hughes organization but they all denied the validity of the book. He made another call to Frank McCulloch, *Time* magazine's New York Bureau Chief. Their conversation revealed that no-one on *Life* had suggested that before public announcement of the book McCulloch should look over Irving's work.

Phelan then rang Morris Helitzer of McGraw-Hill stating his doubts as to the genuineness of Irving's book. He told Helitzer how he had worked with Noah Dietrich on their proposed book and with their joint first-hand experience of Hughes they were experts on the subject. The reporter also expressed his willingness to check the manuscript. His offer was turned down as McGraw-Hill explained they had handwritten letters from Hughes as supporting evidence.

McCulloch and Phelan resigned themselves to the fact that they had been beaten to the post by a newcomer in Hughes reporting. Of course, Phelan's disappointment on hearing the news would have turned to outright fury if McGraw-Hill had let him see Irving's manuscript for he would immediately have recognized the majority of the work as being his very own words taken from the original transcript of the Dietrich tapes.

During December, Jim Phelan was in Las Vegas continuing to check out his own sources regarding the Irving/McGraw-Hill book and learned that his own draft had been read by one Perry Lieber. Lieber was Hughes' PR man in Las Vegas and he told Phelan that the copy of his work had come from Gregson Bautzer. Dietrich in turn found out from Bautzer that Meyer had been to see him. None of them, however, knew of the connection between Meyer and Irving.

Then, nine days after the official announcement of Irving's book, Frank McCulloch received a telephone call from Richard Hannah of Carl Byoir and from Perry Lieber asking him if he would talk to Howard Hughes over the telephone. McCulloch was not given any time to find out about the book as Hughes' representatives insisted that the conversation with Hughes had to be that evening. When the voice came over the line McCulloch had no doubt it was indeed Hughes, who then spent 30 minutes denouncing the book and its author, Irving.

Later that evening, Irving telephoned the *Time-Life* building and Frank McCulloch told him Hughes had declared him 'a phoney'. Irving was cool – he merely asked how McCulloch knew *he* had not been talking to a phoney. End of conversation.

Irving and Suskind were dining that night with Irving's lawyer, Martin Ackerman, and despite his initial calm Irving became upset after the call – he had never expected Hughes to speak out personally.

Next day McCulloch read part of the manuscript for the first time and found enough authentic stories and intimate anecdotes that fitted in with his own knowledge to make him feel that it was genuine. (There was no way, of course, that McCulloch could have known that Irving had used material originating from Noah Dietrich.) The telephone call from Hughes the previous day was then accepted as another of Hughes' deflecting ploys.

However, Chester Davis, the Hughes Tool Company's general counsel, who had been present when the call came through still maintained the publishers had been fooled. So, in order to reinforce their evidence McGraw-Hill decided to have their original Hughes letters examined by more hand-writing experts and decided upon Osborn, Osborn and Osborn, a well-established firm. They seemed ideal – especially when their verdict arrived endorsing Alfred Kanfer's earlier decision!

In fairness, the conditions for comparison were far from perfect. They had to take photographic samples of Hughes' handwriting from Nevada (which even the authorities were not completely sure were genuine) and compare them with the samples at McGraw-Hill's offices. There, both sets of letters were photographed and the ultimate comparison had to be between two photocopied examples of Hughes' papers. Certainly not ideal conditions – but the difficulties were not included in their report of affirmation.

Before returning to Ibiza for a family Christmas, Irving

submitted to a lie detector. The test ended abruptly with Irving leaving for the airport but not before the lie detector had shown that he had been very nervous when answering any questions about money. An unfinished test, though, was not much use in coming to any conclusion on Irving's integrity. In January, 1972, *Life* had the documents studied by a finger-print expert but so many prints showed up (though naturally none of them Hughes'), it was considered irrelevant. Irving's luck was still holding even after twelve busy months crossing the Atlantic. Meanwhile, Mrs Edith Irving, too, had been doing quite a lot of air-commuting herself during 1971.

As early as May 13th, 1971, she opened a current account in Zurich with the Swiss Credit Bank. To do this she needed proof of identity; a passport was accepted, plus specimen signature, and not forgetting some money, in this instance $229. Later that day, having successfully opened the account she returned with a more substantial amount of $50,000.

Edith then opened up a second account in Zurich, this time with the Swiss Bank Corporation, with an identity card as proof of her persona. In later months she busied herself walking from bank to bank, withdrawing money from Swiss Credit and crossing the square to deposit cash in Swiss Bank Corporation. A little strange perhaps but not quite so strange as the fact that the first account was in the name of H.(Helga) R. Hughes and the second in the name of Hanne Rosencrantz!!

Each time Edith Irving had used forged documents as proof of identity. For the H. R. Hughes account, Clifford Irving had altered an old passport which his wife had reported lost, by changing the numbers and sticking in a picture of Edith complete with dark wig and glasses. For the second bank account, Edith simply stole the identity card belonging to her first husband's second wife during a visit to them in Germany. As often happens, the second spouse did have some resemblance to her predecessor. Again a switch of photographs and lo and behold Hanne Rosencrantz was reborn!

All worked well until December 28th, 1971, when Edith withdrew the remaining $325,000 from the Swiss Credit Bank ready to add it to the $425,000 across the road in Swiss Bank Corporation. To her consternation she was informed that there was now another account for Hanne Rosencrantz opened three weeks earlier, with the same address and birth details as her own. Purely by coincidence her first husband's wife had picked the same bank, even the same branch, to start a trust account for her son!

Swiss banks are known for their discretion and without any comment it was suggested that Edith, sorry, Hanne, transfer her account to a branch of the Swiss Bank Corporation in the Bellvueplatz. This she did and as advised used a code name and became Erica Schwartz.

Fortune obviously was still on the Irvings' side and their seemingly inexhaustible luck must have encouraged them to continue with the charade because Irving returned to New York on January 8th, 1972.

However, the roof was about to fall in on the Irvings and the battle to prove or disprove authenticity intensified.

On January 7th a key witness made a dramatic personal 'appearance' to a limited audience. Howard Hughes gave a Press conference voluntarily for the first time in almost 15 years. Irving had achieved the impossible, he had forced the recluse to come out of hiding and face journalists to answer questions. Well, it was not exactly a face to face confrontation, as it was conducted over telephone wires – Hughes in his hotel hideout in Nassau and in Los Angeles seven journalists, chosen by Hughes' associates, surrounded by recording apparatus. Two days later the interview was featured on television, followed by front-page newspaper coverage.

For two hours the billionaire talked, most convincingly about aircraft and rather less so about his personal reminiscences. There was no doubt in the interviewers' minds, however, that this was indeed Hughes. He even said he would be returning to Las Vegas shortly, photographs would be released to the Press and interviews given, all of which would discount the speculation that he was a physical wreck, but the bombshell in the interview was his categorical denial of any communication with Irving. He had never met, written nor spoken to him. The book, stated Hughes, was a fraud!

A super cool Irving, however, kept his nerve – his sole reaction to the recording of the interview was 'A good imitation of Hughes' voice as it may have been three or four years ago.'

In turn, the publishers' reaction was to announce their intention to go ahead and Harold McGraw even showed the counter-signed checks his company had made out to H. R. Hughes to pressmen. Here, surely, was a case of 'none so blind as those who will not see'. *Life* decided to publish their first part of the book in February instead of March. The public was ripe for the story. No planned publicity campaign could have generated half the impact that the claims and counter-claims of the participants had done.

Sensing a hidden story, the mediamen started their own detective work. C.B.S. showed an interview with Clifford Irving filmed in Martin Ackerman's home. Clifford repeated his version of the events and described how both he and Suskind had met 'The Man'. Mike Wallace, the interviewer, had read the manuscript and it was a clincher for him – as it had been for all the others. Ackerman, too, had had a chance to read Irving's material and he challenged Irving on the similarity of his own material to copy included in an interview with Noah Dietrich in the *St. Louis Post Dispatch*. Irving's reply was not to deny the similarity but to point out that as he and Dietrich had talked to the same person, it was highly likely that the details WOULD be the same.

In the meantime, Chester Davis, the Hughes Tool Company's General Counsel had not been idle. He had seen the name of Swiss Credit Bank on one of the checks shown to the press and he determined to track down the whereabouts of the money, as well as to initiate legal action against McGraw-Hill and *Life*, for infringement of Rosemont's right to use the Hughes' name and story. Affidavits by the defendants were submitted on January 18th, together with statements from Irving and Suskind which revealed some details of the deal which had been previously withheld by the publishers from Davis.

On January 11th, enquiries that Chester Davis had started with the Bank began to have results. The Nassau Branch contacted its Zurich headquarters and made enquiries about the account of Mr H. R. Hughes. The staff at the bank were asked about their affluent client, Mr Hughes, – they replied in surprise 'that was no gentleman; that was a lady!' (Helga Hughes, in fact, not Howard Hughes). In due course the bank admitted only that the account could not have been opened by Howard Hughes. This snippet was passed on to New York on January 18th and Chester Davis was fortunate to obtain it because Swiss Banks rarely pass on any information regarding clients.

By January 20th, McGraw-Hill themselves officially filed a complaint with the Swiss authorities and the police there began their own investigations. Shortly, the publishers also learned that H. R. Hughes was female and the money in the account had been withdrawn.

A description was teletyped by Interpol for a warrant for 'Unidentified woman alleged identity Helga Hughes. Between 160-165 centimetres (5 ft. 3 ins. to 5 ft. 4 ins.) about 35 years old, slim, petite person, weight about 45 kgs. (99 lb.).

'Thin face, dark long hair falling straight to the shoulders, possibly brown eyes, speaking broken German, wore midi-dress, sometimes boots, small well-groomed hands, wore various rings.

'The woman is wanted on several counts of fraud committed between May and December, 1971 amounting to 2.55 million Swiss francs or 650,000 U.S. dollars.'

The pressure on Irving now really began to build up. All parties wanted confirmation of his story, the publishers, the press, his lawyer . . . When he announced he was going back to Ibiza to Edith he had more questioning from Frank McCulloch and Bill Lambert of *Life*.

As a result of this meeting the journalists thought it would be worthwhile trying to trace George Gordon Holmes, the man Irving had alleged was his link-man with Hughes and to whom he had handed the last check made out to Hughes for $325,000. He would be the one person who could confirm the meetings had indeed taken place.

Irving agreed with Lambert to send a letter to Holmes in Miami. The U.S. mail authorities promised to help but needed a complaint to enable them to check if their service had been used illegally and in a fraudulent manner. Lambert asked them to watch for the pick-up of Irving's letter to Holmes.

Irving meantime left for Ibiza leaving his letter to be posted. Lambert rang Irving's lawyer, Ackerman, who was more concerned that it was *his* client who might be the one who had been duped. Consequently, the lawyer was quite prepared to make a complaint in order that the U.S. Mail inspectors could act.

Bill Lambert went to Miami and met Lex Callaghan, an agent for the Post Office. However, he found that a letter Irving had written to Hughes in December was still waiting in the now rigged mailbox. Not a promising situation.

Callaghan and Lambert decided to physically go over the ground that Irving had described as his rendezvous – but the timings did not fit. They found a discrepancy in the timings Irving had given for the alleged Miami Newport Hotel meeting. A car hire ticket proved the time he arrived, a hotel entry form the time he checked in, and in between those times he was supposed to have met both Hughes AND Holmes. Only there was no way he could have fitted in the meetings.

Clifford Irving's willingness to provide his doubters with as many points of proof as possible had led him to describe the fictitious 'George Gordon Holmes'. Lambert told Frank McCulloch of this description and McCulloch in turn had been busy checking with John Goldman of the *Los Angeles Times*. They thought they had found the mysterious Holmes, in the person of an ex-Hughes employee called John Meier.

As Irving had by then returned to the States, together with his wife and children, Goldman and McCulloch decided to call on Irving to show him photographs of Meier in the hope that the true identity of Holmes would be revealed. They, like Irving's lawyer, still believed the manuscript to be genuine and that the possibility was that Holmes had been fooling Irving. If they could prove Meier was Holmes, the journalists could expose an even bigger story. They certainly got their big story but it was not the one they were expecting.

McCulloch and Goldman did not know of any connection between Irving and Stanley Meyer, the erstwhile literary agent for Dietrich and of Meyer's visits to Gregson Bautzer. Certainly they did not know of Edith's trips to Switzerland. They did know they wanted Irving to identify Meier and Holmes as one and the same man.

When they called at the Ackermans' house, Mrs Ackerman said they could not see Irving. Consequently, they left a message for him that 'they knew all about *Meier*.' Mrs. Ackerman repeated the message verbally to Irving and Ackerman. Irving's reaction was that if the reporters knew about *Meyer* they must know the basis of his material. Because Irving had received the message verbally he did not realize that McCulloch was referring to John *Meier* and that he, McCulloch, had never heard of Stanley *Meyer*! Having had luck and coincidence working with him for so long, the misunderstanding was a cruel irony. The whole fight drained from Irving – if the reporters knew all about *Meyer* the whole hoax was exposed. The bravado evaporated and Clifford Irving made an instant decision to confess that night (January 27th) to the District Attorney. He did.

On his return, Irving faced McCulloch and Goldman, who had come back for their interview, and he examined their photos late that night – pyschologically a bad time for anyone, especially with the weight on Irving's mind. They, of course, were unaware that he had already been to the D.A. that very evening.

McCulloch and Goldman gave Irving several photographs to study, including one of Meier but there was no reaction from Irving. He did not recognize him. The reporters had drawn a blank, and their hope of having discovered the mysterious link-man was dashed. Then Irving, the man who had so coolly bluffed his way through the American publishing world for over twelve months, but now tired and emotionally spent and believing the game was up, said simply 'Helga Hughes is Edith. Edith is Helga'. The reporters were stunned.

The following day Ackerman, who had all along believed Irving was telling the truth, resigned as his lawyer and a criminal lawyer, Maurice Nessen, took his place. On January 31st Irving appeared before two grand juries, one State and one Federal. The bubble had burst. Not only was Chester Davis on the warpath, McGraw-Hill and *Life* were more than a little anxious to find out what had happened to their money. Maurice Nessen successfully asked for the case to be adjourned in order to have time to prepare and the hearing was put back to February 7th. This meant that while the D.A. knew most of the story the press were still anxious to fill in the gaps. The question now was, if Irving was not with Hughes on his trips (for there was ample proof he *had* been to Miami and Mexico) whom did he see and did he have any companions to corroborate his story?

Various enquiries by the interested parties in finding out the truth had revealed the name, Nina, and further enquiries indicated that a neighbor of the Irving's in Ibiza might be a possible candidate. She was Nina Van Pallandt, a well-known singer on television in the U.K. but hitherto unknown in the States. Unfortunately she was not initially to be found. Meanwhile Richard Suskind was summoned from Majorca to tell his story. A great welcome awaited him. The U.S. tax authorities had filed claims of over £192,000 against him and the Irvings.

To add to Irving's problems, one of the main characters in his book 'Fake', Fernand Legros, had not been very flattered by his portrayal by Irving and asked for all copies of it to be destroyed. He additionally sued for damages of £21 million. Nothing attracts publicity like big money.

Worse still on the 7th of February – the date of the hearing – Suskind confessed that the story of his meeting Hughes was false. The credibility of Irving's story was almost gone.

By now, Nina had also been found and was willing to be interviewed. She told how she stayed as Mrs Clifford Irving at the Hotel Victoria, Oaxaca, twelve months earlier. There was no chance, she said, that Irving could have gone to a rendezvous with Hughes on a mountaintop, as they were together the whole of the time. She confirmed she would also be prepared to appear before the Federal grand jury and testify.

It was then discovered that on the trip in December, 1971, ostensibly to hand over Hughes' check, Clifford Irving had a different lady companion. The U.S. Postal Authorities who had helped track down Nina now also found Anne Baxter – a scuba-diving instructor at the Newport Hotel in Miami. This was the hotel where his check-in time had first given the lie to his earlier statements and which first made Lambert and Goldman suspicious. In fact Anne Baxter and Irving had gone to the Virgin Islands that month, eight days after meeting each other.

The ladies in Irving's life were now in the spotlight. The Swiss authorities had found out that Edith Irving was Helga R. Hughes and demanded her return to Switzerland for their own enquiries. Edith, of course, was busy, together with her husband and his researcher Suskind, appearing before the grand juries, during which Irving did at least deny that John Meier was George Gordon Holmes, which was one less conflicting detail to be sorted out.

The newspapers were enjoying a field day and parts of the manuscript were deliberately published in the hope of jolting some reaction from authentic sources.

One particular story that was leaked into the papers involved Perry Lieber when he was publicity man at Hughes' film company, R.K.O. When he read the details he was startled as he could not remember ever recounting the story to anyone and his reaction was mentioned in a *New York*

Times article. Although Lieber had forgotten that ten years earlier he had told James Phelan the same anecdote, Phelan did remember the incident and on reading of Lieber's puzzlement everything clicked into place. Phelan realized in a flash that Irving must have based his 'authorized' biography on his own manuscript. The last piece in the jigsaw was now in place.

On February 10th, McGraw-Hill received a retraction from Osborn, Osborn and Osborn on their earlier verdict of the authenticity of the Hughes letters and the same day they received a message from Phelan to say he was now sure he knew where Irving had obtained his material.

Next day Phelan flew from California to New York and at McGraw-Hill's offices his own manuscript was compared to that of Irving. At the end of that day the truth was plain. *Life* declared Irving's book a hoax and McGraw-Hill issued a statement outlining the use of the material from James Phelan and Noah Dietrich. Phelan's cryptic comment was 'They ought to rename the Hughes autobiography 'Son of "Fake".'

Naturally, Phelan was anxious now to find out *how* Irving obtained his and Dietrich's material. He was intrigued to find when comparing the two manuscripts that Irving had included a story that had been on the *transcript* of Dietrich's taped session but not in their *written* manuscript. As far as he knew the transcript had only been seen by two other people apart from Dietrich and himself. Therefore, Irving must somehow have obtained the transcript and used that as his source. Further detective work by Phelan narrowed the suspect down to Stanley Meyer. However, none of the investigative journalists following the story managed to locate Meyer before he appeared at the grand jury hearing. Nevertheless, he testified to meeting Irving and showing him the transcript and the mystery of the true source of Irving's background material was finally revealed.

During March the Irvings and Suskind appeared before both grand juries. Although Suskind was named in the allegations he was not charged as a co-conspirator.

It was June before sentences were passed. Clifford Irving had confessed the conspiracy on March 3rd and his wife followed suit on the 5th. By American law the defendants were able to confess their parts to the juries and, therefore, did not have to stand trial.

Edith Irving served only two months in the States; the bulk of her offenses had, of course, been committed in Switzerland where she ultimately served 14 months of her two year sentence on charges of fraud and forgery. Her husband served 17 months of a $2\frac{1}{2}$ year sentence starting in August, 1972, after Edith had left the U.S. jail.

When both had finished their sentences it was the end of their marriage. They were in debt to the tune of £500,000.

Edith has continued her painting and has managed to make a living under her own name, having exhibitions in Paris, Barcelona, New York and Zurich.

Clifford Irving is still trying to sell his 'original' story but, meanwhile, has published his own book of the story behind the hoax called 'Project Octavio'. He has also plans to write a book of his time in Danbury Prison, Connecticut, as prisoner No. 00040, where he issued clothing to new inmates.

Noah Dietrich and Bob Thomas' book was published in 1972 as Noah's reminiscences and James Phelan also wrote a book about Howard Hughes' secretive last years – called 'The Hidden Years'.

The central character in the melodrama – the mysterious and eccentric living legend – ended his days a very sick, lonely and no doubt miserable, old man. The publicity of the hoax forced him and his 'Mormon Mafia' to leave Nassau and seek refuge and much sought-for peace in Nicaragua. His last four years were spent in further isolation and in paranoic fear of germs and disease. No will has ever been found that has yet been proved genuine – but it is unlikely that Osborn, Osborn and Osborn or Alfred Kanfer would be called in to pass comment on any signature purporting to be that of Howard Hughes!

Indeed, had Clifford Irving really managed to have met Hughes and talked to him and listen to him express his opinions, fears and even hopes, it is possible that Howard Hughes would have benefited from at last facing the world that he had shut out for nearly 20 years.

And so ended one of the greatest publishing hoaxes of all time. The supreme irony being that Clifford Irving – who had had the colossal nerve to attempt to bluff his way through this outlandish fabrication – failed because of his own confession. And that was triggered by a simple mis-understanding over the sound of a man's name.

The con-man had been conned – by himself!

THE IRISH CATTLE JOB
by Elliott J. Mason

I flew into Dublin on a Spring morning in 1977 to interview a young Irishman, who, if the figures of the Irish Department of Agriculture were to be believed (in this case they weren't!), must have had a cattle farm on a scale approaching an over-ambitious Texas rancher.

In fact, I discovered you could have put all the cattle he owned on a truck – which is in fact precisely where his herd actually did live!

It all started when the Irish Government, intending to boost cattle exports, introduced an export premium on cattle. A sum of money was payable as a bonus to every cow exported from the Emerald Isle. Now, 'exported', of course, included to the U.K. and the U.K. starts in Ulster – just across the border.

Our young broth of a boy decided that the call of country life was too strong to resist and this was a business for him. Admittedly, his training as a motor mechanic didn't appear a perfect background for ranching but nothing ventured. . . .

His first stop was a little unconventional. He avoided the stock auctions, didn't waste time negotiating for lush pastures – instead his first purchase was a cattle truck – and especially a nondescript truck – no flashy advertising for him.

He then purchased ten cows. Young and healthy was his criterion and the vendor might have wondered why he was so insistent that they were especially strong and docile. No neurotic cows for our new rancher.

The next step was to acquire and file the necessary paper-work for the export of ten cows. Simple. The authorities were only too pleased to co-operate to boost the export drive and every little bit helps.

Papers complete, our boy takes the wheel and heads north. The Eire border authorities being more interested in gun-running than cattle shipments duly stamped the papers – thereby qualifying the nascent cattle baron for the export bonus and through the border he drove. For about ten miles. Then, making a sharp left turn he took a series of smaller and smaller lanes until, after an hour, he was back again on home soil.

Later that afternoon, the cattle truck rolled up at another border post and the procedure was followed all over again – and over the next fourteen months, again – and again. . . .

This fanciful exporting might have continued for a long time – with the aid of registration number plate changes – if he had not had a minor accident at a border patrol post causing a rather obvious scratch on the truck and damage to a post sign. An especially alert official was surprised to see the same truck roll up later in the day – with what appeared to him similar looking cows on board. Maybe the cows had become dizzy by now with the circular motion. Certainly they had had less exercise than normal.

Well, the game was up when our export expert appeared with his cargo the next day. But retribution has not yet followed, for the authorities now know what he did, but due to a confusing trail of aliases – do not know how many times he did it. The current position is that the lad has offered a refund of modest proportions with the authorities counter-claiming for many thousands of pounds more. During this stand-off situation more details cannot be revealed. . . .

KEN HOWARTH
AND THE COPPER MINE CAPER

by Richard Milner

All thieves considered, Ken Howarth is the most agreeable con-man I have ever met. Within minutes, he was practically an old friend. Within a week, he had bought me lunch three times. This must surely rank as a British record for optimistic hospitality to an investigative journalist. It was only with extreme difficulty that I managed to pay for the wine on our second outing. We were at a friendly neighborhood Sicilian restaurant called the Mondello in Theobalds Road, London, WC1, which he seemed to enjoy almost as much as his favorite Savoy Grill. He should have been a diplomat.

Kenneth Howarth of E. J. Austin International is perhaps the boldest City trickster of our times. He came to be known as the 'Crock of Gold' man, which is my fault. I first focussed attention on the Austin saga back in September, 1969. 'It has elements of oddity, disaster and almost unbelievable luck', I commented in the *Sunday Times*. 'It is not as bullish as some enthusiastic stockbrokers would like to believe, for there are certain ambiguities and contradictions that would raise the hackles of any conventional analyst. But above all it is the story of one man and his search for the crock of gold at the end of the entrepreneurial rainbow.'

Like any good con-man, Ken Howarth tackled this criticism head on. At the next shareholders' meeting of Austin International, he insisted that there really *was* a crock of gold in them thar hills. Or to be more accurate, a crock of gold, platinum, silver and copper. He even produced some samples to show round. Not actual nuggets, as it happens, but mini-ingots of refined metal. In fact, he was a classic gold-brick merchant but on a grand scale. He valued the gold brick at upwards of $1,000 million. In the interest of E. J. Austin, however, he was prepared to sell the company his half for a mere £6½ million.

It is a measure of Howarth's persuasiveness that he very nearly induced merchant bankers Morgan Grenfell to cough up £1 million to finance his multi-metal venture in California, that John Ormond of Surinvest was buying Austin shares like a man with four hands and that stockbroker Christopher Spence of Spence Veitch was convinced that his clients were on to a gold mine – or was it a platinum mine? For a while he had the City of London very excited indeed. He was a man of conviction. He is now a man of several convictions, having collected a handful at the Old Bailey in May, 1975.

Watching normally astute City men fall over themselves in blind eagerness to buy a gold brick is, of course, extremely amusing. Dedicated cynics ascribe all investment decisions to two basic motives – greed and fear. And there can be no doubt about the motivation of those who jumped into Austin International with their eyes shut. Those who lost their shirt deserved to lose their trousers as well. In a sense, perhaps some of them did. It would be difficult to imagine an affair when the City threw caution to the winds with such zest and ended with its corporate dignity flapping around its ankles.

What makes the Austin International affair so exceptional is that the whole thing was quite incredible from the start. Ken Howarth had a record of erratic business enthusiasms, though nobody except the *Sunday Times Business News* suggested that this might be significant. His ventures in California and Cyprus depended on an amazing 'secret process' invented by his partner, Wayne Chambers, a horny-handed Oklahoman mining engineer whose track record was if anything even more enigmatic. And even before the gold brick hit the Stock Exchange, at least one erstwhile associate was already disgruntled. To wit Alfred Hinds, jail-breaker, penal reformer and latterly mine-owner.

James Kenneth Howarth, who first featured in the Directory of Directors with no fewer than 19 directorships in 1969, had actually set foot on the executive ladder ten years earlier. He had joined the board of a company known as Barrow Haematite Steel (BHS), then a subsidiary of the trouble-torn Arusha Industries group whose products included Klaxon sirens and Webley air pistols. And by the time Harley Drayton's associates secured control of Arusha (renamed General and Engineering Industries) in 1962, Howarth had become managing director of BHS. Its profits had bounded to a peak £221,000 in 1969 but had slipped back to £163,700.

Then a fresh-faced 32-year-old, Howarth was keen to impress the main board, even a shade too keen, perhaps. At one point, for example, he was seized with the idea of exploiting the BHS slag-heaps and came rushing in to one of his executives with ore samples. 'Everybody knows that those kidney-shaped loomps are haematite', he was informed briskly. 'That's no way to take a sample'. But it took more than that to put down Ken. And in later years, he was dealing with directors who had no more notion of how to take a sample than they had of flying to the moon.

But in 1968, Ken Howarth's industrial career was rudely interrupted. That June the U.K. ferro-manganese cartel was broken up. His Mostyn works was badly affected. Profits of Barrow Haematite Steel plummeted to a mere £13,794 and results went from bad to worse. General & Engineering chairman Martin Rich decided to put BHS into liquidation. Four days before the creditors' meeting, Howarth prompted his first mining sensation by disclosing to the *Barrow Evening Mail* that BHS had located a massive new iron ore field. There was just one small snag. It was underneath a large body of water.

Chairman Rich was not over-impressed by this last-minute underwater discovery. Barrow Haematite was put into liquidation in March, 1964 and disclosed a deficiency of more than £560,000. Howarth was determined to salvage something from the wreck. Within three months of the winding-up order, he had bought the BHS iron foundry from the liquidator and incorporated his own business, Kenarth Engineering. But although he persuaded the Board of Trade to back Kenarth with a £25,000 debenture, this business collapsed in September, 1966. It showed an estimated deficiency of just over £59,000 and the Board of Trade lost some £5,000-odd.

Financially battered but enterprisingly undeterred, Ken Howarth came south to seek his fortune in the City of London. Early in 1968 he joined financier Olivel Jessel to help run multifarious interests ranging from unit trusts to (of course) mining. He was originally slated to become managing director of a South African subsidiary but, as Jessel commented, 'He was almost too good'. (What exactly he meant by this cryptic remark is perhaps open to question.) For a while, however, there was plenty of wheeling-and-dealing to be getting on with. And then, in the spring of that year, Ken had a real stroke of luck. He ran across James Derrick Slater.

Howarth had gone round to the Hertford Street head-quarters of the reputed Mr Asset-Stripper with a proposition from Jessel. (For those unfamiliar with City practice, it should be explained that these financial wizards often got together to shuffle round other companies' affairs.) Slater didn't fancy the deal but he did have a use for the dealer. There was this little company up in Cheshire called E. J. Austin Contractors Supplies, which was in building, property and a certain amount of trouble. Slater Walker Securities had bought a 20% share stake in Austin and needed a bright chap to sort things out to Slater's advantage. Ken Howarth was ready, willing and – up to a point – able.

As things turned out, Jim Slater did not retain his interest in Austin for very long. Just long enough, in fact, to sell the company a firm of timber importers, Sharp

Brothers & Knight, that he had recently acquired. This didn't do much for E. J. Austin Contractors Supplies, admittedly, but it suited Ken Howarth. He joined Austin in July, 1968, Slater sold out at the year-end and in May the following year the 'new broom' had swept chairman David Bollen out of office and installed himself instead. From being a Slater nominee, Howarth was now his own boss at the head of a publicly quoted company. And going places in a tremendous hurry.

Austin shareholders caught the first strong whiff of change in August, 1969, when the company's name was formally changed to E. J. Austin International. For it was no longer a mere bits-and-pieces group based in provincial Altrincham. In a few short months it had been transformed into an international operation, its dim brick-colored U.K. past replaced by an exciting golden future in faraway places such as Cyprus and California. It was about to become a world leader in metals like chrome and platinum, not to mention copper, gold and silver. From being a Stock Exchange wallflower, it had suddenly become everybody's darling. And the figures *were* very exciting.

Ken Howarth had discovered (or rather re-discovered) chrome ore in the Troodos Mountains of Cyprus. 'There is evidence of surface deposits for at least five years' mining at the maximum rate of extraction of 300,000 tons per annum,' he reported in a circular. 'Any specific profit forecast at this stage could be misleading *but* a profit of at least £3 per ton of ore mined should be reached; and it is anticipated that this venture will contribute to the group's profits in the current year.' Howarth, you will note, had not actually *made* a forecast. But since Austin had a 55% stake in Apsiou Chrome Prospecting, any gambler with a slide rule could figure out that Cyprus was worth around £450,000 a year.

This would have been a real shot-in-the-arm to Austin (suddenly) International. To clear the decks, Howarth had brought in accountants Deloitte Plender & Griffiths to prepare an in-depth report on the group's financial position. This turned out to be a mildly agonizing reappraisal. Profits for the past year would not reach the £460,000 boardroom estimate, Deloittes reckoned, but would be 'in the region of £200,000'. But profits would pick up to £500,000 in the current year, Howarth and his colleagues forecast, *without* counting anything from the two new mining ventures. And if Cyprus chrome could double Austin's profits, what could shareholders expect from California?

What Howarth had discovered in the San Jacinto hills of California was not entirely clear but sounded distinctly promising. It was a 40-acre prospect with 'extensive above average mineralization in the form of copper, silver, gold and platinum'. Possibly he did not want to reveal his entire hand immediately. Perhaps he aimed to test stock market credulity with chrome before throwing precious metals into the pot. Or maybe he simply felt that it would be imprudent to disclose at this point that he and Wayne Chambers had personally bought the 'other half' of this metalliferous acreage and planned to become multi-millionaires by selling their plot to Austin.

That was the situation in the late summer of 1969. Ken Howarth was winging round the world in search of lucrative lodes, his mysterious partner Chambers was keeping his process secret and knowing chaps in the City were telling each other that Austin International was the hottest thing since chicken vindaloo. It seemed almost too good to be true. Hell, it *was* too good to be true. By some intuitive logic, I *knew* that there was some kind of hocus-pocus going on – and decided to investigate. And the whole amazing metallurgical bonanza soon began to develop almost as many holes as a Gruyère cheese.

For a start, there was the question of Wayne Chambers and that 'secret process' for extracting metals cheaply from complex ores. Howarth obligingly produced his partner. Chambers (then 53) was not type-cast as an eccentric inventor. Eccentric, certainly, but hardly inventive. He looked more like a Klondike pick-handler who had come into money, a rough diamond with a sand-blasted face and a taste for flamboyant haberdashery such as ten-gallon hats and lurid shirts. Against the elegant scarlet and gold decor of the Savoy Grill, he stood out like a moustache on the Mona Lisa. And his exposition of the secret process was as clear as mud.

Chambers sketched a diagram of linked boxes on the back of a used envelope. 'You put a certain chemical in the first tank and the copper comes out', he explained in an Oklahoman rasp that cut through the Savoy's discreet lunch time mumble. 'Then you put another chemical in the second tank and the silver comes out'. When every conceivable metal had been leached out of the first batch of ore, apparently, you simply recycled this chemical goulash and did it all over again. By this time, half a dozen tables had been brought to a gastronomic standstill. 'I mix local dirt with the liquor', he concluded. 'You just can't analyze it – it's like Coca-Cola'.

It could be argued, of course, that Wayne Chambers was under no obligation to reveal his secrets to the first journalist who asked. Fair enough. On the other hand, surely any genuine inventor would take pains to ensure that such a revolutionary process (however vaguely described) at least sounded moderately plausible? Quite apart from the Oklahoman's cracker-barrel approach to metallurgical science, the idea that he could perpetually re-circulate (and add to?) the ingredients in his cauldron without affecting the magic formula seemed inherently lunatic. And I already knew that there were some non-chemical problems.

According to the authorized version, Howarth had originally run across Chambers about six years earlier. In the Kalahari desert of all places, where apparently they were both looking for manganese. And they had bumped into each other again almost as soon as Ken joined the Austin board in mid 1968, this time in the more civilized ambience of the Mayfair Hotel. Ken Howarth gave the impression that this was a purely chance encounter and that it was only after sinking a couple of Screwdrivers for old times' sake that he learned Chambers had developed a wonderful new process. But this version of events did not quite fit the facts.

Wayne Chambers had been hawking his secret leaching process round town for some time. It started in December, 1967 when one Ronald Rietti was asked to help out. And through a South London garage owner, Chambers was introduced to the Mason & Barry 'situation'. By any standards, this was a fairly desperate situation. Mason & Barry was a publicly-quoted U.K. company headed by the optimistic Jonathan Huntingford, operating a run-down copper mine in Portugal and on the verge of total collapse. It planned to acquire a worked-out silver mine in Mexico in exchange for a massive issue of shares. Goodness knows why.

The idea seems to have been that the Chambers process might turn the Mexican operation into a money-spinner. Or at least that the overall Mason & Barry situation could be made to look like a *potential* money-spinner, foreshadowing in a quite remarkable way the financial conjuring trick that Howarth attempted to perform with Austin International. But Mason & Barry was too far gone and lost its Stock Exchange quotation. The owners of the Mexican silver mine (whoever they were) vanished south of the border and jail-breaker/penal reformer Alfie Hinds seized control of the Mina de Sao Domingos in Portugal to embark on but another legal wrangle.

Which might seem irrelevant, except for one rather important point. Ronald Rietti was a promoter and did not believe in letting opportunities slip through his wallet. So Rietti formed a partnership with Wayne Chambers to exploit the process early in 1968, several months *before* the old mining hand renewed his acquaintance with the younger ore enthusiast Howarth. And it was Rietti's company, Felday Investments, that sold the exclusive Portuguese license to Hinds. With the result that Mason & Barry had to hire Hinds to leach out a guesstimated £1 million worth of copper from the spoil heaps at its Portuguese mine. Though he had knocked about a bit in the financial twilight, Alfred Hinds was rather nervous about this particular deal. 'When I first met Chambers at Lisbon airport, he was wearing a white ten-gallon hat and a bright green shirt', he recalled. 'He frightened me to death'.

But Ronald Rietti was not content simply to give the Chambers process a trial run in Portugal. Through the good offices of a friend and business associate, he had arranged for a demonstration in February, 1969, at the Royal School of Mines in London. (The R.S.O.M. is embarrassed to recall this occasion but, if it lets out academic premises for private hustlers to peddle a secret process, embarrassment is probably the least it can expect.) This attracted the interest of (among others) London Metal Exchange dealers Henry Gardner & Co, a subsidiary of Amalgamated Metal Corporation.

'(Rietti's company Felday) signed an agreement with Gardner, for instance, under which the London metal dealers would have the right to sell all metal produced by the Chambers process', my colleague Charles Raw wrote later. 'Gardner had seen the Chambers wonder machine at work under laboratory conditions. It worked all right on a concentrated copper solution, but the Gardner men remained pretty sceptical. Still, they had nothing to lose as they were not being asked to put up any money'. (Two points should be noted. First, Chambers was *not* working on a complex ore. Second, Gardner signed *something* on the dotted line.)

Falling over backwards to be fair, Raw added: 'The unique Chambers process does not seem to be as untried as reports have tended to suggest, though it does seem to be unproven. A test machine has been set up for demonstration in London at the Royal School of Mines and elsewhere. One machine was in the form of a four-foot tank in which there are some wheels made of a special alloy. The ore is mixed with a solution and put in the tank and as the metal sticks to the wheels it is wiped off by blades, falls to the bottom of the tank and is removed by a worm screw. The secret, though, lies in the solution which Chambers uses'.

As later analysis proved, the solution that Chambers used turned out to be almost pure eyewash. In so far as any scientific principle was involved, it was fairly straightforward. If you put a metallic solution in at the top of a tank, it is likely to settle out at the bottom. (So, copper was precipitated by electrolysis. What did you expect – whipped cream?) The *secret*, of course, had nothing whatever to do with metallurgy. It was that Wayne Chambers and his partner (or partners) had contrived to give the amazing process valuable credibility by staging this demo in the prestigious Royal School of Mines and securing what could be mistaken for a seal of approval from Amalgamated Metal Corporation.

When Ken Howarth symbolically transformed E. J. Austin Contractor's Supplies into E. J. Austin International in August 1969, however, no outsider could prove that Chambers' complex new-fangled process was plain old-fashioned hokum. What they could have established, though, was that there was considerable dispute over the ownership of the process. Wayne Chambers obviously had a claim, Ronald Rietti formally had a claim through Felday Investments, Austin International apparently had a claim and even Alfred Hinds had at least a partial claim. Moreover, something called World Wide Metals had been set up to exploit the process in the United States.

Rietti had promoted the Chambers process widely if not too well. After incorporating Felday and selling Hinds the Portuguese license in early 1968 he had somehow been pointed towards E. J. Austin up in Altrincham. They had despatched their newest boardroom recruit Howarth (who claimed to be a metallurgist) to check out the process with Chambers. Howarth became enthusiastic, joined the board of Felday and some time later attempted to simplify the situation by putting this company into liquidation. This not unnaturally upset Rietti, who had seen Chambers first. It also ruffled the composure of A. Hinds, Esq. and Henry Gardner & Co.

With a good Savoy Grill lunch inside him, Wayne Chambers brusquely dismissed these legal technicalities. 'Nobody can run this damn process except me and Ken', he asserted confidently. And there seemed no doubt in his mind that the Chambers/Howarth/Austin combination was about to make a goddam fortune out there in California. 'Hell, I could make copper at 20 bucks a ton if I had to', he remarked. This was a fairly startling claim, as the world price of copper was around £700 per ton at the time. (Still, it had been a damn fine lunch and I had been asking a whole bunch of damn fool questions.)

Like the men from Henry Gardner & Co, I was pretty skeptical about the Chambers process. But there was no way that I could turn my skeptical disbelief into scientific disproof. That's the wonderful thing about a secret process. By definition you can't put it to the test! You either believe in it or you don't, like palmistry or fork-bending. But although I was unable to analyze Chambers' magic formula, I could and did check what was actually happening on the ground in Cyprus.

Precious little, it seemed. Ken Howarth had become geologically interested in Cyprus some three months *before* his excited reunion with Wayne Chambers. He had met a Louis Michaelides in March, 1968 at a hostelry known as the Go-Gotel in London's Bayswater Road. Michaelides was managing director of Apsiou Chrome Prospecting, which had established that there were deposits of chrome and copper in the Troodos Mountains but was short of the necessary cash to dig it out. As a newly-hired Jessel employee, Howarth was not in a position to help. But when he joined the Austin board that May, he began to motor.

Before July was out, Howarth and Chambers flew to Los Angeles. Together they looked over the 40 acre property at Corona in Riverside County which Chambers had surveyed some four years earlier. It seemed full of Western promise. Later Austin incorporated a $20,000 Nevada company, E. J. Austin Research & Development of America. It acquired rights to the Chambers process in a cash-and-royalty deal, occupied the property on a letter of intent and started magnamometer tests. Twelve months later, total capital costs were estimated at £250,000 and Ken Howarth (privately) reckoned its profit potential at up to £1 million a year.

By August, 1968, Howarth and Chambers were in Cyprus to spy out the lay of the lode in the Troodos Mountains. Pilot tests were encouraging. Another new offshoot, E. J. Austin Research & Development (Cyprus) was set up. It signed a joint 55/45 deal with Apsiou Chrome Prospecting to exploit the 55 square miles. Though a £200,000 concentrate plant was involved, Ken Howarth reported in the following August that this venture should be self-financing after the £100,000 spent so far.

So even before Jim Slater pulled out of E. J. Austin Contractors Supplies at the end of 1968, Howarth had set the stage for its astonishing corporate transformation. A normally shrewd stock market operator like John Ormond of Surinvest might perhaps have asked himself why the financial maestro had decided to sell his 20% Austin share stake after unloading Sharp Brothers & Knight, instead of staying on what promised to be an excitingly profitable ride in chrome, copper, gold, et cetera. In the death, Slater's withdrawal was well-timed. Surinvest laid a bundle on the Altrincham flier and lost an estimated £650,0000.

Ken Howarth had tremendous zest. He positively revelled in his self-appointed role as Austin's roving international director, jetting around the world to Los Angeles, Limassol, Lisbon and wherever with a fine disregard for jet lag and cost accounting. Three months after he became £20,000-a-year chairman, he still remarked with naive pride that he had logged 27,000 miles since joining Austin. And he never lost his childlike enthusiasm at discovering fresh ore-bodies. After a trip to Jamaica, he carted back a sample of bauxite from a property development site. (Fortunately, he did not pursue this opportunity to get into the aluminium business.)

Wayne Chambers, on the other hand, was more relaxed. He had already knocked around the world a good deal and perhaps the novelty had worn off. One mining site, after all, tends to look pretty much like another. When not actively engaged in flimflamming analysts, financiers, metal dealers, newspapermen and prospectors or hacking round deserts, mountains and spoil heaps, his revelling was more conventional. While actively pursuing Austin's chrome prospects in Cyprus, for example, he spent so much time and money (up to £300 a night) at the Bamboo Club that he finally bought a half-share in the joint. (And for all I know, it may have proved his most rewarding investment.)

On the face of things, however, Chambers had not done much to unlock the profit potential of the Troodos Mountains. Eugenios Cotsapas of Apsiou Chrome Prospecting, who was also a director of E. J. Austin Research & Development (Cyprus), seemed quite surprised that chairman Howarth had managed to predict the life of the chrome mine, the maximum extraction rate and the minimum profit per ton. More than a year after Chambers had first arrived in Limassol, the Apsiou venture was still not in commercial production. There were 'veins scattered all over the area', Cotsapas reported, but no decision had yet been made whether to opt for surface or underground mining.

In these circumstances, Ken Howarth's indication that Austin/Apsiou would be able to mine up to 300,000 tons of chrome ore a year at a profit of at least £3 per ton was clearly grossly misleading. This would have been about 12 times the annual throughput of the biggest chrome producer in Cyprus. And the venture could hardly contribute to Austin profits in the 1969/70 financial year without any extra capital expenditure. It had accumulated some equipment 20 miles away at Moni for £20,000, not a purpose-built crushing mill for £200,000. It was hardly surprising that Mr Cotsapas was surprised.

Towards the end of December, 1969, Austin shareholders took a hefty blow in the balance sheet. Financial results for 1968/69 were rather worse than expected. Pre-tax profits came out at £222,000, in line with the Deloitte's report. But that was before special property losses of nearly £104,000, provision for a £90,000 construction loss and (significantly) an item of £62,400 for the costs of overseas operations. Right down at the bottom line, in fact, the group had incurred an overall net *loss* of more than £168,000 compared with a profit of close on £95,000 the previous year. It was not the kind of performance that earns the chairman a vote of thanks.

With belated caution, Ken Howarth back-tracked from his forecast that profits of Austin's U.K. operations would recover to £500,000. The property division would take longer than expected to make its 'substantial contribution' to results, he reported, and profit margins in other sectors were under pressure. What with the credit squeeze and economic restrictions, the group's finances were strained and (though this cash bind was expected to be 'of limited duration') it planned to raise £500,000 by issuing convertible loan stock. And just to be on the safe side, £1 million had been written off the balance sheet – almost halving the group's net assets.

But Howarth still had that hole card in California and early in the New Year he played the El Sobrante mine for all it was worth. To be strictly accurate, of course, he played it for several millions *more* than it was worth. But according to some experts, sheer nerve is the essence of Five Card Stud. Austin's U.K. interests in building, property, and window-cleaning had been laid out face up and didn't amount to much. Its Cyprus chrome venture had been exposed by the London *Sunday Times* as something of a joker. Everything depended on what Howarth could turn up in the Sunshine State. And it turned out to be the wildest card of all.

The action started with a telephone call from stock-broker Chris Spence to Derrick Pease, a managing director of merchant bankers Morgan Grenfell. Would someone from Morgan's like to see Austin International's 40 acre site at Corona? Pease suggested Henry Gorrell-Barnes, one of the bank's investment managers. Together with Howarth and Chambers, Gorrell-Barnes was flown out to Los Angeles on January 8th. He spent the weekend with friends, was whisked out to the site on Monday and flew back to London the following day. Two days later, Austin director Edward de Guingand formally announced that the company had struck practically everything and that Messrs Howarth and Chambers proposed to swap their El Sobrante half for £6½ million worth of Austin shares.

Leaving aside the question of how Austin's executive chairman and his non-executive American partner had managed to lay hands on 50% of this valuable California real estate without informing other shareholders, the proposed share-exchange offer looked at first blush like a pretty good deal for Austin International. From the figures that were released, any City analyst could work out that the two international adventurers were not pressing for the highest possible price. It was clear that only a couple of generous, open-hearted and very wonderful people would ask such a relatively piffling sum for half a mine guesstimated to earn £10 million a year. Or was it?

Stripped to essentials, the quite staggering value placed on the El Sobrante prospect hinged on four basic claims. First, that 300,000 tons of ore had already been stock-piled. Second, that this averaged 3% copper and contained up to 27 ounces of silver and 60 ounces of platinum per ton. Third, that the ore was accordingly worth around $5,000 a ton or some $1,500 million in all. Fourth, that the constituent metals (plus a smidgeon of gold) could be extracted very cheaply by the Chambers process. If these remarkable claims were true, Austin could afford to parcel up its other businesses and give them to charity. Today Altrincham, tomorrow El Dorado!

But *were* the claims true? By a strange coincidence, the crucial assay report on El Sobrante had been signed by Hugh E. Whirry of Whirry Laboratories on the day before Henry Gorrell-Barnes of Morgan Grenfell took off for Los Angeles. This was a very encouraging report. It showed copper values ranging from 1.99% to 5.27%, silver from 9.9 to 27.1 ounces, gold from 0.1 to 0.31 ounces and platinum group metals from 11.7 to 60.1 ounces per ton. These results however were based mainly on ten boreholes drilled to a depth of only 60 feet, which most experts would consider insufficient to 'prove' reserves.

Precisely why Ken Howarth flew Gorrell-Barnes half way round the world for a day trip to the El Sobrante mine and Corona was not entirely clear at the time. It seemed at first to be prompted by Austin International's need, after the resignation of its advisers Keyser Ullmann, for a merchant bank to back its claims. What did not emerge until later was that Austin also needed someone to cough up £1 million in a hurry, which would enable the group to develop its multi-metal prospect without having to pass the hat round shareholders for the necessary cash. (After two dud profit forecasts, their response might have been less than enthusiastic.)

Howarth's gamble very nearly came off. Henry Gorrell-Barnes, though an old hand at dissecting balance sheets, was obviously out of his element in the San Jacinto hills. 'I'm not a mining expert', he admitted later. 'It looked just like any other mine. There was a crushing machine working with concentrates coming out. It was very confusing'. Gorrell-Barnes seems to have been given something of a run-around. He did meet Hugh E. Whirry but, rather surprisingly, 'only to say hallo'. Despite the confusion, however, he was rather taken with the project. When he returned to London, he recommended 'in enthusiastic terms' that Morgans should provide the finance.

But Morgan Grenfell had been in the merchant banking business for a long time and didn't fancy taking a £1 million plunge without testing the water more thoroughly. Nobody had heard of Hugh E. Whirry, he didn't seem to be a front-rank geological analyst and the corporate finance department prudently decided to take a second opinion. Before long, Morgan's had made up its mind. 'We have not been, are not now and have no intention of being advisers or backers to the company', managing director Derrick Pease reported flatly. 'The purpose of the trip, from the bank's standpoint, was simply to assess El Sobrante as shareholders in Austin International'.

This was not generally known when Ken Howarth took the chair at Austin's annual meeting on January 19th, however. And to those who made the trip to the Bowden Hotel, six miles outside Manchester, Howarth looked the very picture of confidence. Despite the company's vicissitudes, its shares had jumped from a 1969 'low' of 62½p to nudge 95p before the Stock Exchange quotation suspended on January 16th at the board's request. He asserted that there really was a 'crock of gold' at the end of the Californian rainbow. And from the black silky recesses of a gunmetal sample case, he produced his lipstick-size ingots of gold and platinum and silver. It was an adroitly theatrical touch.

At this point, the ferrets of the U.K. financial press finally woke up and started rushing off in all directions. The Investor's Chronicle telephoned Hugh Whirry in Los Angeles, who obligingly reported that Austin's lucky strike was even better than he had first thought. Its ore was now showing 40 ounces of silver per ton. More enterprisingly, the Sunday Telegraph instructed a local correspondent to go and knock on his office door at 2609 North Main Street. Mr Whirry had shut up shop for a while, as it happened, but the Telegraph stringer meticulously described the scruffy interior visible through his fly-blown window. It didn't look like a first-class laboratory.

Howarth was not offering any more free trips to El Sobrante, even to concerned investors like John Ormond of Surinvest. (By now this young City gun-slinger was by no means certain that his 18% stake in Austin International was quite such a sure investment but trying to convince himself that it might work out as a copper mine.) So the *Sunday Times* despatched its New York correspondent Cal McCrystal out to the West Coast with instructions to hightail it for the hills and find that goldurned mine. It turned out to be a rather taller order than anyone at Thomson House imagined.

After some alarms and excursions, he cabled back: 'Security guards with grim faces and walkie-talkie radios patrol the miles of fencing encircling the El Sobrante mine, 50 miles east of Los Angeles. They have been instructed to turn away all visitors anxious to test the extraordinary claims of the mine's new owners that vast deposits of platinum and other precious metals have been found and stockpiled. Yesterday they even prohibited officials from the County Assessor's department from entering. These officials had only just learned of the El Sobrante mystery and after some difficulty in locating the site below a ridge in Temescal Canyon they drove over a hazardous mountain dirt track to see for themselves'. 'The security guards, having seen their credentials, turned them away from the 40 acre property', McCrystal added, 'and told them to apply in writing to the owners for permission to enter'.

His own excursion to the El Dorado of the 20th Century was not without its difficulties, which he chronicled in a style by John Buchan out of Ernest Hemingway. 'Finding the mine was not easy. It is hidden away behind 3,000 foot peaks which this week were shrouded in fog. A journey on foot through gullies and up steep boulder-strewn slopes carries the danger of rattle-snake bites. And the only routes accessible by jeep are blocked off and guarded'.

But it takes more than grim-faced guards and rattlers to deter our Cal. 'Brusquely ordered away by the guards, I managed by an extremely circuitous route to travel by jeep to a high ridge overlooking the mystery mine', he reported. 'It is a gaping hole almost half way up a steep hillside. From my vantage point, a small amount of sand-coloured material appeared to have been dumped near the entrance. On the canyon floor, a new-looking flat-topped building had been built. On the hill facing the mine is a long caravan and car-port. *Apart from the security guards, there was no activity. During the time I watched, no-one entered or left the shaft'.*

Nobody would dispute Ken Howarth's right to protect Austin's property, of course, though it was difficult to see what he was protecting the site against. It is impossible to high-jack a mine, after all. And if anyone did plan to make off with a few pounds of rough platinum, they would not find it easy to load up the necessary ton or two of ore and get away undetected. What was particularly significant about Cal McCrystal's account, though, was the apparently small ore stockpile and the absence of any mining activity. It was possible that the lads were taking a day off. It was equally possible that they had staged a special demonstration for Morgan Grenfell.

While security guards were keeping nosey parkers off his patch in California, Howarth was running into flak in London. Not from people who thought that El Sobrante (Spanish for 'the left-over' or 'the surplus') was a multi-million charade, oddly enough, but from businessmen who reckoned that he and Wayne Chambers might be on to something really good and were determined not to be left out!

At the height of the speculative hysteria over Austin International, some optimists quite seriously believed that the weather-beaten Oklahoman could trigger off an international currency crisis single-handed by producing gold for less than $5 an ounce.

But who *was* this mystery man Chambers who could apparently transform every slag heap from Arkansas to Zambia into a fortune? Wayne Chambers had worked on several old mines in Nevada, Mexico and Alaska. He was a bit of a loner, shutting himself up virtually in solitary confinement while he formulated solutions to extract valuable metal from uneconomic ore. (No amazing successes were recorded.) His home, just 10 miles down the road from El Sobrante at Fontana, was unostentatiously middle-class, apart from the gold Cadillac parked in the driveway. His professional reputation was . . . problematic. Twelve months earlier, he had approached a local rock quarry official with a project 'that turned out to be a farce'. The official declined to expand on this terse remark.

Despite the hysteria 6,000 miles away in London, the reaction of the copper mine's neighbors was somewhat less supercharged. For example, experts at the American Cement Association, which had a research center at Riverside, when told about Howarth's remarkable claims for El Sobrante, simply burst out laughing. Gold and silver had been found recently in the mountainous area of Riverside County known as El Sobrante de San Jacinto. But only in small quantities. The last significant discovery in Southern California had been in around 1964, when a retired bricklayer struck both in the old Good Hope Mine. But that was over in the Gavilian Hills, a range several miles beyond the San Jacinto ridges.

Gold is a historical part of California's rich pattern. More than $1 million worth of bullion was extracted from Good Hope Mine, for example, in the gold rush from 1874 to 1900. Even today small men can still, very occasionally, make it big. It's a local variant of the Great American Dream, which gives the odd pensioner an active interest in life and a handy excuse to get away from the wife for whole days at a time. And just as the retired bricklayer hit pay-dirt in them thar Hills, so retired plumber Wesley Collins (the Austin prospect's previous owner) might possibly have picked a good spot in El Sobrante. *Except* for those platinum assay figures. Nobody had ever found that much platinum *anywhere*.

For an impartial analyst, Hugh E. Whirry certainly went overboard for the prospect. Though he did not appear to have grasped the name, spelling it variously El Sebrinte and El Sobrinte, he made up for this in sheer exuberance. 'An orebody of this proved extent and with the possibility and probability of such additional ore at depth with the probability of its increasing in richness at greater depth', he burbled, 'makes this one of the best mining prospects I have seen in California'.

Straying rather from his remit, he also put in a few good words for the mining gear and the secret process. 'The mill is of high quality equipment, well arranged to do its job of processing the ore', he added. 'In making my assays, the same process was used as that for which the mill is set up: that is the new process worked out and perfected by Mr Wayne Chambers. In these days of high inflation, the remarkable cheapness of his extraction and recovery of copper and silver is something very much to be praised. *The process is in my opinion worth many millions of dollars to any user licensed to install it.* I discovered that the ore from the Cyprus mine is also amenable to this same process. It should therefore add millions of dollars profit to that operation. . . .'

Chambers had apparently brought a couple of bags of 'samples' back from the Troodos Mountains in Cyprus. In almost miraculous fashion, Whirry assayed Group 1 at up to 51.3% copper with gold (up to 6.7 ounces per ton) and platinum (up to 3.3 ounces) thrown in. And Group 2 was even better. It assayed up to 49.9% chrome with a platinum content of up to 12.8 ounces per ton. For some reason, Ken Howarth did not disclose these figures at the time. After the previous *Sunday Times* exposé, even a mining novice like Henry Gorrell-Barnes of Morgan Grenfell might have smelled a rat. (Cyprus was supposed to be a chrome mine, wasn't it?)

But the platinum values disclosed for El Sobrante and the neighboring Austin prospect were even more spectacular. El Sobrante ores apparently showed up to 60.8 ounces of platinum group metals per ton, never dropping below 11.9 ounces, while the Austin stockpile assayed up to 61.6 ounces and 'random samples through vein downhill' averaged 36.4 ounces per ton. To be on the 'conservative' side Whirry's report estimated the Austin stockpile at 30,000-

40,000 tons instead of 300,000 tons. But by this time, even the most credulous reporters were treating Howarth's optimistic figuring with considerable reserve. And those platinum assays really blew the gaff.

The theoretical arithmetic of the situation was positively mind-bending. If Austin/El Sobrante had 300,000 tons of ore averaging 30 ounces of platinum per ton piled up at Corona, this was equivalent to approximately *six times* the entire United States stockpile of this precious metal. All Howarth and Chambers had to do was extract the stuff and they would be rich beyond the dreams of Aberystwyth. As Dr Douglas Morton of the US Geological Survey, who doubled as assistant professor at the University of California, remarked 'I said there was supposedly over a billion dollars worth of platinum in that stockpile. And if there was that much, they wouldn't be wasting their time talking to me.'

But as Dr Morton told Judge Charles Lawson at the Old Bailey trial of James Kenneth Howarth in 1975, 'For the geological environment, the values purported for platinum were just ludicrous'. Platinum is an odd metal. Although alluvial platinum from Alaskan rivers can pan out at 85% pure or even better, crude ore with a platinum content of 60 ounces a ton is something that prospectors would sell their souls for. And the major Rustenburg mine in South Africa is commercially satisfied to extract platinum from its ore-body at a mere *quarter-ounce* per ton, helped by the inter-mingled nickel. Douglas Morton was right. This amazing San Jacinto extravaganza was just plain ludicrous.

Howarth's financial credibility was not helped in February, 1970 by disclosure of how he and Chambers had acquired El Sobrante. Both 40-acre sections had, it emerged, been acquired on the instalment plan. Austin bought its half for $250,000, paying $150,000 cash down with further repayments of $3,000 a month. But it acquired this prospect not from the estate of Wes Collins (deceased) but from the hands of Wayne Chambers (very much alive), who had bought the so-called 'east half' from his widow

Mrs Maxine Collins. Howarth and Chambers had acquired the other half for $250,000 on much easier terms, $3,000 down and $1,500 a month for the next 14 years!

To confuse the issue still further, the original (El Sobrante) deal had been carried out by a Howarth/Chambers company known as Magpie Investments, officially based on the Oklahoman's home address in Fontana. And the money for Austin's purchase was channelled through another such Bahamas-registered outfit. It was not easy to establish whose money was being used for what deal, though it rather looked as if Howarth and Chambers had managed to finance the easy-payments purchase of their half by overcharging Austin for its piece of the action. However, their prospects of laying hands on £6½ million worth of Austin shares were by now receding fast.

Whatever other City institutions may have felt about this tangled California situation, Lloyds Bank finally decided that enough was enough. Ken Howarth was removed from his executive position with Austin International on March 6th, 1970, and on the 16th the bank appointed a Receiver. With remarkable swiftness, the Board of Trade announced that Austin would be officially investigated. And on April 3rd, barrister John Lloyd Eley and accountant Dennis Garrett were appointed Inspectors. For a change, the Board of Trade was not worried about the effect of such overt action. Austin was found to have debts of more than £1 million. It was almost all over bar the counting.

Even so, Howarth incredibly kept right on pitching for El Sobrante! He had to, for, thanks to some hefty purchases of Austin shares, he was into his London stockbrokers for a daunting £135,000. Less than a month before he was ejected from the Austin chair, however, he managed to persuade Chris Spence to lend *Chambers* $70,000 for this miracle mine in return for the American's joint guarantee on the combined ($165,000) loan account. And in late March, the cheeky devils tapped poor Spence again to peddle dollar shares of El Sobrante Mining Corporation in the U.K. Amazingly, the Bank of England granted permission. Spence sold $100,000 worth and sent the proceeds to Chambers via the Bank of America, Foothill Mango branch. 'Spence has told us that when he arranged for the sale of these shares he remained convinced that the mine was valuable and a commercial proposition', the Inspectors later reported, 'and that Chambers was a person he could trust'.

Seldom was trust more badly misplaced. Wayne Chambers was not a member of the Stock Exchange and did not subscribe to its worthy motto 'Dictum meum pactum' ('My word is my bond'). Indeed, he seemed to prefer the unauthorized version 'Dictum meum rectum'. For over the next few months, this simple Oklahoma engineer ran everyone pretty ragged.

Further eccentric efforts were made to secure a 'promising' (but more authentic) geological appraisal of El Sobrante. First, a Los Angeles engineering geologist was asked to have a go. He hired the unqualified Barney Eglit to act as 'resident geologist', recommended three-phase development and spoke encouragingly of a 'supergene-enriched zone' discovered at depth by core-drilling methods. Dr Morton of the US Geological Survey did not find this scientifically credible, either, though it was difficult to be categorical. Because Chambers, contrary to traditional practice, did not keep core material on site.

Several assay reports were submitted. Most showed low metal values but one dated June 2nd was quite remarkable, indicating a quarter-ounce of gold and up to 43 ounces of silver per ton. 'Five samples were assayed on this occasion', Messrs Eley and Garrett noted, 'and these were described by a partner of the firm as what appeared to be treated ore or ore that had been altered in appearance and certainly different in structure to all previous samples brought to the laboratory allegedly from the site'.

Whoever gave this ore the treatment, unfortunately could not be established.

Then, in 1970, Ken Howarth and Wayne Chambers fell out. Howarth tried to put El Sobrante Mining Corporation into receivership, complaining that (as the owner of 501,000 shares) he was dissatisfied with Chambers' administration. Chambers hit back, asserting that (contrary to their 50/50 agreement) Howarth hadn't put a cent into the company whereas he had chipped in more than $316,000. (Howarth had tried previously to flimflam more than $316,000 out of Austin with a false bill for road-building, flood repairs and so forth but he later claimed to have been robbed of exactly this sum in an abortive Mexican gold deal.) Anyway, Chambers won. And when the Austin receiver proved unwilling to keep up the $3,000-a-month payments, Wayne foreclosed on its 40 acres.

It was not until February, 1972 that the report on Austin International by HM Inspectors John Lloyd Eley and Dennis Garrett was published, by which time Ken Howarth had prudently emigrated to the United States and his erstwhile associates in the City of London were doing their best to forget about him. This was a detailed, fascinating and genuinely hard-hitting document. It baldly accused both men of theft. Howarth had stolen £43,360, by their reckoning, not to mention the £10,640-odd spent on his house, and Chambers had 'in all probability' stolen upwards of $200,000. Both had engaged in a deliberate conspiracy to defraud.

What made this (by then) Department of Trade and Industry report so remarkable was not so much the way that the Inspectors had painstakingly checked through the figures. (They noted for example, that in the 13 months to January 31st, 1970 Ken Howarth had claimed a grand total of £21,600 expenses including £8,912 disbursed in the United States, and that the E. J. Austin board, which had always seemed complacently happy to give their wandering executive whatever he wanted, had in fact authorized only £18,700 worth of this impressive outlay.) But the strong point of these official investigators was honest to goodness common sense.

Their down-to-earth approach was typified by the brief summary of their impressions of El Sobrante and the 'east half' at Corona, which had dazzled and/or confused other visitors. 'On our visit to the property', they reported, 'we were struck by the fact that whereas all the apparent constituents for a working operation were present, that is to say a stockpile of rock, a mill and the Chambers processing plant, *there was absolutely no sign that any output of metals on even a modest scale was being or ever had been produced.* And they added: 'A few fruit-preserving jars containing copper powder were shown to us as being the product of the process'.

That Ken Howarth's 'crock of gold' had dwindled to a few jars of powdered copper did not, admittedly, come as any great surprise. But the fact that they were *fruit-preserving* jars reminded us that HM Inspectors were not dealing with (say) Consolidated Gold Fields but with an altogether more modest enterprise. Former owners Mr & Mrs Wes Collins, let's face it, were more accustomed to bottling fruit than refining gold. And the Inspectors shed a clear light on the two left-over mysteries of Austin International. How did Howarth almost fool Morgan Grenfell? And what exactly was the Chambers Process?

Henry Gorrell-Barnes of Morgan's, as he frankly admitted, is not a mining expert. He had seen the Chambers process in operation out there in the San Jacinto hills or, at least, he *thought* he had seen it in operation. 'He has told us that he saw a grey sludge turned into silver and copper and was convinced of its effectiveness', Messrs Eley and Garrett reported. 'He was given to understand that crushed material from the stockpile had been introduced into the processing machinery, but never actually saw any transfer of material into the process'.

From Howarth's viewpoint, Gorrell-Barnes was not supposed to know what went into the sludge. That would have ruined the whole trick.

But John Lloyd-Eley QC and Dennis Garrett FCA soon discovered what Wayne Chambers had up his sleeve.

'Invoices from chemical suppliers in the USA to Austins US show that in early January just prior to Gorrell-Barnes' visit to the site, 1,200 lbs of cuprous chloride, 25 lbs of silver nitrate, 1 oz of gold chloride, 100 sacks of half-ground salt, 4 lbs of copper sulphate and 2 barrels of copper powder were delivered to the site', they noted with meticulous precision.

For that crucial demonstration on January 12th, 1970, in other words, the California ooze was guaranteed to be copper-bottomed. And Morgan Grenfell were almost tempted to buy it.

'These materials have been explained by Chambers as catalysts to start his process working', the Inspectors added, 'but we take the view that they were delivered so that they could be introduced into the tank and provide the copper which was to be extracted'.

(When those invoices were discovered, Chambers must have known that the game was up but you have to give him credit for continuing with his bare-faced effrontery.) With cool, scientific detachment, the Inspectors' paragraph ends: 'It is within our knowledge that cuprous chloride is soluble in a salt solution and that a simple process of electrolysis would deposit copper particles on the electrodes'. Q.E.D.

In fact, Wayne Chambers' conjuring trick was not particularly complicated or original. Back in 1722, for example, Geoffrey the Elder had described some of the dodges used by false alchemists purporting to turn base metals into gold. 'They often used double-bottomed crucibles or cupels, lining the bottom with oxides of gold or silver, then covering it with an appropriate paste', he writes. 'They also sometimes made a hole in a lump of coal and poured gold or silver powder in it. Small grains or tiny ingots of silver were hidden inside lead, and reappeared when the lead was heated in a cupel. Gold that had been albified (whitened) in mercury was passed off as tin or silver. When mercury containing a quantity of zinc was passed over the red copper, the copper took on the color of gold. The nitric acids used in these operations contained gold and silver dissolved in them beforehand. . . .'

But the Chambers *process*, theoretically at least, was more than a simple matter of electrolysis. It was formally summarized in three brief provisional patent applications by Wayne Chambers. These several patent documents were handed to David Neylan, principal scientific officer at the Metropolitan Police forensic science laboratory. And with the air of a Jockey Club steward asked to officiate at a Donkey Derby, Neylan did his best to make sense of the oddities and contradictions of the 'Secret Mining Process' for which E. J. Austin had paid Wayne Chambers and Ronald Rietti £28,270. In the end, he gave it up as a bad job. 'The details of the patent application are a mixture of elementary old-fashioned chemistry and sheer chemical impossibility', he concluded. 'All the papers show a familiarity with antiquated chemical jargon together with a total lack of understanding of the subject'.

Though Ken Howarth was being investigated by Scotland Yard in the Spring of 1971, it was $2\frac{1}{2}$ years before he was busted and four years had elapsed before he appeared at the Old Bailey. He used the breathing space to advantage being energetically involved in a number of bizarre international capers. During this period he was associated with a wide range of businessmen – from US millionaire Nicholas du Pont to Dutch bank swindler Walter Voss.

In the summer of 1972, for example, Howarth was characteristically trying to do three things at once. He was acting as financial adviser to US millionaire Nicholas du Pont, he was promoting an idea called Le Grand Club International, designed to attract US bank deposits offshore by offering 'free' Caribbean holidays instead of interest. And he was attempting to raise extra funds by cashing a $200,000 certificate of deposit from the Bankers Deposit & Finance Corporation Ltd, of the Virgin Islands, guaranteed by W. J. Voss of Intercambio International Bancario of Panama.

But a re-excursion into platinum dealing in 1971 had been frustrated when a West German firm checked with the Union Bank of Switzerland. 'These people are very without belief and very unfriendly', it reported to Howarth. 'If you will make with us business in platinum and other metals please note that it must be very serious and with full trust'. Possibly influenced by Wally Voss and his business associate Petronella Gruyters (alias stripper Lady Cadillac), Howarth seems to have transferred his attention from imaginary metals to bogus banking including his very own Uniman Banking Corporation of Panama.

Come 1973 Ken Howarth surfaced again, still with Nicholas du Pont, but also claiming to represent a consortium of Swiss bankers headed by one Dr Icklé with upwards of $100 million to lend on very attractive terms. Two young London wheeler-dealers Adrian Nash and David Michaels took the bait, flew to New York and started non-stop negotiating. Howarth was pretty choosey, however, about the borrowers. Rothschilds were OK, he conceded, but a major UK property group was dismissed out of hand. For some reason, he was keener to lend to an offshoot of E. Alec Colman Investments – particularly if there was a guarantee from Jim Slater.

It was not until Nash Michaels Associates had practically sewn up $40 million worth of loan business to earn themselves a prospective commission of $1,690,000 (then worth £684,000) – that the penny dropped. Michaels suddenly remembered my *Sunday Times* article about Howarth's unorthodox banking activities. As a result, my colleague Lorana Sullivan contacted the amiable fraudsman. He was quite happy to talk over old times, claiming to have been made 'the absentee whipping-boy' for Austin by J. Slater, Esq. and it seemed that the Colman 'deal' was intended to settle this personal score. Meanwhile, I telephoned Dr Max Icklé, former head of the Schweitzer National Bank foreign department. 'I do not know these people and I am not involved in such a transaction', he said. 'Sometimes people are misusing names to make things a little more creditable'.

But not even Ken Howarth could stay loose for ever. In November, 1970 he was arrested by the police in New York and charged (a) with conspiring to possess $40,000 worth of stolen securities and (b) with making false statements to the US Immigration & Naturalization Service. Each carried a maximum penalty of five years' imprisonment plus a $10,000 fine. Instead, he was deported to London. But by a strange coincidence, the passengers in the adjoining seats on the flight back were Detective Inspector Derek Brown and Detective Sergeant Mervyn Atkinson of the Fraud Squad. When the plane touched down at Heathrow, he was promptly arrested again.

Which brought the absconding chairman of E. J. Austin International in 1975 to the dock at the Old Bailey, facing no fewer than 13 charges of fraud ranging from dishonestly attempting to obtain some £6½ million worth of shares from his company to dishonestly obtaining a £30,000 loan from his stockbroker. (His 'evil influence' Wayne Chambers escaped prosecution.) Like El Sobrante, West Court Two is an afterthought. It is a small and rather crowded room over the road from the regular Old Bailey, an ironically drab setting for the not so grand finale of a colorful City fraud that for a few exciting weeks had almost everyone counting potential Californian profits by the million. On May 15th, 1975 Howarth was found guilty on 11 counts and sentenced to five years imprisonment.

Wonderful prospects in faraway places are always tempting, of course. And there is something rather special about the idea of extracting precious metals from cheap rock. But as El Sobrante showed, there can be big differences between the preliminary report and the final survey. 'I did not see any platinum', Dr Morton told the Court. 'I would have settled for anything silver and shiny at that point'.

It is a risky business, as Ken Howarth always knew. 'In mining, you sometimes think you'll get millions of tons and it turns out to be a few thousand – or the other way round', he once remarked.

He never said a truer word. Next time, Ken, the lunch is on me.

THE IRISH TRADE-MARK TOUCH

This case is included because it perfectly illustrates the blurred line between the con-trick and a nice legitimate bit of sharp business.

Back in the 30's an especially enterprising Irish lawyer observed that the big American consumer goods companies were beginning to 'invade' Europe. Companies like Procter and Gamble, General Foods, Kelloggs were setting up European subsidiaries to market their products in the old world. Naturally they always tried to use the brand names and basic pack designs with which they had built their companies in the US. It was reassuring for the ex-patriot management to see the familiar names and it saved money on design and advertising to have this standardization. (The only exceptions were where the US name turned out to be a term of abuse in the foreign language.)

Equally naturally, they started their operations in the biggest potential markets – England, Scandinavia, France – and everywhere they set up they registered their brand names as protected Trade-Marks.

Eire was, of course, a low priority for immediate development – and here was the opportunity our sharp-eyed lawyer saw. He began unobtrusively to register as *his* trade-marks every single top American brand name he could find. Over the years he built himself a handsome collection.

When the advance guard of the American marketeers arrived in Eire to capture the 'hearts and minds' of the local peasantry with their superior products, they were more than a little miffed to discover that their old and trusted names couldn't be used – unless, of course, they bought the name from the innocent-eyed country lawyer. They always did.

BERGMAN –
THE CASE OF THE FRIENDLY RABBI

by Fred Lawrence Guiles

New York and San Francisco have long cherished a
particular kind of rogue – the scoundrel with generous
impulses. The robber barons of the nineteenth century might
be shunned in their home communities, but they could move
to either coast and build mansions, be accepted in the best
clubs, endow museums, and feel assured that posterity would
measure the good along with the bad. These two cities had
and have forgiving souls. Felons can return from prison
to either place and pick up the pieces of their lives, in some
cases as though they had only taken a winter holiday in
Florida.

In January, 1977, a tall, very pale man, an apparition of
a man who appeared to have been brushed with marble
dust, stepped from a car onto the pavement in front of an
apartment house near the corner of West 100th Street on
New York's Riverside Drive. It was a blustery day and the
man did not stop to look about him, across the little park
of trees to the West Side Highway or the Hudson River. He
sought only the warmth and relative comfort of his over-
sized apartment. He had seen enough of weather to last him
several lifetimes. Having just emerged from three and a half
months in a Federal penitentiary during the icy heart of what
had gone on record as the coldest winter in a hundred years,
he needed more pampering than his limousine had afforded.

His name was Rabbi Bernard Bergman, and at sixty-five
years of age, that time when most Americans are receiving
gold watches and testimonial dinners, he was now listed in
official documents as an ex-con. Because of his 'excellent

public works,' which it seemed had consisted chiefly in appropriating funds intended for the aged and poor, the Federal government had granted him the favor of spending his prison term in an open facility where the gates were never shut, and where an astonishingly low figure of less than two per cent annually skipped out to freedom through them. But the benevolent Bureau of Prisons had not counted on the new ice age, which had arrived in November, halfway through the Rabbi's stay at the Allenwood Pen, and there was still snow on the ground when he left. Below zero temperatures were a common occurrence, and it didn't matter that there were 4,000 acres on which to walk. Few ventured outside except to move from one building to another. It was a time of huddling close to any available heat and bundling at night into heavy bedclothes in the barracks where the inmates slept. Those who decried the 'injustice' of handing down a sentence of less than four months for the theft of close to three million dollars were too chilled in their own homes and apartments to complain further. The few who knew that the Rabbi was doing his time in the desolate snowy wastes of Pennsylvania began to worry that his 'light sentence' might turn out to be a more devastating ordeal than the elderly, unhardened firsttimer could endure.

But Rabbi Bergman was made of stern stuff. His face was austere, at times forbidding, as though chiseled from granite with only a little tuft of beard sprouting from his lower lip to suggest that he was made of flesh. His pallor might have come from incarceration, yet he had been just as pale before his last stay of sentence was denied and the handcuffs went on, the traditional humiliation when spiriting a man from freedom into enforced confinement. There were two or three stays granted by the generous Federal judge.

Only two years earlier, there were few Jewish New Yorkers who had not heard of Rabbi Bergman, and not as a thief of public funds and 'a trafficker in human misery' but as one of the most successful fund-raisers for Jewish causes anywhere; as one of a three man presidium of the world

Mizrachi movement, an organization devoted to the advancement of orthodox Jewry. He raised money for Soviet Jews, and there were few political leaders partisan to the cause of Israel and Zionism who had not at one time been the recipient of campaign funds from the Rabbi. Richard Nixon and Rockefeller, too, had received contributions. There was nothing small-time about Rabbi Bergman.

And many of the politicans were grateful. Indeed, their gratitude was such that when the Rabbi finally went down, crashing resoundingly since he was, after all, quite a big man, numerous clay toes were squashed.

Bergman was not just a man of means; he was a millionaire several times over. In 1973, his own accountant (later sentenced himself for false entry style bookkeeping, a system much frowned upon by the authorities) officially confirmed that his employer was worth more than $25,000,000, an impressive figure especially when one realizes that it grew from such modest 'scratch,' as sourdoughs in the Yukon would say. With an initial $25,000, or about what a semi-detached might go for in one of the less desirable sections of Flatbush, Bergman acquired a home in Jerusalem, real estate all over New York, New Jersey and Connecticut. A little collateral seemed to have gone a long way. But most of it was in nursing homes, and that was a fatal miscalculation.

They say that old age and chronic illness were handled better in America during the 19th century. Then there was no thought of allowing one's parents or grandparents to die in an institution. It was mostly managed at home, where advanced age was respected. Movies, often with Martha Scott, showed us charming rural villages where everyone cared and even went on caring in the cemetery. If, in fact, it was not unusual for a bedridden, old family member to be confined to an ugly upper chamber and only be seen at feeding time or for an occasional scrub-up, still there were the lucky ones whose families sent the children up for some conversation with grandma. Many youngsters genuinely liked their grandparents and felt an awe in their presence.

Then there was no shoving them down subway steps and grabbing their purses or clubbing them from behind as they made their way upstairs to a flat with no elevator.

But in mid twentieth century America, human values had deteriorated. Divorce was the norm and there were fewer children being brought up by both parents than at any time since the founding of the Republic. Religious ties had eroded. Younger members of families were moving out of nests earlier. Dropping out. The emphasis was on the individual and his needs, rarely on the family. Books on how to be selfish, intimidate others, and say 'no' proliferated. Every promotional gimmick devisable was being used to make the nation youth-conscious. Nearly half the population would make a major move every three years. During a housing boom in the nineteen fifties, there was some emphasis being placed by builders and architects on an 'in-law suite or apartment' in larger homes. By the mid sixties, this had become as quaint as the Keeping Room of the 18th and 19th century Colonial house.

As families disintegrated, the elderly were among the first victims. Slick evangelists tried to reverse the trend but these men were part of the ghastly machinery, packaging morality like frozen peas. The government realized that something had to be done, and it very quickly was.

The name of the legislation was Medicaid, and in operation it meant that any elderly person could enter a nursing facility, either public or private, and his or her care would be underwritten by the government. It was restricted to the truly needy. If you had as much as $1,800 (£1,000) in the bank or in bonds, you were too rich to qualify. For those who had built up a nest egg, large or small, against old age and its terrors, they could enter a nursing home, where a semi-private room might average $1,000 a month, including meals, medications and all services, and find that in two years or less, as much as $25,000 had been consumed by room and board. Then, under the Medicaid laws, they were automatically drawn into the program, where they would remain until they died.

It suddenly became more profitable to build a nursing home than a chain of pizzerias. The elderly were up for grabs, and heads of large nursing home syndicates, such as those controlled by Bernard Bergman, regularly employed 'head hunters,' whose job it was to comb through patient registries at local hospitals and determine if any of the older patients could be persuaded to move into a particular nursing home upon discharge or, if senile, taken there willy-nilly amid a flurry of paper-work they did not understand.

Once in a nursing home, it was next to impossible to get out again. When you are in a wheel-chair or you walk with a cane or an aluminum walker, it is quite unlikely that you are going to return to keeping even a bed sitter or a one-room flat.

There are several options open to the ambulatory old. There are 'retirement villages,' some of them such as Rossmore's Leisure World very comfortable indeed with one and two bedroom cottages into which you may bring your own things; golf courses on the property; elegant dining out accommodations or convenience kitchens in your cottage; shuttle buses forever making rounds of the vast acreage; security guards who challenge any stranger and patrolled walls surrounding the entire village. If you prefer to remain in your old home or apartment, it is unwise to venture out since there are young hoods from about twelve up who do nothing but prey on the aged. To resolve that considerable problem and to help those who become chronically ill at home, there is a food program known as 'Meals on Wheels,' whereby most of their weekly dinners are supplied at cost, delivered to their doors still hot from special warming trays.

For at least a hundred years or more, the nursing home was for many elderly an emotion-charged subject. There were attractive, well-managed Homes run by the Masons, by the Eastern Star, by the Presbyterian, Baptist, Methodist, Catholic, and Unitarian Churches. There were Jewish Homes by the hundreds. The cautious laid plans as early as their thirties for admission into one of these Homes since there was a long waiting list. Those who called the turns in their lives by flipping a coin looked upon Homes as 'institutions' where they would be deprived of all their rights and possessions. 'They confiscate everything, you know.'

By the mid-nineteen sixties, the Homes began to look attractive even to retired madams. Street crime had turned America's cities into battle zones. Grocery deliveries skyrocketed, but a favorite gambit of a hood was to pose as a delivery boy. Visits to a doctor's office became a matter of concern to offspring since you could count on mom's having her purse snatched at least once every two years and being knocked down in the encounter at least once every four years. The only legitimate beneficiaries of all this mayhem were dentists to replace knocked-out teeth, oculists to repair broken frames and shattered lenses, and those doctors the ladies were on their way to or from in the first place.

So with the advantages of urban living reduced to near zero, nursing homes suddenly looked far more inviting. The trouble was that until Medicaid came along, few could afford them.

Once the law was enacted, the Homes became the fastest growing industry in America after the computer. It became a symbol of hope even though often encased in ochred brick with a design that was more penal than residential. Nursing home guests quickly overcame their surrender shock, that trauma that grips anyone who realizes he is now institutionalized. Many came to look upon their new accommodations, however colorless and ungracious, as shelters from an impossible world outside. They made friends within the Home. Many resumed religious ties cut as far back as childhood. Bingo was rampant; bridge was pursued as in the heyday of Culbertson; occasional movies were shown; carolers sang at Christmastide; and there was the constant babble of someone's television from morning 'till night. By 1975 in New York City, it was costing the government between $15,000 and $20,000 a year for *each* Medicaid patient.

It would be gratifying to report that for all of that money, and it totalled hundreds of millions altogether, the elderly were getting the finest care that money could buy. In actual fact, doctor visits were infrequent in many Homes to the point of negligence, and in one, the cost of food for each patient was only 32¢ a day.

But skullduggery, while deplorable, rarely succeeds indefinitely unless the Church or organized crime is involved. Governments fall, embezzlers are jailed, cheats are exposed. In 1974, the Watergate Trial held America enthralled. Many found its revelations hard to accept. This sort of thing happened in Latin America, in southern Europe, wherever the sun shone on the heads of crooked politicians. After the fog of doubt began to lift, there was very little in American government that was not scrutinized.

Scandals were not new within the nursing home industry, but now it seemed that every Federal and state agency was taking a magnifying glass to its faults and omissions. One name kept appearing again and again. *Bergman. Bergman. Bergman.* A spot check by the Social Services Department auditors in New York City found that Social Security checks forwarded by the post office to nursing homes from the patients' former addresses were simply dropped into the bank account of the institution as 'profit,' likewise funds belonging to patients who had died. Bergman's nursing home records all but defied examination. Ledger entries failed to correspond with bank checks; rents were grossly inflated. Investigators began to run a tally of sums misappropriated by the Bergman syndicate. It began to exceed two million dollars.

As accusations mounted, so too did the outcry from the Rabbi's friends. It was, said a professor of law who had known Bergman for years, a case of character assassination. Bernard Bergman had many fanatically loyal friends. Perhaps today, as he fights to keep his nursing home empire together, they are still his friends. Bergman was a man with a hundred decent traits, a genius for making and keeping friends. It seems such a pity he turned out to be a crook. He was a good loser. When an investigator said his homes were fire traps and slapped him with a violation, he accepted it stoically. There was no fuss in defeat, that smokescreen so many guilty ones throw up about themselves.

In shadow, he rather resembled the sinister Sidney Greenstreet, that huge actor who so urbanely attempted to dispatch the likes of Humphrey Bogart to their doom but not before offering them a drink to their taste and some civilized chitchat. Bergman only looked sinister at bay, when live television cameras recorded his agony at having to take the 5th Amendment before a joint congressional (state and Federal) investigating committee. Then he looked like a highly-bred animal caught in a rude trap.

To know Bernard Bergman was to love him. Friends said that so often about the Rabbi, if you were in America on a first visit from Tibet, you might believe that, upon meeting this elder of Zion, the phrase had been invented to describe him. Nothing upset Bergman more than meeting someone who didn't like him, and there was a good deal of Old World charm about him. His chief pleasure was sitting across from a friend in a good bistro or coffee house where he could chat and watch people. The paradox was that this eager curiosity about nearly everyone resided just behind a face that reflected a melancholy common to rabbis obsessed with the Diaspora.

Bergman enjoyed the role of benefactor to society's unwanted. To him, they were not nameless. They were human beings who hurt more than most because of the inroads of age. He was old himself. He was one of them. Perhaps it was the magnitude of his empire that made him forget to have fire exits checked or fire-retardant doors installed, roach-infested storage rooms fumigated, or communicable ill isolated from the other guests. When Medicaid was billed by Bernard Bergman for nurses who did not truly exist, when losses were shown on income tax statements when in fact there were profits of sometimes 40% on his investment, that did not harm those guests in his care. Or so he must have believed. How could billing and book-keeping possibly matter to them? Had a single patient ever come to the admissions office asking what Medicaid was being billed for his or her care? Most of his 'guests,' as long-term patients are called, were women because they, with few exceptions, lived longer, and few women are preoccupied with audits and financial accountability.

He was so generous with his time *and* with his money, you could very nearly forgive him for his crimes against the helpless; almost as one forgave Alfred Bernhard Nobel for all the deaths and suffering wrought by his munitions because of his peace prizes. (Nobel and the Rabbi shared a name, too.) Bergman gave away hundreds of thousands – to the cause of Zionism, to Soviet Jews needing money for transportation and for funds to tide them over, to the United Jewish Appeal. His checkbook was always open. Due as much to this as to his Henry Ward Beecher style of public speaking, he was often called upon to speak at Jewish dinners. In September, 1974, when the Jewish press asked him for a statement on the eve of Rosh ha-Shanah (the Jewish New Year), Rabbi Bergman said: 'We live in a generation where the spirit is losing the battle . . . bringing with it all the ills of crass materialism.' The man had the tongue of a post-industrial revolution prophet. He could lie in his teeth and be believed.

Everyone knew he was rich, but there was no opulence about him. His homes in Jerusalem and on New York's no longer fashionable upper West Side were filled with large, comfortable furniture suited to his huge frame but with no eye on decor or what visiting friends and dignitaries might think. There was something almost deliberately unattractive about his personal accommodations. Perhaps something to keep the little dogs of conscience from nipping.

Besides, Bernard Bergman had come a very long way from his ghetto origins in Hungary. Born there in 1911, he was the only son of Shlomo Bergman and Gitel Leifer. There were rabbis on both sides for generations. Bernard's father died when the boy was five years old, and when he was nine, his mother married a cousin, Isak Leifer. His own name was changed to Leifer.

During the last great Jewish migration from central
Europe, the Leifers settled in Brooklyn. The year was 1929,
not a good year for America or for the western world. But
there was a personal gloom within the Leifer household
more insidious than any caused by hard times outside.
Young Bernard and his stepfather could not stand each
other. Bernard returned to Hungary, then – a step ahead of
the Nazi armies – settled in Czechoslovakia, where in 1937
he married Anna Weiss, the daughter of a family whose
fortune had been made in homes for the elderly. They moved
to Palestine, where he studied religion and was ordained a
rabbi. It was there he changed his name back to Bergman
and his stepfather was, in effect, dead for him, but not quite.
Family ties were strong in Bergman and even for the despised
Leifer he would reach down with a critical assist when
Leifer needed it most.

Like many of his decisions, this name-changing was
timely. In 1939, Isak Leifer was arrested in France for
attempting to smuggle 17 pounds of heroin concealed in
religious books from Marseilles to New York. Stepfather
Isak drew two years in a French prison, but was extradited
to New York and was lost to public view. Sometime in the
1950s, his stepson helped him back to respectability by
giving him small shares in various nursing homes then under
his control.

Bernard's mother Gitel pleaded guilty in New York as an
accomplice to the drug-smuggling attempt and received a
suspended sentence because of her many family responsibilities. At almost the same moment mother Gitel was
free to leave the courtroom, son Bernard was opening
a session of the Congress with a prayer. At that time,
he was chaplain of the Home of the Sons and
Daughters of Israel, a nursing home on East 12th Street in
Manhattan.

The post was obscure, but the rabbi was not. Adored by
the guests in the 12th Street home, he was admired all across
the city for his wisdom and compassion. Good works, real
or fancied, radiated from him. So impressed were the head

of the nursing home, Joseph Halpern, and his wife, Mollie, they bequeathed the bulk of their $60,000 estate to Bergman. But luck was not as constant as his nimbus and Mrs Halpern's sister contested the will, and when the suit was finally settled, Bergman received only $25,000.

Still, that was enough. The following year (1950), he was elected head of the Zionist organization, Hapoel Hamizrachi. It seemed a wise choice. He had a real gift for persuading people to hand over large contributions to this partisan cause.

Another benefactor in those early years of building a formidable public reputation was the owner of *The Jewish Morning Journal*, an influential Yiddish daily in New York. He asked Rabbi Bergman to become its editor and publisher. Two years later, the finances of this newspaper sank so low, it was sold at a considerable loss in moribund condition.

With his $25,000 in heritance and other funds never publicly accounted for, buildings were bought in New York and New Jersey. Mortgages were easily obtained from leading banks to renovate these structures into nursing homes. The plan was simple. Buy an old building with a great many rooms, install additional plumbing facilities, an institutional kitchen, a nurses' station on each floor, and then the doors were swung open for the old, mostly enfeebled and ill and, more often than not, cast out.

What lay ahead for many of them, while not precisely a page torn from Dante's *Purgatorio*, was an assault upon the body and sensibilities only by degree an improvement over war camps. A staff doctor at Kings County Hospital in Brooklyn testified before a Commission on Living Costs headed by Assemblyman Andrew Stein that elderly patients brought from nursing homes to the hospital were dehydrated, ulcerated, grossly infected, in shock, and suffering from a general lack of medical attention. Where was the money going besides to the several bank accounts and favorite philanthropies of Rabbi Bergman? The State Welfare Department ran a check on nursing home owner Charles Sigety, whose homes went by the corporate name of Florence Nightingale – no saint or samaritan was safe from these men's obsessive need to stand with great humanitarians! It was found that Sigety had billed Medicaid in 1972 for $40,571 for foreign travel, social club dues, opera tickets, wine and liquor. While Sigety was relaxing from the rigors of juggling his books, Mrs Esmeralda Santiago told investigators that her grandmother lived in filth and neglect at the Gramercy Park Nursing Home in one of New York's most exclusive residential areas until she was sent to a hospital, dying. As at Auschwitz, the dead were often the lucky ones.

Andrew Stein, once aroused, spent nearly all his waking hours pursuing the men who were hauling in these shipwrecked members of society for profit. Stein was extremely young, only 29, but Andy was a Jew who had everything Bernard Bergman had lacked in his own youth – money from his father, Jerry Finklestein, publisher of the New York Law Journal and for a long time a member of the City Planning Commission. Young Stein had changed his own name not because of domestic shifts as with the Bergman-Leifers, but because it sounded less ethnic in the exclusive clubs he was joining in Manhattan. He was barely twenty-five when he was first elected as a Democrat to the New York State Assembly – from the East Side's 'blue-stocking' district, the same political turf that had produced John Lindsay. And Andrew Stein was almost as handsome as Lindsay, marred from fashion model looks by a piercing glance, sharp enough to penetrate nearly any defense. If looks could kill, Andy Stein had them.

His stiletto glance belied his compassion. From his earliest days in the Albany Assembly, Stein was interested in problems of the dispossessed; first in nutrition and then in conditions at Willowbrook, an infamous institution on Staten Island for the retarded. By 1973, he was already looking into the nursing home industry.

One of Bernard Bergman's homes interested Stein and other investigators particularly. It was a tall, grim pile of stones built in the Victorian era (1884) as the New York

Cancer Hospital. Now, because of its neo-gothic architecture, it was known as the Towers Nursing Home. In 1971, it had been called unfit with 'atrocious' conditions by a Social Services employee named Amalia Crago, and she ruled Bergman 'unfit' to run any nursing home. But someone overruled Amalia Crago and literally overnight the objections were withdrawn. Who, Andrew Stein wondered?

There was a distressing pattern emerging. A home would be cited for numerous violations or its license withheld after an inspection; then word would come down from above and violations would be erased or a license granted. It happened so often during the period that Nelson Rockefeller was Governor of the state, and there were so many meetings between Bergman and other nursing home magnates and Rockefeller henchmen that a special state prosecutor appointed in 1975 felt compelled to mention the fact that corruption within the industry was 'rife' during that administration. It came as something of a shock to discover that a man so wealthy that his candidacy for president was immaculate as far as corruption was concerned, a man above even the possibility, allowed criminal neglect of the helpless by his political aides. The mystery remains, although there is no doubt that it did Rockefeller permanent political damage.

When the state (Andrew Stein Commission) and Federal (the Senate Commissions on Ageing and Long Term Care) were joined, Senator Charles Percy of Illinois glanced at the facts and said he would move to turn over the investigation to the Justice Department. He found that he and his colleagues were not simply looking into the kind of care being given the aged and infirm, they were staring at a ledger of shocking crime.

There was nothing new about appalling and substandard facilities within New York's nursing home industry. As far back as 1960 when Rockefeller was Governor, a two year investigation was completed by Civil Court Judge Louis Kaplan and forwarded to Mayor Robert Wagner, Criminal fraud was proven, but instead of prosecutions being mapped out by the city, the offenders, principally Bergman, Hollander and Sigety, were awarded increases in rates for welfare patients. It was very much a case of the murderer getting the chair and finding it to be a rare Louis XIV antique sent around to his home where he was sentenced to live rent-free. Judge Kaplan waited months and nothing happened; not even a reply was forthcoming. So he tried again two years later when the same old names and charges cropped up again, and once more nothing happened. That 1962 report revealed that without the city court's knowledge or consent 'the Welfare Department had given the nursing home industry two rate increases, totalling 45%, before attempting to recover any sums allegedly defrauded from the city by operators.'

So it was obvious that Bernard Bergman was a power. His money had bred it, but his own stature in the Jewish community sustained it. Or perhaps it was the other way around. He was pushing the same levers that have kept organized crime in control of scores of American cities, and of several state governorships – helping politicians to power with contributions and encouragement in the right places and, if absolutely necessary, outright bribes. In the case of Assemblyman Albert H. Blumenthal, Bergman allegedly attempted the latter.

The Blumenthal-Bergman relationship was the strangest aspect of the entire case. It was a situation so intricately interwoven with lies, deceit, evasion and occasional indignation and outrage, even today it is impossible to know with any certainty exactly what transpired. Suffice to say, the men's paths crossed at a critical juncture and Blumenthal is out of politics today. Perhaps that was one of the saddest results of the investigation since Blumenthal was a good man, apparently incorruptible.

Albert Howard Blumenthal, a New York liberal and the Albany Assembly majority leader, was indicted in December, 1975, charged with accepting a bribe from Bergman to pave the way for a license to open the Park

Crescent Nursing Home. That opening had been resisted by state and city inspectors on the ground that the building's renovation did not conform to the plans they had approved and that its hasty opening would endanger patients. Further, the authorities considered Bergman unfit to operate it, in light of his past record of violations and alleged fraud. Blumenthal testified that he had been approached by a lawyer for Bergman who asked that Blumenthal put in a kind word for the nursing home magnate. Blumenthal said he then had called Assemblyman Stanley Steingut, who knew Bergman well, to inquire about Bergman's reputation. State officials said that after that inquiry, Blumenthal accompanied Bergman to Albany, where before the head of the agency looking into the matter, he vouched for Bergman's good management of the notorious Towers Nursing Home, which in less than two years would be closed for a string of violations and was at that very moment being denounced by Miss Crago as 'atrocious' in its handling of patients. Blumenthal allegedly said 'the Towers is spotless.' A further revelation disclosed that Blumenthal was grouped with Attorney General Louis Lefkowitz (under Rockefeller) and Assemblyman Steingut in being 'very interested that Bergman project be approved and believed him to be a "very fine gentleman".'

Whatever was said, the machinery was still working. Almost before Bergman could get back to Manhattan, a four hour journey by car, Albany officials ordered their New York City office in charge of nursing homes to waive minor structural deficiencies and let Park Crescent open. Sometime later, according to testimony from Andrew Stein, young Assemblyman Stein was asked by democratic leader Steingut not to investigate nursing homes owned by Bergman. Steingut had been Rabbi Bergman's friend as far back as the early fifties and it is not surprising that he would feel protective toward him. But Steingut called Andy Stein 'a god-damned liar!'

So it was one politician's word against another's. And it was a little like David with his sling-shot at this point.

Steingut was running for the speakership of the Assembly in Albany. Despite the daily revelations in the press about his links with Bergman, Steingut won by a landslide. His only concession to public opinion was to surrender posts in the management of two insurance companies doing business with Bergman nursing homes. The lone dissenter to the Steingut appointment was Andrew Stein. It must have seemed painfully clear to Stein that the arrogance of political power-brokers did not die with the Watergate scandal. From Steingut's side came charges of headline-seeking against Stein. There was truth in both points of view.

The election of Steingut must have been reassuring to Rabbi Bergman. He became bolder in his fight to save his empire. He told the editor of a Yiddish weekly, 'Only God in heaven knows that I am not guilty.' He filed a lawsuit in Federal District Court, alleging that his constitutional rights were being violated by Assemblyman Stein, Assistant Welfare Inspector William Cabin and John Hess, a crusading New York Times reporter who was conducting his own investigation of nursing homes. Bergman said these men were bringing to bear upon him an 'unremitting barrage of unfair, inaccurate, maliciously false and prejudicial reports . . . innuendos and anonymous allegations of improper and criminal acts by the plaintiff.' He sought a million dollars in damages as well as an injunction. He then made himself unavailable to appear before the Stein Commission by flying to his home in Jerusalem. He later said that he had been advised to leave the country by his lawyer, the Metropolitan Nursing Home Association, and his children 'until the tumult' subsided.

But the tumult surrounding Albert Blumenthal was even more dramatic. His fight to clear his name began with considerable fanfare. Trumpets blared. Passions were stirred. As his rousing speech ended in which he mentioned that his good name was all he really had earned in public life, he was given a standing ovation. There was only one man sitting down in fact – Andrew Stein.

As much as any politician can be, Blumenthal was in public service because he had a real compulsion to ensure that government served and was not unfeeling. By all accounts, he seemed an exemplary politician, fighting for all the right causes. He led a five year and successful fight to overhaul New York State's abortion laws. While that did not endear him to the Catholics or fundamentalists, feminists and girls in trouble everywhere had cause to acclaim him. Throughout his political career, he had an intense interest in improving the educational system within New York City, where he was raising four children of his own.

Blumenthal was at the peak of his political power when he was indicted as an alleged perjurer and bribe-taker. Special State Prosecutor Charles Hynes, named by Governor Hugh Carey to do nothing but investigate the nursing home industry, gave priority to looking into Blumenthal's relationship with Rabbi Bergman. The West Side liberal, whose future seemed so bright, began slipping into those murky waters of ambiguity that once nearly enveloped Senator Ted Kennedy after Chappaquiddick.

Then on April 13, 1976, the unexpected occurred. New York Supreme Court Justice Aloysius J. Melia suddenly dismissed the indictment against Blumenthal. Melia scathingly attacked the probity of Special Prosecutor Hynes, declaring that Hynes had exceeded his jurisdiction, provided gross speculation and unduly coerced the grand jury. The Justice had been convinced of all this by defense counsel Louis Nizer, perhaps the most gifted and strongest criminal lawyer in America. Blumenthal had needed – and got – the best.

Albert Blumenthal had his day, briefly. A fellow Assemblyman did a tap dance in the legislative corridor; some wept in joy, including Blumenthal, and another sent out for champagne. 'It feels so good to be right,' said Lt. Gov. Mary Anne Krupsak, putting into words either her relief to know that her belief in Blumenthal was not misplaced or, as people sometimes do, expressing someone else's thought under the impression that emotion has made them mute. 'You're so decent,' she told the weeping Assembly-man, clutching him to her bosom.

Blumenthal phoned his children in school, and his father, who like his son wept in relief. He told reporters that Justice Melia's ruling had condensed the whole world 'into a minute.'

Not coincidentally, on the same day Blumenthal won dismissal of those charges, the state legislature voted to grant Special Prosecutor Charles Hynes nearly two million dollars more to continue his probe into nursing homes. It was an irony that went unnoted by the press. The legislature was joyous over Blumenthal's apparent vindication, but they wanted no-one to think, especially Bernard Bergman, that they were letting his kind continue bilking the government and exploiting human misery.

Five months after Blumenthal's victory in the State Supreme Court, Special Prosecutor Hynes issued a memorandum that was buried in the back section of the daily press. He alleged that Blumenthal had been scheduled to receive a partnership and a percentage in a manpower training contract at a Bergman nursing home in addition to his usual legal fee in return for his help in obtaining the license. Justice Melia was not asked to comment, and under American laws of justice, Blumenthal could not be charged again since he was already cleared. He eventually resigned from the legislature, the most lamentable loss in terms of public good caused by the Bergman case.

But it is difficult to feel any compassion for Assemblyman Stanley Steingut. Clearly, he was made of sterner stuff than Blumenthal. Obviously, there was considerable help and advice given Steingut by the most powerful men in New York State.

Once the investigators had exhausted the long roster of political protectors of the Rabbi, they turned all of their attention on his method of operation. The most remarkable fact to emerge from this scrutiny was that only one nursing home was on the records as being owned by Bernard

Bergman. He had been careful to keep his name from the legal ownership of nearly all the nursing homes in his syndicate. When the probe spilled over into neighboring New Jersey, the owner of one nursing home accused of fraud was Bergman's half-sister. Many in New York were owned by Stanley, Bergman's son, or Anna Weiss Bergman, his wife. There were brothers-in-law nominally operating others and, in some cases, trusted friends. Finally, the investigators made a huge map showing all private nursing homes in the Greater New York metropolitan area, including New Jersey and Connecticut, and they drew lines between every home with a tie to Bergman back to his headquarters on Riverside Drive. They found that 'all roads lead to Bergman.'

Bergman's lawyers yelled 'Foul!' and by now they had won a wedge of sympathy among civil libertarians. The latter group, usually drawn to liberal causes, was disturbed by the manner in which people with no credentials whatsoever were stepping into committee rooms from out of nowhere to allege that an aunt or a father had been maltreated in a Bergman Home. They were alarmed that his *modus operandi* was being ventilated in the press as something sinister when the truth was that very few corporations as vast as Bergman's had ownership revolving upon a single individual who could be personally wiped out if an adverse situation should develop. The investigators were publicly airing a massive, complicated business operation with the heat and rhetoric of district attorneys. It was reminiscent of Senator Kefauver's televised hearings on organized crime during the nineteen fifties – an investigation, incidentally, that no American congressman, justice official or President has been bold enough to repeat even though the Mafia is now stronger, in more complete control of politicians beyond number and cities by the hundred than ever before. Kefauver aroused the nation and the various Families were shaken, but only Frank Costello suffered, and he eventually died in his own bed in a comfortable apartment on Central Park West.

The investigators shut down the 'open door' phase and closed the books on individual tragedies. They began amassing a catalogue of alarming fact. The shuttered Towers Nursing Home had made an actual profit of nearly a million dollars during seven years of operation from 1966 through 1973 and not a cumulative loss of far more than a million as it had claimed to the New York Health Department. Special Prosecutor Hynes began referring to 'accounting shenanigans' wherever Bergman, Eugene Hollander (the second largest owner of Homes after Bergman) or Sigety Homes were involved.

Eugene Hollander attempted to be cleverer than Bergman. Rather than advancing himself as a political friend and philanthropist, he assumed the role of Educator. He and his advisers worked out a deal whereby he tried to give Touro College, a school founded by his friends possibly at his instigation, $145,000 a year income by selling the school four nursing homes and leasing them back with Medicaid paying the rent. He actually sold four homes to Touro College at a tentative price of $29 million and leased them back at a rent of nearly a million and a half. Because Touro had no capital funds to speak of, Hollander accepted notes from it for nearly $20 million in lieu of the purchase price with the right to seek the rest at some future date. Then he attempted to explain why the college undertook this $29 million commitment without approval of its trustees board. It was a simple matter, he told investigators. He *ran* the trustees board as its chairman with such esteemed figures as Mayor Abe Beame, Senator Jacob Javits, State Controller Arthur Levitt, former Attorney General Louis Lefkowitz, Assemblyman Steingut, and former congressman Emanuel Celler on the board.

As it became evident that Bernard Bergman, the man of unassailable good works outside the nursing home field, was about to be destroyed, he publicly announced: 'I must cleanse my reputation.' If most public utterance from the Rabbi evokes bearded tribal elders in lofty towers, it has to follow that he hoarded his real charm for private ears.

His announcement came too late. His crumbling role as a Jewish leader was dramatically evident when Israeli youth met in an extraordinary session to discuss the harm being done the Jewish image by certain Jews in America in control of the nursing home industry. The young Israelis suspended Rabbi Bergman from his post on the three-man presidium of the world Mizrachi movement.

Meanwhile, fellow magnate Eugene Hollander, having rocked the academic community with his disclosures about Touro College, pleaded guilty to New York State and Federal charges of bilking Medicaid of hundreds of thousands of dollars to pay for paintings by Utrillo, Renoir and Mary Cassatt. Eugene Hollander was not your run of the department store thief, with his need to be involved in higher education and have the finest cubist and impressionist art on his apartment walls. He promised to make restitution of over a million dollars and agreed to get out of the nursing home business.

But Rabbi Bergman was flintier. This Jewish aristocrat who would have been at least an advisor to the court in the days of Solomon, was on legal quicksand and he knew it. The Special Prosecutor felt he was ripe for 'plea bargaining,' a device in which a defendant is allowed to plead guilty with the understanding that he will co-operate with the prosecution in explaining all details of the crime. It differs slightly from the more nefarious act of being a stool pigeon or 'fink' in that you are only incriminating yourself. However, often the plea bargainer becomes a fink as well.

Eugene Hollander was sentenced to spend five nights a week in jail for up to six months and was fined $10,000 in addition to his promise to make restitution. Plea bargaining suddenly looked very attractive to Rabbi Bergman. Headlines screamed the next day: 'BERGMAN PLEADS GUILTY.' It was a one day sensation, but it did not resolve the case of the friendliest rabbi in town. True to character, Bernard Bergman, though a crook, declined to become a fink.

As a vital condition to pleading guilty, he insisted that son Stanley and wife Anna would be immune from prosecution. Once the process began, he held back so much vital information, Special Prosecutor Hynes threatened to reopen the case. Bergman had agreed to make restitution, but when the Prosecutor learned that he had come up with only a quarter of a million when he had defrauded Medicaid of two and a half million, everything seemed about to unravel.

Bergman finally talked, but apparently he confined his incriminating testimony to smaller fry like Albert Blumenthal. He testified that he had bribed Blumenthal. The Assemblyman was aghast and called the unexpected blabbermouth 'a liar.'

Prosecutor Hynes was not happy with the way the Bergman case was winding up, but he let the numerous omissions and hedging pass. When Bernard Bergman was sentenced by Federal Judge Marvin Frankel to what the Judge called a 'stern' sentence of four months, he noted that Bergman had an 'illustrious public life and works' and was then 64. The public was outraged and the entire case blazed furiously for days in the newspapers. Frankel was denounced by nearly everyone for giving Bergman 'a slap on the wrist' when the misery the Rabbi had wrought had caused pain, death and heartbreak to thousands of people. A *New York Times* editorial said that in light of his four month sentence, Bergman joined the ranks of formerly respectable white collar criminals who have received sentences which make odds on such crime look rather good and added that the criminal justice system was far from even-handed.

Justice Frankel, undeterred by criticism, continued to be Bergman's ally by granting him a delay in serving his sentence. In July another delay was granted, but possibly smarting under near libellous charges concerning his own integrity Justice Frankel denied a third appeal for delay in September and ordered Bergman into prison.

Bergman went quietly into jail in late September, 1976, and was gratified to learn that he would be doing his time at

Allenwood, a penitentiary in northern Pennsylvania, called a 'minimum security' facility by the Bureau of Prisons. It was a vast, hilly farm where inmates were free to walk on their free time 'as far as the cemetery,' a wry restriction that actually allowed them to walk nearly a mile without seeing a guard.

Gordon Liddy, the principal break-in expert at Democratic Headquarters during the Watergate caper, was the most celebrated inmate. He held occasional press conferences. Rabbi Bergman stayed out of touch with everyone but his lawyers and family. He still faced a year's sentence in New York State for the bribery attempt, but that bothered him less than public opprobrium. Never again would he be the leading speaker at a fund-raising dinner. Few would ask his opinion on anything. Could there be any punishment greater than that for Rabbi Bernard Bergman?

EPILOGUE

The nursing home industry was compelled to purge itself of nearly all the practices exposed by Hynes, Stein, Senator Frank Moss and others. It can be said that they did little of this voluntarily, but Medicaid began withholding reimbursements on such a scale, numerous Homes faced bankruptcy. In the second year of his investigation, Special Prosecutor Hynes had uncovered frauds totalling $50 million. Dozens of nursing home operators had been charged with criminal fraud and many convicted.

Flagrant abuse and neglect was subsiding, but not nearly fast enough. In some instances, Homes were being given advance warning of inspections by a 'friend' within the inspecting agency. The old established Homes were still functioning as well as ever, with an emphasis on individual concern and a home-like environment. A handful of newer Homes were attempting to do the same.

But not nearly enough thought or genius had gone into the problem of caring for the aged and infirm. No-one seemed to have any sensible alternative to the Home. And the wise elderly were still trying to avoid the saddest con game of them all – their own children making the Home sound like the Plaza with constant room service.

HARRY CLAPHAM –
THE RIGHT REVEREND RIP-OFF

by William Hastings

The Reverend Harry Clapham looked as if he had walked out of the Pickwick Papers.

Portly, bluff and hearty, and with snowy white hair flowing over his collar and a bald patch in the crown, he was to the members of his South London parish, the kindest man in the world.

But this vicar with a golden tongue was, in fact, one of the greatest swindlers of all time.

He ran the biggest begging organization ever built by one man. Police believe that by 1942 he had received more than £200,000 from charity appeals most of which he kept himself. At today's rate that fortune would have amounted to almost £2 million.

The story of the Rev. Harry Clapham began in 1888 in a humble home in Bradford. Everyone in the neighborhood lived in great poverty. Harry Clapham got a job at 14 as a warehouse boy and later became a shop assistant. He joined the Salvation Army and would travel the West Riding mill-towns singing hymns and preaching the Gospel.

When he was 26 he went to Canada where he studied at the Montreal Diocesan College and McGill University. He became ordained and would go into the great pine forests of Canada and preach to the tough, hard-drinking lumberjacks.

He returned to England and became the vicar of a church in Wellington, Shropshire, and when he left in 1925 to come to London his parishioners presented him with £119, a generous gift in those days.

142

The Rev. Clapham became the vicar of St Thomas's Church in Lambeth. His stipend was £400 a year but he had a wife, son and daughter to keep, and the church restoration fund was desperately low.

But he plunged into his work with great gusto. One parishioner said of him: 'I pray for the vicar every night. He is the kindest man in the world.'

Another said: 'We idolize him.'

But the vicar did not like being hard up and he developed a 'kink' which took the form of a love of money for money's sake.

It was while visiting a hospital patient that the Rev. Clapham hit upon his fantastic plan to make money – and lots of it too. He saw an official opening letters containing subscriptions to the hospital. There was a huge pile of checks and postal orders on the desk. The vicar's heart leapt. He bought from an agency a list of people known to respond to charity appeals. He circularized them telling them of the plight of his church and to his great delight obtained more money than was needed.

Now the vicar really got going. Police later estimated that he was buying 1,000,000 envelopes a year. He sent out, they believe, 200,000 appeals a year for 14 years.

Working in the vestry was a staff of people sending out pamphlets describing his work for the hungry and needy of the parish. Most of his workers were volunteers but one old man was paid sixpence for every 500 envelopes he addressed.

The pamphlets tugged at the heart strings and depicted the poor of the parish lining up for food. They told of how clothes were given to the waifs and strays, coal to the aged and bread to the hungry.

His book-keeper and secretary was a former school-teacher, Miss Constance Owens, who took to wearing a sister's uniform and became known as Sister Connie.

It is believed only $2\frac{1}{2}$% per cent of the money which flowed in went to charity. The remainder went into 91 different hush-hush bank accounts, building societies and defense bonds. He also bought nine houses.

Now, with tailored suits and a gold watch chain across his portly tummy, he began riding around in expensive, high-powered foreign cars complete with radio sets and other extras. He took several holidays a year on luxury liners to the West Indies, Canada, the Holy Land and other places. When asked by a friend how he got on so well he said: 'God has blessed me, I have been left some money.'

In order to cash much of the money he persuaded his brother Willie in Bradford to come to South London and buy a sub-post office. He said he would put up the money and his brother could pay him back. Now he had somewhere to cash his postal orders and checks without raising suspicion.

But the golden bubble was about to burst. People, including the Charity Commissioners, were now highly suspicious.

The vicar sacked his assistant curate, the Rev W. A. Hewett for alleged disloyalty. The curate said later: 'What I saw and heard at St Thomas's could not fail to excite suspicion in my mind. 'When I thought about two expensive holidays in less than a year, a house with luxurious furniture – better than I have seen in a bishop's palace – when I thought of two cars, a television set and the splendor of the Christmas parties put on by the vicar, I considered I was morally right in coming to the conclusion that the vicar was living above his official income.'

Scotland Yard was called in. When they went to the church they were amazed to find the bustling activity in the vestry. There were filing cabinets, index cards by the thousand and stacks of stationery and ledgers.

So complex was the situation they had to call in a private accountant, for this was in the days before the Yard's Fraud Squad was formed with its huge team of experts.

The smooth-talking vicar parried off all questions regarding his financial transactions. But the detectives began by playing a cat-and-mouse game and then they struck. They found he had applied to the Cholmondeley

Trust as 'a poor clergyman' anxious to be helped with the education of his son at Cambridge.

Rules of the trust provided that candidates must not have an income exceeding £400 a year from all sources.

It was typical of the Rev. Clapham. He had thousands and thousands of pounds hidden away but still was greedy enough to ask for a few more pounds.

It was a case of obtaining money by false pretenses and the Yard stepped in. When arrested, all his old magnetism left him. He said: 'I think I know who is responsible for this: someone who is jealous of me.' He had £150 on him.

In June, 1942 as most of his parishioners made their way to the air-raid shelters the Rev. Harry Clapham went off weeping to Parkhurst Prison to begin a three-year sentence.

An Old Bailey jury had found him guilty on 21 charges. He was ordered to pay £1,000 towards the prosecution. There was a clamor by MPs to get the money he had embezzled back. The Treasury considered the matter.

But then Harry Clapham's health began to deteriorate rapidly in prison. He had been sacked by the Archbishop of Canterbury. Because of his failing health he was allowed to leave prison. Sister Connie was waiting outside for him, and he went to live in a bungalow in the country which he bought for £3,000.

He died in 1948 leaving £9,000. He left most of it to his faithful secretary as 'a small token of my gratitude for services rendered and sacrifices made.'

But there was no hint in the will what had happened to the rest of the money.

The former vicar with the unsatiable lust for money took this secret to his grave.

IVAR KREUGAR –
A MATCH FOR ANYONE

by Elliott J. Mason

Ivar Kreugar is probably the most unusual fraudster the world has yet seen. He created the largest scale fraud ever – and looking with a historical perspective, accomplished it above all with a supreme sense of self-confidence and a suave and reassuring manner that inspired near fanatical loyalty from his employees and charmed over $460,000,000 – £200,000,000 – from a galaxy of top banking names and from the stock market investors of America especially.

The scale on which Kreugar operated can hardly be exaggerated. He created not only the biggest commercial company the world had then seen, he literally rescued whole state economies during the 20's, was hailed as the economic messiah and was the confidante of ministers and presidents – including President Hoover.

Yet his whole gigantic commercial edifice was primarily built on fraud. Not, paradoxically – in a story shot through with paradoxes – that it essentially need have been, for his basic concept was viable. Ivar Kreugar, however, set himself a visionary goal and rather than fail to achieve his grandiose schemes he resorted to continuous deception and even forgery on a mind boggling scale. One of his more ambitious schemes was to create a 'Euro currency' and the fact that some observers believed that he, as a *private* individual, could actually create such an institution speaks for the scale on which he operated.

But let us start the story at the beginning. Kreugar was born on March 2nd, 1880, in Kalmar some 200 miles south of Stockholm, Sweden. His father had begun his working life in a machine factory in a nearby town and had acquired, by the time Ivar Kreugar was ten, some three small match factories in the area. Sweden had, at that time, become predominant in matchmaking due to the invention in that country of the safety-match. As a boy, Ivar Kreugar is reported to have been rather studious and certainly reserved. He was an extremely intelligent boy and although intellectually very able would even in those days improve his examination results by cheating.

At the turn of the century, in 1899, he graduated from High School as a mechanical engineer and set sail for New York. Interestingly, he had very little success at this early stage, taking jobs in New York, Chicago, on the Illinois Central Railroad, then to Denver and finally back to New York. After an adventurous interlude in the jungles of Mexico working on a building project for a New York company, he returned to the business capital of America and from there set sail back to Sweden in 1902. However, he remained restless and in February, 1903, he returned to the United States – where amongst other interests he read extensively the biographies of the free-wheeling early American entrepreneurs.

On this visit Ivar Kreugar was considerably more successful and having taken a job with the Fuller Construction Company, was able to learn the latest American construction techniques. He put these techniques into practice with another American firm of builders, the Trussed Steel Company, and subsequently with a British firm with whom he worked in South Africa. Returning to Sweden, in 1908, Ivar, who had accumulated a moderate amount of capital in South Africa through investing in a restaurant and gold and diamond shares, formed a partnership with a friend named Toll. This partnership specialized in the construction of buildings using the then new steel-reinforced concrete process. Among a number of projects, they bid for and were successful in gaining the contract to build one of the tallest buildings then planned for Stockholm. Kreugar was particularly keen on this contract, not only from the profit standpoint, but because it would enable him to create the image and reputation that he was seeking. The combine offering the contract, suggested a penalty clause of $1,200 (£400) per day, for every day that the building was overdue on its scheduled completion date. Kreugar agreed but only on condition that his own company would be paid the same bonus for every day that completion was ahead of schedule. The investors were more than agreeable because no-one had ever succeeded in completing on time let alone ahead of schedule. Nevertheless, by using American construction techniques, including arc-lamps for all-night work and by covering the construction with tarpaulins which with heating enabled the workers to work around the clock, the building was completed in the then unheard of time of $1\frac{1}{2}$ months – 2 months ahead of schedule. The contract having been completed – Kreugar and his partner, Toll, took not only the profits but an additional $70,000 (£23,000) as the bonus for completing ahead of schedule. By 1910 Kreugar and Toll had accumulated capital of over $2,500,000 (£800,000) and this had almost doubled within the next year. The company grew rapidly to become the best construction company in Sweden and immediately prior to World War I had branches in Finland, Germany and Russia. It should be remembered, as the later history of the Kreugar empire is unfolded that at this point Ivar with Toll had created an extremely successful and sound construction business and he was already a wealthy man.

To everyone's surprise, immediately prior to the First World War Kreugar decided to give up active participation in the construction company and go into the match business. He left Stockholm and took over the family factories in Kalmar – news which was welcomed by the banks because the financial situation of his father's companies was by no means sound. In fact the whole Swedish match business was extremely fragmented and generally in poor shape. It was at this time that Ivar Kreugar conceived the grandiose scheme which was the start of his enormous business empire. The concept was blindingly simple, even though its execution required the most complex financial manoeuvres. Kreugar decided to create a monopoly in the match business. He was not a man to move slowly and by 1915 he had persuaded, cajoled – some say threatened – several smaller factories nearby to either sell out or combine with him. From this group of nine match companies was created the Kalmar Trust or the United Swedish Match Factories. Ivar Kreugar's target then was the Jönköping Vulcan Combine – the largest match-making concern in Sweden.

Ivar Kreugar gained control of the Vulcan combine in the Winter of 1917 by the blunt device of cutting off raw material supplies to his rival. He did so by purchasing the firm of Hamilton and Hansell – a firm that supplied the essential phosphorus and potash for the manufacture of the match-heads. Having obtained control of this company, he stopped supplying the potash to his rival and 'starved' them into submission! By mid-1917, Ivar Kreugar, by combining the Jönköping – Vulcan Company with his own United Swedish Match Factory Organisation, had created a new combine which then totally monopolized the Swedish match-making industry. He called his combine 'The Swedish Match Company' and became its first president. The operation had been planned much like a general plotting a battle campaign and his initial objective was to create additional profitability from a more efficient, streamlined organization. So far an uncomplicated and far-sighted strategy.

It was about this time, however, that Ivar Kreugar, probably more by accident than design, stumbled upon the enticing leverage power of a holding company situation. His first move was to create a company which he called Kreugar and Toll Building Company. This acted as a holding company (i.e. a company whose function was not to trade but to 'hold' or invest in shares of other concerns). It controlled the shares of Kreugar and Toll, the actual operational building firm. Kreugar then used the capital of Kreugar and Toll Building Company Limited (K.T.B.)

to purchase slightly over one quarter of the stock of The Swedish Match Company. He was already beginning to create the smoke-screen of interlocking company deals and holdings that was to enable him later to perform the accounting conjuring tricks and share manipulations that ultimately created the most widely quoted shares in the world. Within a few months, Ivar Kreugar issued his first 'annual' report on K.T.B. He declared profits of £800,000 and a dividend of 20% – an extraordinarily high and attractive dividend for the time. Following this attractive profit and dividend declaration, Ivar offered Kreuger and Toll shares to the public via the Stockholm stock market and a year later made two capital issues, raising the share capital to $30,000,000 and the reserves to $40,000,000. The share launch was a total success, and the public clamored to buy the stock which raised continuously in value. Ivar Kreugar maintained this simple formula from start to finish – the profits of his rapidly increasing number of companies were significantly dependent on inter-company transactions – trading between sister companies and only Ivar knew the full details – therefore his valuations ultimately made up the profits that his compliant and bemused accountants 'reported'. These profits – always exciting – in turn resulted in increased demand for Kreuger company shares which rose in price. This in turn enabled Kreuger to offer the public even more shares for fresh cash injections into his companies – which in turn gave him the liquid cash to pay out continuously high dividends next year which made his shares more attractive which made new issues of shares even easier which . . . ! And so the merry money go round continued at ever faster and more stratospheric levels!

It was a formula to be copied again and again – often by men, like Bernie Cornfeld of I.O.S., who also started legitimately and were sucked into the funny money paper cyclone by the euphoria of their initial success.

Only 15 years later did it become clear that even at these early stages the dividends were being paid not out of solid profit earnings but at least in part from capital. However,

Ivar Kreugar's personal control of the combine ensured that his valuation of the assets and profits were final, and no-one except him could penetrate the deliberately confused figures of his company reports. Thus by the end of 1918 less than two years after the creation of the K.T.B. Holding Company, Kreugar was reporting profits of $8,000,000 (£2,500,000) and a dividend of over 20%. He was already cavalier in the details contained in his company reports. For over half the combine's profits were listed as 'earnings from various transactions'. His posthumous psychological biographer, Dr Bjerra, compared Ivar with a great painter creating illusory reality not with paint and canvas but pen and balance sheet!

By now his reputation and the phenomenal success of his shares in the stock market were beginning to open up to him the huge lines of credit which were the foundation of his extraordinary confidence trick.

By 1919 Kreugar had already ceased becoming a producer of matches. He had become a manipulator of money. We shall never know, precisely, how much of the manipulation was deliberate deception, how much was self-deception and how much was the fact that his combine had become an unstoppable juggernaut with its own inexorable forward motion. Certainly Ivar Kreugar consciously sought to promote his image as the world's top financial 'wheeler and dealer'. He built a huge office building which was known as the 'Match Palace', in Stockholm. Aptly named, it was more like a palace than an office building with massive marble columns, a fountain in the middle of the reception area and an extremely impressive office for the President. Kreugar's office was sound-proofed with discreet mahogany panelling, sumptuous carpets and rich decorations. On his desk were a battery of telephones and on the floor was a useful button which the 'Match King' could depress with his foot to cause one of the telephones to ring. Kreugar used this device to hold imaginary conversations with important heads of state, financiers and even kings – all to impress his visitor who thought he was overhearing a private conversation. Alternatively, he could use the device to telephone himself in order to excuse himself when an interview had become tedious or inconvenient.

Kreugar began to live the lifestyle as befitted Sweden's most famous multi-millionaire. A succession of women trooped through his life and bachelor pad and he established mistresses in most of the capitals of Europe. Nothing, however, diverted his attention for long from his task of building up his fast growing financial edifice. By 1921 he was ready, he announced, to increase the capital of K.T.B. even further to a combined issued and reserved capital of $130,000,000 (£43,000,000) and this was to be done by issuing a further 80,000 shares in the combine. The shares were eagerly taken up by the public and the fresh money injected into his company was used to set up subsidiaries and factories over half of the world. To ensure the continuous flow of new capital, the Swedish Match Company shares were listed and floated on the principal Stock Exchanges of the world. The money available to him through this capital and through the enormous bank borrowings which his reputation and signature were now able to command, enabled him to seriously contemplate and finally execute the last stages of his master plan to control the total world match market.

Where match industries in certain European countries were protected by tariff barriers, he had no option but to conquer from within, in other words to purchase control of that match company within the borders of the country of operation. He did so through a mixed tactic and inducement, bribery and outright threats. Kreugar had not hesitated to employ on his own payroll, men whose job it was to compromise, blackmail and even to physically threaten competitors whom he wished to acquire. More than once he used his previously successful stratagem of cutting off vital raw materials and, knowing the moment at which his rival would be financially unable to continue operation, he would make a psychological and successful bid. Using a mixture of all these methods, Kreugar by 1922 had obtained monopolies not only in his native Sweden, but in Finland, Norway, Denmark and Belgium and was already making inroads into Southern Europe.

His principal problems, however, in completing the Western European monopoly were the countries in which making matches was a state monopoly. Here, clearly no normal commercial ploys were likely to succeed. In applying himself to this problem, the solution which Ivar Kreugar conceived must rate him as the world's most grandiose con-man. Again, the scheme was in principle simple but on such a colossal scale that only a man physically incapable of fear would have conceived it. Interestingly, Kreugar did have unusual physical abilities – he would for example endure dental extractions without anaesthetic and all his friends both male and especially female found him unemotional.

His strategy would be to advance loans to the governments of the countries that he wished to penetrate, in return for the monopoly. For a private concern to contemplate loaning a government money was an undertaking which had only been attempted once in history. It is ironic that those to whom the proposition was put neither saw the parallel, nor if they did, drew the obvious conclusion. The only other occasion that this tactic had been employed was in England in the 18th Century when the South Sea Company had, in return for a monopoly in trade to the South Seas area, undertaken to take over the National Debt (which at that time was running at £150 million). Almost every schoolboy knows that the result was the 'South Sea Bubble' and the complete collapse of the embryonic British Stock Market.

Kreugar knew, of course, that such an audacious scheme as he was contemplating required phenomenal sums of money and only one country in the world offered access to such cash – the United States. And so it was that in the Autumn of 1922 Ivar Kreugar boarded the liner 'Berengaria' and set sail for New York.

His plan was to obtain the money from American bankers plus the public by the flotation of a completely new company called the International Match Corporation. This company would invest its money in the following way: (1) all proceeds would be paid over to individual national governments in the form of loans, (2) these loans would of course command interest, (3) in return for the loans, the country would grant to the International Match Corporation a monopoly for making matches within that country, (4) the combination of the interest payable on the loans and the guaranteed profits from a monopoly situation would enable the International Match Corporation to pay out higher than average dividends. Moreover, and here was the sucker bait, the whole operation would be 'gilt-edged' because not only were profits assured from a monopoly situation, but the only people with whom the International Match Corporation would be dealing would be reputable and accredited national governments. The scheme appeared totally foolproof and secure. Some of the monopolies were so tightly worded that in some countries laws were passed to prohibit the use of lighters (punishable by fine) and to this day travellers in one South American country have to declare the possession of a lighter to customs officials!

Kreugar however knew that his reputation, although solid throughout the whole of Europe, had to be re-created all over again in America.

Consequently, he went to some trouble on his voyage to America to create the necessary image so that his arrival in New York would not go unheralded.

At an early stage during the voyage the passengers on the 'Berengaria' were annoyed to find out that for a period of twenty-four hours at a time the complete wireless facilities of the ship had been taken over by a certain Mr Ivar Kreugar who apparently was so busy that he needed the total telegraphic resources of the ship. Indeed, day and night throughout the whole trip stewards would troop backwards and forwards to his state cabin bringing messages and taking replies. Consequently, when the reporters assembled at the end of the ship's voyage in New York to interview the personalities on board – a normal procedure at the time – Kreugar had become the center of attraction. He was able consequently to expand his plans in detail to a full assembly of the American press. One particular incident guaranteed him 'front-page' in every paper. He had been asked by an American reporter what it meant to be the 'Swedish Match King' and during the reply, in which he made full use of the opportunity to explain his plan, he was interrupted by a reporter, who was about to light a cigarette and, grinning, had turned to Kreugar to ask him if he had a match. It was the perfect moment for the showman. He turned to the reporter, with a quizzical smile, and said 'I'm sorry, gentlemen, I never seem to have a match with me'. The 'Match King' without a match! – it was the sort of copy that news editors love and Kreugar got his headlines in all the important papers.

Within weeks, he had managed to sell his scheme not only to the New York bankers (some of whom, including a Rockefeller, were to be included on his board of directors) but also the American public.

In 1922 alone no less than $150 million was collected from flotations and loans in America and transferred to Kreugar and his combines in Europe. Much of this and subsequent borrowings was paid directly into two companies, Union Industrie AG and Continental Investment Corporation, from the main share company in the USA the International Match Co (IMCO). The amazing fact was that Kreugar's partners in IMCO were a highly respected company of American brokers named Lee Higginson and Co and their reputation added the necessary authority to the exciting prospects of the famed financial genius. Altogether, the partnership of respectability and hyper-fraud took the American investors for a staggering $88,000,000 – worth perhaps $400,000,000 at today's values. Yet despite their status the sophisticated financiers at Lee Higginson exercised almost no control over the destination of the funds disappearing rapidly eastwards. Apparently Kreugar's charisma and the regular dividends allayed all suspicions. A Rockefeller board member returning from a 'fact' finding trip enthused 'I have never been more impressed by anything than by this organization'. The august New York financiers would have had a fit if they had taken even the most cursory look. The money siphoned off from IMCO into the Zurich corporations often as not ended in a shell company rejoicing in the unlikely name of A. B. Russia (in practice Mr Kreugar's personal bank account) or in one of several banks owned by the imaginative Swede. Not that Kreugar's intention was to steal the money – he merely figured that once in his private control he could re-issue the cash and control it on his complete personal whim. It is hardly surprising that Ivar grew somewhat disdainful of these experts he was fooling so easily. In a rare unguarded moment he remarked to a man, who came to regard Ivar as a 'latter day Conquistador' that, 'Every period has its own gods – its own high priests . . . instead of being fighting men we've chosen new high priests and we call them accountants. They, too, have holy days, the 31st of December, on which we are supposed to confess.' But as we know Ivar didn't believe in confession – at least in his business life.

In his private life Ivar was not especially extravagant – if you don't count five or six mistresses permanently installed in apartments around Europe – and his most eccentric extravagance was his weekly standing order for 1,000 lilies of the valley with his Stockholm florist. But personal wealth had long since ceased to be a motivation.

Over the next two years Kreugar had negotiated loans from either International Match or Swedish Match of over $300 million to a total of 20 countries and through the medium of these loans had come to control some 65% of the whole world match production. This much was factual However, there were other loans which he claimed to have made (and which went to build up the legend of the un-faltering financial wizard) which were in his imagination only – albeit used most effectively for publicity purposes and to continue to justify continuing borrowing. Ivar Kreugar devised an extremely effective method of bolstering his image and credit-worthiness with the top financiers of Western Europe. If it was a complete con trick – well by now who cared?

One particular example served to show his technique. In 1924, he was able to claim to key bankers in Paris that he had advanced approximately $5 million to Spain and in return had a contract signed by the Prime Minister dated January, 1925, which gave him the match production rights. However, to prevent this being checked, he warned his banking backers that if any details of the loan and its terms ever became public there was a serious and real possibility of war! In the same way, he was able to boast of and show contracts of a similar deal with Poland. It was precisely this type of 'contractual' arrangement which created the necessary high powered image with the European banks and allowed him to secure his massive borrowings while at the same time the deals were, by definition, impossible to check! Kreugar had by now perfected the combination of artistic (one belated investigator called it poetic) accounting, allied to a series of exciting sounding but uncheckable deals. He ensured that only he knew anything of substance about his empire by impressing a signed vow of secrecy on his employees, complete with a $25,000 fine for breaking it, and by operating what the CIA now call the 'need to know' principle. Each employee only knew enough to conduct his part of the Empire – no more.

There's no doubt that his match empire was profitable in the trading sense but the phenomenal growth of his combine was accomplished by deception. As soon as he acquired a specific and tangible asset he would borrow on the security of that asset, thereby acquiring more funds to acquire yet more assets on which he could borrow more funds . . . etc, etc. Where Kreugar undoubtedly overstepped the mark from the very beginning, beyond even the normal giddy spiral of 'leverage', was that he would not borrow just *once* on the security of each asset but often two or three times and would pledge the same asset to several banks! In this way the multiplier effect of his borrowings became quite enormous. Through the bank borrowings and share issues he had by the late 1920's built up an empire which consisted of 160 match factories in 35 countries, including the UK. Perhaps even more important to his scheme the network of holdings, cross-holdings, loans, inter-company loans and borrowings were such that nobody, especially his accountants had any real idea of where the profits originated or indeed where the money was going. He therefore could manipulate the figures from his company report almost at will. Moreover, by issuing only non-voting shares he had come to control $600,000,000 worth of assets with 1% of the shares.

From the reputation created by the apparently quite fictitious early deals with Spain and Poland, Kreugar's empire made genuine loans and genuine monopoly deals with many other countries and it seemed that the cash would revolve merrily forever.

As we have seen through this book, however, no system whereby the dividends are being paid out of capital and not out of genuine profit can expect to continue forever and just how long the Kreugar empire would have survived on the cash carousel is anybody's guess. It was perhaps Kreugar's bad luck that at the very height of his powers, when the cash flow was so immense that he could probably have forestalled any major problem for many, many years, came the Wall Street crash. The drying-up of credit all over the world inevitably hit the highly-geared companies first and hardest and despite his immense reputation and resources, Kreugar was no exception. Ironically, it was the seemingly 'gilt-edged' loans to countries that precipitated his downfall because, as money grew tighter, many of his international clients began defaulting on loan repayments or alternatively on the share due to the International Match Corporation of local match profits.

Worse still many of the loans that he had negotiated were on an instalment basis and if the International Match Corporation did not continue to keep making the loans, the countries, with whom he had deals would have had the excuse to curtail the monopoly arrangement. He was therefore caught in a trap, made worse by the fact that to once miss paying a dividend or interest would destroy the all important confidence on which the whole edifice was built. He had to keep continuing to dole out loans to countries with which he had made new arrangements, but was finding it difficult to extract the funds due to him from the countries with which he had already completed arrangements.

The search for new funds therefore grew faster and more desperate. He was daily transferring millions of pounds from one bank to another. Every time he transferred in a deposit, he would obtain a receipt from the bank. He would then use that receipt as collateral to borrow more funds from a new bank! On one particular occasion he resorted to the really desperate expedient of walking into the office of the president of a very large international bank in Brussels and throwing on the desk a huge bundle of currency. 'There are 400 million francs for deposit', he said to the president, 'I would be grateful for a receipt'. The bank president was only too flattered to have received a visit from so eminent a gentleman as the 'Swedish Match King' who to the outside world was hailed as the 'Savior of Europe'. Kreugar really was loaning money, albeit out of necessity, to governments throughout Europe to keep their economies functioning. The president signed the receipt immediately without the 'necessity of checking'. Within a couple of hours however it was found that the bundle contained not 400 million francs but 5 million. When Kreugar was contacted he apologized profusely and said that this must have been the mistake of one of his accountants. He refunded the receipt, of course, and took a new one but not before achieving his objective. For in the intervening two hours he had already raised a further loan from another bank on the strength of the receipt for the 400 million francs!

This was by no means a unique trick in these desperate times. It later transpired that in 1931 he personally, with a confederate, forged the names of the Director of the Italian Reserve Bank and indeed the Finance Minister of Italy on completely bogus Italian Government stocks and bonds. It was hardly a small time forgery because the face value of the bonds was over £28 million – a sum of money which was desperately needed by Kreugar to shore up his now crumbling empire.

It was in the Winter of 1931, however, that Ivar Kreugar made his fatal mistake. He journeyed to New York to raise much needed money by selling out his share in the Erikkson Telephone Company of Sweden to the International Telephone and Telegraph Company of New York. But, for once, the sheer magnetism and reputation of Kreugar was insufficient to enable him to flimflam his way through the accounts of the much raided Erikkson Company. By early February, 1932, the auditors of I.T.T. had made a thorough investigation of the Erikkson Telephone Company's account and found a discrepancy in an inter-company loan between the Erikkson Telephone Company and the Swedish Match Company – a discrepancy that came to a little matter of £7 million. Kreugar simply could not bluster his way out of the 'accounting error' – nor refund the missing £7 million and on February 19th, 1932, the stunned New York financial world learned that the I.T.T./Erikkson merger was off. By this time, those in the know had come to realize that the reason for the failure of the Erikkson Company deal was a severe liquidity shortage within the Swedish Match and International Match Corporation structures and the true run on Kreugar began. The American banks pressed for repayment of the loans – so Kreugar went to the Swedish National Bank to demand a further £2 million loan. Although the Swedish National Bank was already into Kreugar's companies for an earlier £2 million, they tentatively agreed but only if they could have access to the books. Kreugar accepted their request, maybe out of desperation, maybe out of a belief in his ability to baffle the National Bank auditors as he had almost every other auditing company for the last fifteen years.

Meanwhile, on this his last trip to New York, he was using millions of his own personal money in a desperate attempt to keep up the price of his shares – by buying his own stock. This above all lends credence to the belief that Ivar Kreugar had not embarked upon his colossal con-trick for monetary greed – remember he was already a wealthy man before he even went into the match business – but out of a desire for recognition. Even at this stage – if he were a true con-man – he could have silently disappeared and remained one of the wealthiest men in the world. Instead, he decided to return to Europe to face what he must have known would be a series of at least embarrassing, and possibly humiliating interviews. Before he left New York he wrote two suicidal notes – but delayed posting them. One contained a philosophical if – to be honest – hypocritical musing on capitalism. 'Once we begin to go into deep water we soon get out of our depth. What sort of a foundation does this world rest on? Forests draw their nourishment from roots and earth, the seed grows in the corn, man springs from man. All that is certain but what is certain about money, which after all holds the world together? It depends on the goodwill of a few capitalists mutually to keep to the agreement that one metal is worth more than another.'

His journey from New York to Europe on the 'Ile de France' cannot have been happy. However, when he reached Paris he heard worse news. The Swedish Bank auditors had been far from satisfied with what they had found and, in particular, were asking awkward questions about the Italian bonds which had been put up as security for a series of inter-bank loans. Kreugar realized the end had come and that his empire was about to crash. He retired to his apartment on the Avenue Victor Emmanuel.

The papers of March 13th, 1932, carried a simple report. On the morning of the 12th of March the man acclaimed as the financial 'Savior of Europe' had ended his life with a bullet through the heart. The reaction to the news was instant and traumatic. The Swedish Parliament itself met at midnight on the Sunday for a hastily convened session to discuss the implications. In Switzerland the Bank of International Settlements called an extraordinary general meeting and in Paris the Premier consulted with the Swedish Ambassador. On Monday morning the New York Stock Exchange had one of the most severe drops in its history.

Even this was nothing compared to the shock when bit by bit the real story emerged. The rapid dissolution of the Kreugar empire, commencing with initial defaults on New York bank loans, became a flood as the scandal of the forged Italian Bonds became known. The Swedish Foreign Minister himself flew to Rome to interview Mussolini, his Finance Minister, and the Director General of the Italian Bank. Once the Italian bonds were certified by the Finance Minister and Mussolini as forgeries, the rush was really on to investigate the whole of the paper edifice of the Kreugar empire. The more that was discovered, the less backing there appeared for the house of cards.

After intensive investigations, the Kreugar and Toll holding company was declared insolvent and when all the figures were added up it was found that the deficits of the Kreugar empire were larger than the whole Swedish National Debt. Final claims totalled £234 million – something like a billion pounds at today's values. Less than 10% of the liabilities were ever met from the assets of the company.

Even in death, however, Kreugar managed to put on a show. Newspaper reports for months afterwards speculated that it was not suicide but murder and a theory was seriously investigated that the man with the bullet hole in the chest that lay on the bed in the flat in Paris, was not Kreugar but a double and Ivar Kreugar himself had disappeared with a large proportion of his wealth to Sumatra. Certainly in 1939 Kreugar's previous personal tobacconist confided to a newspaper reporter that long after the 'Match King's' supposed suicide he had received from Sumatra an order for a large consignment of custom-built Havana cigars for which only Kreugar himself knew the exact specification. . . .

THE LORD'S APPOINTED

It's not so often that two 'chosen instruments of the Almighty' get jailed – but it happened in 1971 in York Crown Court, England. Two men were sent down for several years on the evidence of a local wealthy but aged widow. Admittedly they didn't look too religious in the cold light of the court day – but then their bizarre con on the widow was initiated in the middle of the night, and the visions that they had were more in the area of personal comfort than a better society.

According to the widow, she was first introduced to the two defendants as being the gentlemen who would give her advice and instructions on how to best invest her wealth to benefit her fellow man. During the months following their first meeting they did indeed give her advice and over £45,000 was invested by her in bogus charities invented by her new found investment counsellors, until her bank manager had a discreet word with the police and the whistle blew.

But, pressed the defense, why did she trust these two helpful investment guiders in the first place – since they were complete strangers to her until the beginning of the year? Simple, she explained, they were introduced by God himself. An impressive reference, you must admit. And how precisely was the introduction effected? 'Well, He telephoned me in the middle of the night,' she explained patiently, 'and said "This is God speaking" and then He told me to invest part of my wealth for the benefit of those less fortunate – He also mentioned that my advisers would call the next morning.' With the assistance of a few more midnight electronic communications with the Almighty the business was completed.

The case is ludicrously simple but it shows that sometimes the most outlandish schemes can (nearly) work.

MAUNDY GREGORY –
EARLDOMS COME EXPENSIVE

by Tom Tullett

He was a confidante of Kings, a guardian of state secrets, a suspect in a strange and still unsolved death riddle and a confidence trickster of exceptional ingenuity.

His name was Maundy Gregory and his beginnings were humble. Perhaps that was the spur, for his life style later became grandiose in the extreme. He lived a life of luxury, he was a lavish spender while he found easy victims, and he died in a German concentration camp during the second world war.

This man with the unusual name was the elder of two sons of a Hampshire clergyman, born in 1877. He was privately educated and was sent to Oxford but failed to get a degree.

By all accounts his family was poor, so much so that when his father died his mother had to go to live in a home for widows of the clergy.

But although the family lived in comparative poverty he was brought up in genteel surroundings so that he was well-mannered, quietly spoken and always quick to cultivate anyone who might be of use to him.

Maundy Gregory's first job was that of a junior schoolmaster, but not for long. He could see little future in that career and he decided to go on the stage. If he knew then what he was going to do later it was a brilliant choice. He was a competent actor and he got parts in West End productions although he was by no means distinguished. Like most actors of the day he issued little notices to newspapers in the hope of getting business and, for a while, did fairly well.

Later he became an assistant theatrical manager and, emboldened by his success, launched out on his own as an impressario. It was a mistake for he was under-capitalized. He got quite a good musical show together and it opened to good notices and should have done well. But he was short of cash and when he could not afford to pay the musicians they walked out. The show folded and that was the end of the stage aspirations of Maundy Gregory.

On the credit side, however, he had learned a great deal. The stage had provided his apprenticeship. He was suave, confident and well-dressed. He was set for his future of gulling the unsuspecting, of fleecing his victims of their cash on the promise of an award in the Honours List.*

He dealt only with the wealthy who had ambition and who were not in the least fussy about how they achieved those ambitions. Like all good con-men he had an air of oozing confidence, of charm and wit, and he was never in a hurry. He was kind and considerate, generous with his compliments and equally generous with gifts. He believed in casting his bread upon the water, knowing he would be amply repaid later.

By now he had all the appurtenances of a gentleman, manners, dress and speech. He was distinguished, arrogant and he caught the eye. He always sported a diamond watch-chain across his ample stomach and his suits were tailored to perfection. He was ready for his next move, that of an Honours Salesman. Although his name was unfamiliar to the general public he was becoming well known in the highest places in London. His circle of acquaintances was select and it embraced a host of the most notable people of the day.

Princes and prelates, peers and distinguished commoners, statesmen of high rank, leaders of the arts and the sciences, all alike came within his ambit. Yet to all he

---

* The Honours List is published annually in England and announces those on whom the Monarch has bestowed titles – such as Peerages. An 'Honours Salesman' is one who uses his influence to ensure his friends appear on the Honours List.

was a man of mystery. Exactly his position in the scheme of things no one really knew.

By some he was assumed to hold high position in the Foreign Office, by others he was regarded as the head of the Secret Service and, again, by others to have some indefinable influence in affairs.

He was to be seen in Whitehall, entering his palatial offices in Parliament Street, between the old Scotland Yard and the Prime Minister's home in Downing Street. What better place for a con-man to set-up in business?

Within his offices, where he edited an anti-Communist periodical called the *Whitehall Gazette*, Maundy Gregory received some of the most famous people who wrote articles for his publication. These included foreign royalties, ambassadors, high civil servants, judges and senior barristers.

This office was part of the necessary build-up to the business of an Honours Fix 'broker', a business where a knighthood cost £10,000, a baronetcy £30,000 and £50,000 to £100,000 for a peerage.

The trappings did not stop there. Those who were invited to these offices were received by a uniformed attendant looking like a messenger from any Government department. The atmosphere was quiet, even grave and, after a period of waiting, mysterious lights would flash on the reception desk, indicating that Maundy Gregory was ready to receive.

The double doors were thrown open to reveal a lofty apartment, furnished with exquisite taste and in the middle sat Maundy Gregory in a large chair upholstered in crimson leather.

On the massive desk were telephones, bell-pushes and a series of colored lights which flashed from time to time. An extra refinement was a Morse 'tapper' key which he used to summon his secretary or any other members of the staff.

Maundy Gregory did not forget a thing. He even had red despatch boxes similar to those used by the Foreign Office and other departments. And around the walls were magnificent portraits of many of the crowned heads of Europe, Eastern potentates, generals and admirals.

This man, who has been called the Prince of Fixers, never neglected an opportunity to improve his sphere of influence. Sovereigns and rulers driven into exile by revolution found in him a counsellor and financial help which won him their gratitude and fullest confidence. Ex-King George of Greece came to London a fugitive and impoverished and Gregory became his friend.

The Montenegrin Royal family, dispossessed of their country by Serbia, entrusted what remained of their fortunes to Gregory, and gave him power of attorney.

It appears the major part of Maundy Gregory's wealth was acquired by the 'sale' of Honours and his opulent life style not only resulted from this exotic con-trick but enabled him to pull it off.

One of his treasured possessions was a heart-shaped rose-colored diamond which once belonged to the Empress Catherine of Russia, and which had passed through the hands of a kinsman of the Czar murdered by the Bolsheviks. The diamond was brought to England by a diplomat at the request of a grand duchess in straitened circumstances.

Gregory travelled widely and was an avid collector of 'useful' people whom he always invited back to his Whitehall office where he was able to impress them. One of his favorite methods was to be given a message from his secretary saying: 'Mr Gregory. You are wanted by number ten.'

He would pick up the telephone and engage in serious conversation which was guaranteed to give the impression to the hapless listener that he was indeed highly honored to be there at all. In fact, it was just another elaborate trick for Maundy Gregory had gone to some considerable trouble to find himself a private house in the right neighbourhood bearing the number 'ten'. Thus, whenever he wanted he could arrange for the call to come through on cue. It was an extravagant piece of stagemanship but that was part of his make-up. A less flamboyant character might have settled for a hired man to call him when needed.

What was the origin of this man who exercised such power, so much influence over kings and statesmen?

To anyone interested, and if they were not he would convince them they should be, he would produce an authentic document compiled by the College of Heralds which traced his ancestry back to Edward III.

That was another con-trick but done with great artistry.

It was not enough for Gregory to allude to his amazing ancestry. He would produce the College of Heralds document, about four feet long, setting out his pedigree. It purported to show that his lineage could be traced right back to William the Conqueror, that the blood of eight kings was flowing through his veins and that famous figures of history like John of Gaunt, Harry Hotspur and the Black Prince were all among his forbears. His last royal ancestor was shown as Edward III, and the entire family tree was sprinkled with the names of earls and dukes.

There can be no doubt that Gregory found this document most useful when setting-up his victims and, of course, they never knew that his eighty-five year old widowed mother was living in an almshouse in Winchester. She was one of eight widows of indigent clergymen selected to be provided with such a cottage together with a yearly income of £80 a year, plus light and fuel.

He did occasionally go to visit his mother but he was much more likely to spend his time in one of his ill-gotten possessions, like the hotel in Surrey, the flat at Brighton, his bungalow on the Thames, his London house or palatial offices, or the smart Ambassador Club in London's Mayfair.

At his club he had the popular band of Jack Hilton and on most days he would arrive there promptly at a quarter to one to be greeted with two bottles of champagne on ice.

He used that club to attract his victims and spent lavishly in the process. There were great dinner parties, all the guests being household names. On the eve of every Derby race he held the biggest dinner in London.

His most lucrative years were those following the first great war. He explained his absence during the war years mostly with odd and carefully quiet references to some hush-hush job with the Foreign Office. He wanted people to believe that he had been working for the Secret Service and he succeeded.

In fact, in 1914 Gregory was thirty-seven, too old to face the exacting hardships of active service. He was called up in 1917 as a private in one of the Guards regiments. Later he was transferred to a line regiment and tried to get a commission but was turned down. So a private he remained until 1919 when he was demobilized and placed on the Reserve, where he remained until 1930.

It was in 1919 he founded his *Whitehall Gazette* and *St James's Review*. Although priced at half a crown it was mostly given away free. But it was sent to the premier clubs and Government departments and more than covered the cost of publication by carrying illustrated articles on aspirants to titles, for which they paid heavily. This all helped Gregory's main occupation which was to sell Honours.

Gregory's *modus operandi* was simple. He gained, through various contacts, access to the files of prominent individuals who were *already* under consideration for a knighthood or a baronetcy. He then would discreetly check who, among the list, were keen enough for an Honour to pay for it – and how much they were prepared to pay. A letter was then written suggesting a meeting to discuss 'a social matter of a very confidential nature'.

Many victims paid – little knowing that in many cases they would have received the Honour anyway! Not that they were all so gullible. One cautious chain store owner did indeed write Gregory a check for £50,000 but signed it with the title he was expecting, remarking, 'The day I receive the peerage you promise you can cash the check.'

Sometimes Gregory would reverse the procedure, pick a nouveau riche industrialist who he knew would pay for an Honour, and then use his not inconsiderable influence in Lloyd George's administration to wangle him onto the Honours List.

Gregory's skill in ensuring he would sit next to the right people on public occasions was also helpful in furthering his image. The story is told of how he managed to place himself next to a cabinet minister on a picnic river trip and talked right through the journey in, apparently, intimate terms. The minister did not know even who he was but was too polite to demur. For the wily Gregory it was a perfect opportunity for he was subsequently able to impress future clients with his ministerial 'friend'.

By now however many people were becoming suspicious of Gregory. Indeed, they were more than suspicious, they were on to him. Lloyd George was out of office and the Conservatives, under Stanley Baldwin, were in power. In 1925 a new act was passed which was hardly noticed by the public. But it may have been passed specially for Mr Maundy Gregory's 'benefit'. It was called the Honours (Prevention of Abuses) Act, and there is little doubt that it was passed with the express intention of catching him.

Gregory carried on as usual but other people were working for his downfall. Lord Davidson took over the chairmanship of the Conservative Party in 1927 and one of his first tasks was to destroy Gregory, but in a way which would protect the many eminent men who had been involved in his dealings. The scandal of the trafficking in Honours for party funds, (with Maundy Gregory as the middle-man), had discredited the government and it had been publicly said that the royal prerogative was being prostituted for sordid reasons.

Davidson arranged his plan of campaign with Scotland Yard's Special Branch. Even so, it was a difficult job for he had to make sure that none of Gregory's client's names got onto the Honours List. It was decided that the first thing to do was to break Gregory financially – but that involved making enemies of many people – some very well known – who were his clients and who expected Honours in return for payments they had already made.

The method chosen was to infiltrate a spy into Gregory's organization to obtain a list of the clients whom Davidson then made sure did not receive the Honours they had expected. The job was given to a Mr A. J. Bennett, who became the assistant treasurer of the Conservative Party.

Davidson meanwhile deliberately maintained apparent friendliness towards Gregory and lunched with him at the Ambassadors Club some weeks before the Honours List was to be published so as to allay suspicion. He discussed the qualifications of Maundy Gregory's candidates and explained with assumed regret and great expressions of sympathy, how difficult these things were.

Trouble was brewing and in a big way. There had been a good many indignant letters from would-be purchasers who thought they were certain to be named. Most of them thought they were doing nothing wrong and that to pay was the usual thing.

By this time Maundy Gregory was beginning to feel the pinch. He had received a sum of £30,000 from an unnamed person on the promise that he would negotiate a title for him. Not only did he fail to arrange the title but he did not repay the money, on the belief, which had always worked before, that person seeking the title would not dare to sue. Gregory was in deep water for to fail to produce the title and keep the money was fraudulent; and to keep the money on the grounds that the man did not want his name exposed was blackmail. Unhappily for Gregory the nameless would-be baronet died and his executors had no scruples about sueing for the repayment of the money.

For months Gregory tried to bluff it out but just before the case was due to come to court he gave in and paid. There was worse to come.

One winter's morning in 1933 the Assistant Commissioner for Crime at Scotland Yard, Sir Norman Kendall sent for one of his senior investigators, Detective Super-intendent Arthur Askew, a member of the famous Big Five. He was told that Mr Maundy Gregory was to be prosecuted under the Honours (Prevention and Abuses) Act and to go to the Director of Public Prosecutions for instructions.

The Director told him that Gregory was to be proceeded against for having attempted to obtain £10,000 from Lieut-Commander E. W. B. Leake, DSO, a notable figure in sporting and social circles.

Askew, taking with him the Attorney-General's fiat, went to Bow street magistrates' court and applied for a summons and got it. That evening he went with his sergeant to Gregory's house at number ten Hyde Park terrace and there a sedate and dignified butler informed him that Mr Gregory was not at home. Askew insisted on making an appointment for the next morning and duly served the summons, although not without many hours of waiting. When Gregory received the summons he enquired: 'Supposing I do not appear?

'Then I am afraid I shall be back in a very short time with a warrant for your arrest. And then you will have no option,' said Askew.

Maundy Gregory remained calm and smiling and he was still, apparently, unruffled, when he appeared at Bow Street court where he pleaded not guilty.

Lieut-Commander Leake went into the witness box and told how he had received a letter from a stranger named Moffat, asking for an interview. They met and Moffat later introduced him to Gregory. An invitation to meet over lunch was extended and it was there, in the midst of sumptuous food and expensive wine, that Gregory made his proposal.

The officer was told with flattering suave phrases that he had become famous and many people among the nobility thought he ought to have a title. Gregory suggested a knighthood and that it was necessary that certain closed doors should be opened to ensure the title be awarded. And that would require certain arrangements to be made which would, of course, cost money. He suggested £10,000 or, perhaps, £12,000.

Lieut-Commander Peake was new to such proposals and he asked for more details. Gregory was not in the least put off. He told him how he had been instrumental in making similar arrangements for many other people, and quoted the sums he charged for the various titles.

The officer did not like it and laid the whole matter before the authorities. After other evidence the case was adjourned and when it was resumed the famous KC, Mr Norman Birkett appeared for the defense. He explained he had offered certain advice to Gregory and, as a result of that, he pleaded guilty.

Detective Superintendent Askew told the court that Gregory had no previous convictions but he also said that the police had received a number of complaints of a similar nature to the one before the court. In fact Scotland Yard had gathered quite a dossier on the bland con-man.

The eminent counsel made an eloquent plea for his cunning client but the magistrate had other views and he sentenced Maudy Gregory to two months in the second division, fined him £50 and ordered him to pay £52.10s., or a further two months in default.

Gregory must have been extremely relieved but a great many other people breathed more freely at the quick ending to the case. There was to be no scandal, no rattling of skeletons in the cupboards of so many people.

Although a prisoner and on his way to Wormwood Scrubs, Maundy Gregory took it well. But he did not know that once Scotland Yard is alerted they do not let go easily. They now wanted to know the exact circumstances of the death five months earlier of Mrs Edith Rosse, the former musical comedy actress who had long been Gregory's friend.

On the same day that Gregory was sentenced the police were at Brighton interviewing the dead woman's husband,

Frederick Rosse. He was a well known conductor and composer and was musical director of the Waldorf Theatre (now the Strand) when Maundy Gregory was acting as business manager. Rosse married a beautiful girl in the cast of a touring company which played at the theatre and Gregory became a great friend of the couple. He used to stay with them at their bungalow at Staines, a location chosen by Mrs Rosse because she liked to be near the river.

Later the three shared a house in St John's Wood, London, with Gregory occupying the top rooms only. Two years later there was a rift between the married couple, there was a deed of separation, and Mr Rosse left the house.

Mrs Rosse was given a generous allowance, with a minimum of £364 a year. She was a keen business-woman and owned property. Gregory stayed on at the house and when, later, he wanted a house with the number 'ten' she helped him find it in Hyde Park terrace. When he moved there she went too and she died there in September, 1932.

She was 59 and she died in a fairly normal way of a seizure. There was a medical certificate to say she died from cerebral haemorrhage and chronic Bright's disease.

Gregory, as her close friend, attended to the funeral arrangements. He went to some trouble to organize her burial in the tiny riverside graveyard at Bisham, Berkshire, some five miles from Maidenhead. Her personal estate was £18,699, and every penny of it was bequeathed to Maundy Gregory.

The astute Mr Askew discovered that the will was written in Gregory's writing. It read: 'Everything I have, if anything happens to me, to be left to Mr J. Maundy Gregory to be disposed of as he thinks best and in accordance with what I should desire.' It was witnessed by her doctor and housekeeper, and it was dated August 19, less than a month before she died.

This was curious enough but even more curious was that

the will was written on the back of a menu card bearing the name of a well-known Mayfair restaurant.

On the day she died Gregory had been lunching with the former King of Greece when a telegram was brought to his table, calling him to the bedside. She signed this strange will form twice 'Edith Marian Rosse' and it seemed the will was a fact.

There were relatives of Mrs Rosse who were not so sure and Askew found out some other facts which intrigued him. A few weeks before her death Mrs Rosse had confided to one of Gregory's friends that she had destroyed a previous will at Gregory's suggestion. She had also told the friend that Gregory had been pressing her for money and that he had had to mortgage everything he could.

It was decided to exhume the body of Mrs Rosse, a happening of which Gregory knew nothing. By this time he had finished his sentence and gone to Paris.

At the inquest Sir Bernard Spilsbury, the famous pathologist, said that he had found no brain haemorrhage and no sign of Bright's disease and was unable to find the cause of death. There was no trace of poison, although Sir Bernard said there were certain poisons which would have produced the same symptoms. He said the coffin had been flooded in the riverside grave and any traces of poison would have been washed away.

The death certificate was wrong but how Mrs Rosse died remained a mystery. The only person who might have known was Maundy Gregory who had possibly pulled off the ultimate in con-tricks, and was living in fair style in Paris. For when he was released from jail the man who had exposed him, Lord Davidson, on the orders of Stanley Baldwin, paid him a sum of money and a pension to keep his silence.

And keep it he did until he died in a Gestapo hospital in 1941.

MAUNDY MONEY

There is nothing more hilarious than when a biter gets bit. It happened once to the larger than life subject of the Honours Scandal – Maundy Gregory.

Con-men are generally imaginative and bright people with inventive minds. At the height of his success, Gregory took time off from promoting the aristocracy to speculating on the opportunities in the noble sport of Kings. To Maundy betting on one of two horses in a race exposed him to the undesirable chance of losing and his mind dwelt on the possibility of fixing a race or two.

Maundy Gregory was not a man to do things by halves and his concept certainly seemed foolproof. Not for him the twilight world of bribing jockeys, he decided to own all the horses in the race and bet on the *order* in which they finished. This is the highest payout type bet.

He imagined, quite rightly, that it would not be so easy to pull this stroke in England, so, after spending some months building up a suitable string of horses (ostensibly owned by different nominees) he took them to Belgium.

There he entered his horses in the 3:30 race one damp afternoon at a seaside race track. All seven horses in the race belonged to Gregory and the jockeys were briefed as to the precise order in which to finish. It was a flat race so despite the drizzle the plan looked foolproof.

The race started and went according to Maundy's master plan until – a few hundred yards out – disaster struck. A sudden breeze blew a patch of sea mist across the track just before the finishing line. The horses disappeared into the mist and when they emerged to pass the post they had become hopelessly muddled and were in completely the wrong order.

For a man who more than once assured his prospective 'mark' that obtaining him a knighthood was 'a racing certainty' it must have been an especially galling experience.

JEROME HOFFMAN –
TAKE THE MONEY AND RUN

by Michael Gillard

There have been few richer rackets than the offshore fund game. It produced a new breed of slick, share selling dream peddlers who saw the world as their market.

The offshore fund was a Sixties' refinement of the British unit trust or American mutual fund which had first appeared forty years before. The theory is that the unit trust or mutual fund provides the means for small, unsophisticated investors, without the knowledge or time to regularly buy and sell shares in order to maximize income or capital gain, to spread their money and the risk over anything up to 100 different shares chosen by full-time experts. This is achieved by investing directly in the trust or fund which in turn buys and manages the large number of shares with the investors' cash.

The trust or fund is usually open-ended. That means it can sell as many units to buyers as are demanded, unlike a company, where the number of shares in issue is strictly limited.

Subsequently this concept was adapted by several American money managers in the Sixties for investing in property.

The term 'offshore' originated about the same time when investment managers began to look towards tax havens like the Bahamas, Bermuda and Liberia – far from the legally restricting shores of the US or Britain – as bases for new funds.

Offshore funds presented the key to hundreds of thousands of cash caches, many of them illegal, secreted in mattresses, private safes, High Street deposit boxes or Swiss numbered accounts; hoards which were constantly threatened by inflation or revolution or both. It was a perceptive American salesman named Bernard Cornfeld who showed how this cornucopia of cash could be unlocked. The founder of Investors Overseas Services (IOS) and his legion of imitators made use of little known corners of the globe with accommodating laws to the benefit of their bank balances. So successful were they that by 1970, when their afghani to zloty filled money balloon burst, these pied pipers had charmed away perhaps £2,500,000,000 of other people's money. Today, several stock market crises, good-ideas-gone-wrong and plain, old fashioned frauds later, an estimated up to £1,000,000,000 has disappeared.

But while this caused much private distress in the offshore darkness, where the investors' dreams had sunk without trace, most of the dream merchants themselves landed safely and contentedly onshore, their cash intact.

Born out of the money game's two most potent parents – greed and fear – offshore funds found their victims mostly outside the US, where the Securities & Exchange Commission's regulations prohibited offshore investment by American residents, and Britain, where the funds were banned by the Exchange Control rules. Elsewhere, however, buying into many different, fast appreciating shares or properties seemed to offer profit without risk while removing the twin fears of loss and inflation. More important, the offshore concept overcame a primary fear for those who had to live with the spectre of the 'equalization of wealth', and similar inconvenient political theories in the Third World.

Anonymous accounts in Swiss banks had always been the traditional insurance policy against that knock on the door in the middle of the night. Offshore funds extended that security to anyone with two or three hundred pounds cash or the ability to pay a few pounds a month for the next five or ten years. Now the company executive in Rome, the shopkeeper in Dar-es-Salaam, the rice merchant in Saigon, the lawyer in Rio de Janeiro and the hotel manager in Bahrain, as well as princes, presidents and politicians, could sleep more easily at night. So too could the London abortionist and the New York mobster.

Maximum profit, minimum risk, secrecy guaranteed − and no petty inconveniences like the taxman. This was the theory behind the beautiful dream that separated over 1,000,000 investors from £2,500,000,000.

The laws of the offshore jungle were few, succinct and, while the spell lasted, infallible.

Law One: use to the full the largely non-existent company law and enticing tax concessions for non-resident companies in such noted financial centers as Liechtenstein, Panama, Bermuda, the Bahamas, Cayman Islands, Netherlands Antilles or Liberia.

Once incorporated, foreign owned funds registered in these locales were usually required legally to do little more than pay a registration or incorporation fee. Controls over the directors of the fund and their handling of the fund's money were minimal − where they existed at all. The off-shore fundsters hit upon a legal vacuum which they proceeded to fill with other people's cash, safe in the knowledge that they were answerable to no-one. Bernie Cornfeld's surprise arrest by the Swiss police in May, 1973 and his subsequent several months in jail without trial was the first evidence that 'offshore' did not necessarily mean prison-proof. When the unpleasant truth about off-shore funds was discovered by the investors, the dream ended and the nightmare began of trying to recoup their savings. But the offshore sharks had been aware that in appealing to tax dodgers and ilegal investors they were dealing with many who could not tell and so dare not yell.

Law Two: set up headquarters at a prestigious address in one of Europe's main money centers like London or Geneva. Both offered all the commercial advantages with few legal disadvantages.

Law Three: deck the board of the company running the fund with well known and respected names.

This created the necessary aura of respectability and security.

Because the operative word in their credentials would be 'former' such boardroom window dressing didn't come so expensive. They also came eager for the gilt on the offshore gingerbread: bargain priced shares in the all-important fund management company.

All that remained was to add publicity material geared more to optimism than objectivity, recruit an army of money-hungry salesmen with promises of fat commissions and an offshore fund was born.

By 1968 IOS was rising towards its £1,000,000,000 high-water mark. Cornfeld's imitators had left little room for new offshore angles on investing in US shares. However investing in property had been relatively overlooked. The front runner here was Great America Management & Research Corporation. GRAMCO had been the 1966 brainchild of offshore prodigy Keith Barish from Miami, then just 21, and his Cuban partner Rafael Navarro. Two years later Barish and Navarro were on their way to controlling £100,000,000 plus of the public's money through their Nassau-based fund USIF (United States Investment Fund) Real Estate.

It was at this time that another American, Jerome D. Hoffman, decided to challenge GRAMCO's hegemony with a creation of his own, the Real Estate Fund of America.

Hoffman knew property and knew also that land had a powerful selling edge over shares – it rarely went down in value in the long term. Also he realized that there was more to be made from buying land and building on it than in GRAMCO's policy of buying already let office blocks. Another astute piece of Hoffman sales psychology was the knowledge that an ambitious property proposition could appeal to thousands of people for whom the purchase of land or their own home was the first step towards wealth and security; people moreover who knew little about American property and even less of the dangers lurking in offshore funds.

Jerry Hoffman may have had few social graces and a less than engaging habit of punctuating or terminating sentences with a grunting, nasal snort but what the squat, beetle-browed American lacked in appearance and person-ality he made up with his salesmanship. Hoffman was touched occasionally with a promotional genius that lifted him into the Brooklyn Bridge selling class. It was this quality that had already carried him a long way from the Mid-West city of St Louis, where he had been born in 1933, and the small-time property deals of his father, Morris Hoffman.

There were two versions of the Jerome Hoffman story. The first was strictly for boardroom, investor and general public consumption. The second was the truth.

The essential and recurring themes of the authorized Hoffman biography were spelled out in the September, 1969 issue (Number 1904) of his own house magazine, *Fund Forum*. Much of what appeared there, under the headline 'J. D. Hoffman: man of action', was as phoney as the magazine number itself. Like the REFA prospectus, Hoffman's view of Hoffman was based on exaggeration of the trivial and neglect of the important.

He billed himself as a poor boy made good, working his way through Washington University and the London School of Economics. A pioneer, organizing one of the first real estate investment trusts, National Realty Investors. A whiz-kid, transforming Institutional Monetary Corpora-tion from a one-man-and-a-desk outfit into 'an instant success'. An idealist, abandoning the plush Madison Avenue offices of his booming companies to travel abroad and establish a 'new investment giant'. Old newspaper headlines were resurrected, very selectively: 'Man of the Week' – *Real Estate Weekly*, March, 1967. These were mixed with favorable quotes salvaged from even the most unflattering of cuttings. The final ingredient was the human touch. Hoffman the sportsman working out with the baseball greats of the St Louis Cardinals. (Hoffman later demonstrated an obsessive desire to take over the New

York Yankees team but was laughed away, short of first base, in two farcical attempts.)

The truth was both less romantic and impressive.

Washington University is not to be confused with the University of Washington in Seattle but is a less well known institution in St. Louis. The London School of Economics had no record of a Jerome D. Hoffman. It was with somewhat lesser qualifications that Hoffman moved to New York in the late Fifties to become a broker for Brown Harris Stevens, one of the city's largest property firms. Later Hoffman moved on and into his own mortgage broking scheme. This was Institutional Monetary Corporation which he set up two years later. Ingenious in conception and ambitious in execution this gave a startling insight into Hoffman's style and methods of doing business.

Hoffman made his play for the big time in 1966 when, during a mortgage famine, Institutional Monetary Corp. circularized thousands of property owners as far away as Puerto Rico and Guam offering unlimited mortgages. Within a few months this sales drive brought Hoffman to the attention of New York's Attorney-General, Louis J. Lefkowitz. Two years later he alleged that Hoffman's company had received over 600 replies asking for no less than £440,000,000. Only £1,700,000 was actually advanced on the only three of the promised mortgages ever completed. However, this had been enough for Hoffman to rake in fees of over £400,000.

IMC was set up so that mortgage seekers would be impressed by his 60 employees and classy offices. Once impressed the clients were carved up in two ways. First the property owner was charged a £200 fee for an 'inspection' of his property. Then, after a meeting at IMC's office during which Hoffman promised a mortgage, another fee – ranging from £1,000 to £10,000 – was extracted for an 'appraisal' of the deal by a second Hoffman company, Criterion Marketing Report. All this before the customer saw the nature of his mortgage, which was always less than

Hoffman had originally promised or on unacceptable terms. Lefkowitz branded the scheme 'reckless, improvident and fraudulent' and brought Hoffman's activities to the attention of the Post Office, the Securities & Exchange Commission and the US Attorney for Manhattan.

Hoffman denied the Attorney-General's allegations but consented to a permanent injunction banning him from share dealing in New York. A ban was also imposed on a £10,000,000 sale to the public by Hoffman of shares in Institutional Monetary Trust.

All of this might have dashed the ambitions of a man lacking Hoffman's resilience. But it was not for nothing that he would regularly proclaim 'I don't give in easily'. He began planning a comeback away from New York.

Early in 1968 Hoffman met socially New York lawyer John Lang, a partner in Hill Betts, Yamaoka, Freehill and Longcope which had in the past acted for the British Government. Shortly after that he approached Lang about a possible shipping venture that ultimately fell through. Then in September, 1968 Hoffman contacted Lang again. This time he had a new idea – an offshore property fund. According to the attorney he already had letters from several prominent individuals agreeing to become directors of the management company. One of these was to come from Reginald Maudling, Britain's former Chancellor of the Exchequer and deputy leader of the Conservative Party.

Another recruit according to Lang was the chairman of the Automobile Association, Viscount Brentford, a one-time Ministerial colleague of Maudling's and senior partner in the London solicitors Joynson-Hicks & Co.

Although prevented from selling shares in New York this did not prevent Hoffman recruiting big names to sit round the boardroom table of an offshore fund which was not to be sold in the US. Early on he recruited Holmes Brown, the chairman of the New York Board of Trade, who had worked under John F. Kennedy's brother-in-law Sargent Shriver as Assistant Director of the Office of

Economic Opportunity. Hoffman soon added to the REFA roll-call of Washington alumini: Dixon Donnelley, ex-Special Assistant to the Secretary of the Treasury; Charles A. Sullivan, former Deputy Special Assistant to the Secretary of State for Disarmament; Kennedy aide John F. Wood; James G. Morton, ex-Special Assistant to the Secretary of Commerce; Henry J. Kuss, America's chief arms salesman when former Deputy Assistant Defense Secretary.

Hoffman also brought in Robert F. Wagner, three times Mayor of New York and a former US ambassador, together with several other business and legal figures.

From Europe, in addition to Maudling and Brentford, Hoffman brought Paul Henri Spaak, the one-time Belgian Prime Minister and Secretary-General of NATO, plus William Clarke, Director of the Committee on Invisible Exports. All were at one time directors of the management company.

Hoffman's appetite for famous names was insatiable. So much so that 'ghost' directors appeared in sales literature or discussions. One such was Dr Robert Weaver, the first black in a modern US Cabinet when President Johnson's Housing Secretary. He declined an approach from Hoffman but still featured in the REFA prospectus. Hoffman also claimed former Treasury Secretary Henry Fowler had joined REFA but this too was untrue.

However, the roll of those that did join is a tribute to the salesmanship of a man who once aptly summed himself up by saying: 'I'm a promoter – I may not be an honest guy or a virgin of goodness.' Especially as in June, 1968, when he arrived in London, one associate put his finances at little more than £2,000. But then Hoffman was extremely adept at obtaining backing from those who were given directorships on the promise of the hundredfold payout awaiting in the inevitable future crock of gold.

In addition to his old zap and zeal Hoffman had one more new attribute when he landed in Britain – a connection with the Joynson-Hicks law firm who had carried out occasional legal work for him. Hoffman's aim was to get the senior partner Lord Brentford's name and backing for his proposed offshore fund. Although it was an unlikely combination – the American promoter and the Eton and Oxford-educated heir to the Brentford title, who with his father was a fervent supporter of the evangelist Billy Graham's crusades – Hoffman succeeded and Joynson-Hicks became London solicitors to the proposed Real Estate Fund of America. Lord Brentford and his son apparently also advanced loans for initial expenses. But the Brentford name was worth more than money. It gave Hoffman a credibility that was to be vital in putting REFA on its financial feet. Brentford and his son became directors of both the management and sales companies.

It was Lord Brentford who suggested and recruited Reginald Maudling for REFA. The two men had been contemporaries as both Members of Parliament and junior Ministers in the early Fifties. On September 26, 1968 Maudling received a letter inviting him to join the Real Estate Management Company of America board from Brentford. The letter outlined the project, which was highly regarded and warmly recommended by a man Maudling 'knew and trusted'. The peer clearly felt he knew and could trust Hoffman. Maudling therefore replied that he would be pleased to become a director.

The Real Estate Fund of America was an interesting idea into which the Tory politician apparently did not enquire closely enough. Maudling was convinced that further investigation was rendered unnecessary by the Brentford recommendation, the prestigious advisors and the suggestion – untrue – that he might be joined on the board by the prominent US Senator William Fulbright and a top German banker.

Reginald Maudling was to be rewarded in shares rather than salary for his confidence in REFA and its promoter. Maudling became a shareholder in the management company because, in his own words, he was 'hoping to build up a little pot of money for my old age.' It is not difficult to see why Maudling saw REFA as providing that assuring prospect.

IOS was said to have created an army of dollar million-aires from those lucky enough to get shares in the management company through being early directors and executives. Shares in GRAMCO Management soared to over £7 each within a few months of their public flotation in May, 1969. Its parent company GRAMCO International, owned mainly by Barish and Navarro, was then worth around £70,000,000. Merchant bankers Kleinwort Benson, where Maudling was a director, were involved in the GRAMCO share sale at the same time as Maudling was finalizing with Hoffman plans to launch REFA.

The attraction of shares in the management company to Maudling was also increased by one other simple but highly tasty perquisite. The former Chancellor was given his shares. He was quite prepared to pay but possible Exchange Control problems, which would probably have necessitated buying the shares with expensive investment dollars, led to Hoffman offering the shares as a gift, which Maudling accepted. The Tory politician became one of the biggest director-shareholders with 10,000 of the 1,000,000 shares. There was also an option agreement giving the right to raise this holding to 5% of the Management shares. Hoffman baited his hook well. And the prestige Maudling gave REFA made the bait cheap at the price. His world-wide reputation was perhaps the fund's greatest asset and its promoter's strongest card.

For some months Hoffman toyed with the idea of incorporating REFA in the Bahamas. However, the fund was finally set up in Liberia on January 27, 1969. Real Estate Management Company of America and Real Estate Fund of America (Sales) were incorporated there the same day. The three companies were incorporated on Lang's instructions by an American owned resident business agent, International Trust Company of Liberia. Three of its employees were listed as the first directors and subscribed for a nominal one share each.

The companies were nothing more than brass plates – three of many – outside the agent's offices in Monrovia. Any mail was merely forwarded to the REFA registered office in Bermuda. International Trust's attitude towards REFA was succinct: 'We do not have any records nor does Liberian law demand that we should.' There is cold comfort in such hot climates for the victims of offshore frauds. Incorporated in Liberia, legally resident in Bermuda and based in London, the barely contiguous REFA corporate chain reforged slavery's eighteenth-century golden triangle. But this time the westward cargo was investors not slaves, although the number who survived, cash intact, would have brought no smile to the captain of a Liverpool slaver.

Jerry Hoffman was the common link in the triangle. The £4,000,000 that poured into REFA was always moving between companies he alone controlled. Hoffman owned all the Sales share capital and as its Executive Vice President drew a salary of £20,000 a year. Sales passed all the cash it brought in on to REFA minus either an initial or redemption charge. It also received a commission from Management which reimbursed the cost of the sales effort. Another company handled the fund's headquarters administration in return for a 5% fee. The investment of the REFA cash was handled by Management. The money went round and around but came out where?

Hoffman is estimated to have bought or held options on 650,000 of the 1,000,000 Management shares at a cost of just £2,600. These shares were then sold to directors of the management company, salesmen or even REFA investors. The management company made its money partly by charging a fee of 1/12 of 1% per month on the net assets of the fund but mostly in the 5% to 6% brokerage commission it charged on every property bought or sold by the fund.

By means of these commissions Management was free to take a fat slice of the investors' cash – and this is promptly what it did. This arrangement made it in Management's interest therefore to buy the most expensive properties even though this loaded the fund with debt. This is known as 'gearing' – borrowing against properties owned but no more than perhaps 20% paid for – and was common practice for American property companies. Although extremely dangerous for a fund vulnerable to the sudden withdrawal of cash by investors, 'gearing' enabled REFA to expand faster than it could have done relying on its own resources. But more important, through the thinly disguised 'stripping' of the brokerage charge, this created a steady flow of bigger and bigger commissions into Management and therefore Hoffman's pocket.

In the words of the old song, Jerry Hoffman indeed had come a long way from St Louis, when on May 16, 1969 he sat alongside the ex-Chancellor Reginald Maudling and AA chairman Lord Brentford in London's Waldorf Hotel to unveil REFA to the world. Hoffman told the Press he expected the fund to build properties worth £100,000,000 in the first 18 months. 'I think it's quite remarkable that we are bringing together the combined investment and financial facilities of both sides of the Atlantic,' Maudling enthused. The prospectus produced by the company for that occasion was a masterly mixture of glib generalizations, cunning misrepresentations, stunning omissions, blatant lies and the occasional true fact. The entire package, with its glowing promises and confident assurances, was gift-wrapped in enticing quotations from the famous and phoney photographs of Manhattan skyscrapers which REFA did not and could never own. It made powerful sucker bait and was partly the work of a professional advertising man who later admitted, 'I'm afraid we did a lot of things we should not have done.'

Among these was producing a brightly colored leaflet, 'Profit through Construction', which included three pictures of buildings all captioned to give the impression of REFA ownership. Hoardings or signs indicating their name or the builder were cleverly removed. Two were under construction by George A. Fuller whose president William V. Lawson was a REFA director.

The prospectus was stuffed full of emotive statements and mouth-watering success stories from the super-rich like John D. Rockefeller, Henry Ford, and Joseph P. Kennedy. Encouraging homilies about the value of land were contributed by Presidents Franklin D. Roosevelt, Harry Truman and Lyndon Johnson.

One item, however, was not to be found among all this chaff. Any mention of Hoffman's brush with the New York authorities, hardly a plus factor in persuading a potential investor to part with his cash. Of the 12 directors listed in the prospectus, the least was said about the most important. Jerome Hoffman merited just two lines: 'Executive Vice President, Real Estate Management Company of America.' Shortly afterwards he resigned from the management company thereby avoiding any future reference at all.

Hoffman's longest running and most blatant misrepresentation was the construction myth. Maudling reportedly told the inaugural press conference: 'The novel approach of this fund is that we, unlike any other fund, intend to start with construction'. This turned out to be no more than an empty slogan. Nineteen months and £4,000,000 later not one brick had been laid on another.

This myth should have died in September, 1969 when Lawson resigned because there was going to be no business for his construction company. However, despite Lawson's departure, Hoffman continued to use his and Fuller's name so keeping the image alive. Meanwhile investors were still fed the lie. 'We start from the ground up', declared the 1970 edition of the REFA prospectus. Even as late as October, 1970 Hoffman declared the fund was building 14 apartment houses and an extension to another property. Hardly Manhattan skyscrapers.

But this was only one of several similar misrepresentations.

Security for the investor was undermined by Management's own policies. Growth was minimal – just $7\frac{1}{2}\%$ in the first year although a minimum of 10% was promised to large investors.

Very quickly too Hoffman forgot about the pledge to hold 30% of the fund's assets in cash or saleable securities. This was to back up the promise of repayment on demand. In fact all REFA's securities were sold in August, 1969 and the cash turned over to Hoffman.

Very soon even the promised 'mandatory' right to cash on demand was cancelled by a loophole clause allowing the fund to 'temporarily suspend' this right 'during the existence of any extraordinary state of affairs prejudicial to the participating unitholders and the fund.'

Investors in REFA were also enticed by the claim that, unlike IOS or GRAMCO, there were no heavy charges made against subscriptions in the first three years to pay the salesmen's commissions and overheads. This was true. But if the investor wanted his money back in year one he suffered a one-third deduction. Even in year three it was still 6%.

Annual reports were promised but never materialized. This is perhaps not surprising as even some of the Management directors claimed they were unable to discover any information about REFA's finances from Hoffman. Similarly the promised annual valuations of the properties failed to appear and no independent valuation was ever made.

But the investor did not seemingly just have to rely on Hoffman's word. Could not auditors like Peat Marwick Mitchell be trusted to check the books? Surely banks such as Marine Midland Grace Trust in New York and Bermuda's N. T. Butterfield were reliable enough to hold cash and property deeds, and Wall Street wizards like Lionel D. Edie and brokers Blair & Co were there to invest the money. Would not lawyers such as Hill Betts, Joynson-Hicks and Appleby Spurling & Kempe (the fund's lawyers in Hamilton, Bermuda) see the law was obeyed?

Alas, it was not always on these names from the prospectus that the REFA investor ended up relying. And where it was, there may be some justification for criticism.

Peat Marwick departed on September, 1969 but were replaced by the equally reputable Arthur Young. The original depositary custodian Marine Midland Grace had already left the scene by then. However, this did not mean all the cash collected by Sales went to N. T. Butterfield as was suggested. First it was re-routed to the Geneva branch of the US-connected Foreign Commerce Bank. Later the cash flowed to the little known Investment Bank in Zurich following the purchase of that bank by Hoffman, Wagner, Brown and Hoffman's attorney Milton Zeiberg. For the final two months of the fund's life the property deeds too may have rested in Hoffman's bank.

By these unannounced manoeuvres REFA fundholders, never the most protected species, were stripped of even the elementary offshore security of independent custodians for the fund's cash and assets.

As for Blair, Hoffman's own brokers, they ceased to trade in August, 1970 due to insolvency. Edie had resigned three months before because there was no longer any cash to advise on investing.

So much for the supposed safeguard of relying on prospectus promises and reputations where the offshore fund game was concerned. Despite the presence of so many notables, or maybe because of this, it had been agreed from the start that Hoffman should run the fund. Lord Brentford later reminded him: 'Crispin and I believed that it was in the best interests of potential investors that the day-to-day management should be delegated to you as the originator of the project and the person in whom we, and I believe my co-directors, had every confidence.'

That was their second mistake.

For Hoffman's ideas of management were influenced as much by his own paranoic suspicions as by his desire and need to ensure the figureheads became no more than that. James Morton recalls only two Management board meetings while he was a director, neither of which he attended.

John Wood found that a director's role was to sign proxy forms for unattended board meetings in faraway Bermuda because the Management board and the executive committee only ever met there and only then by proxy in most cases.

But this was not an impression Hoffman wanted to disclose publicly. So he deliberately fostered the view that Maudling in particular was not just a beaming, friendly face on the prospectus but a 'daily, active President.'

Later Maudling specifically denied this description. His position was that being President of the management company was a part-time post not concerned with day-to-day operations. However, this merely emphasizes the dangers in active politicians' involvement in commercial ventures and his own misjudged oversight in being too busy to check how he and REFA were represented to the other directors and the world at large by Hoffman.

The reason Hoffman cultivated the Maudling connection was that it held the key to REFA's success and survival. By his association with the fund the politician endowed REFA and its founder with a respectability neither could have achieved otherwise in Europe. Just how influential this may have been was summed up by Anthony Fetherston, managing director of REFA's early advertising agents who went bankrupt when Hoffman did not pay their bill. 'People like me, small businessmen, are entitled to expect that if a man like Maudling puts his name on I'm entitled to give them credit. It was good enough for me if he thought Hoffman was sound. A man like Maudling has every means at his disposal to find out whether this man was sound or not.'

At a higher level too Maudling's presence had influence. Morton, who met him for the first and only time at a dinner party given by co-director Charles Sullivan, was impressed by the ex-Chancellor's reputation and this was a prime factor in his decision to join REFA.

However, Maudling's most valuable service to Hoffman

was overseas. His prestigious name opened to Hoffman
some of the more influential doors in Europe and the
Middle East. Maudling was the ace in the credibility pack
and no one was more aware of that than the man who had
picked him to head REFA. No opportunity of exploiting
the link was wasted. Both salesmen and clients could not
fail to be impressed by Hoffman's ability to conjure up
Britain's former Chancellor as an apparent friend and
supporter.

The Summer of 1969 found Maudling and Hoffman in
the Middle East. The oil rich sheikhdoms of the Persian
Gulf were wide open to the prowling predators of the off-
shore jungle. And Maudling, through the Tory Party's
policy of maintaining Britain's military presence East of
Suez, had no shortage of high-powered contacts there.
REFA salesmen became regular visitors to Kuwait,
Bahrain and the smaller Gulf emirates.

But it was in Europe that Hoffman relied on Maudling
to beat the REFA drum loudest and longest.

Originally the fund was not to be sold by legions of
high pressure salesmen, the method employed by IOS and
GRAMCO. Instead REFA was to be sold through leading
banks. Hoffman looked to Maudling to establish this sales
network. He was well equipped for the role. As a director
of one of London's best connected merchant banks, a
former Chancellor, number two in the Tory hierarchy and
a pro-European, Maudling had the entrée to most of the
top banking parlors on the Continent. Maudling used
these personal contacts to soften up the tightly-knit European banking establishment for Hoffman – a feat the
American would have found impossible alone.

Kredietbank Luxembourgeoise agreed to act as the
custodian bank in Europe because of the involvement of
Maudling and Spaak. Before doing so the bank checked
with Maudling but not with the former Belgian prime
minister. That was a pity. Had they done so they would
have discovered that Spaak had resigned in March and
did not know Hoffman was still using his name. When

they discovered this, Kredietbank pulled out of the agreement.

Just how valuable an asset Maudling was to Hoffman was shown at the American Bankers Association's international monetary conference in Copenhagen in June, 1969. Maudling had attended the two previous get-togethers which were a magnet for Europe's banking elite. On this occasion the REFA president was able to preach the gospel according to Jerome Hoffman.

On his return, the first President wrote several letters to drive home his initial sales message. One letter went to Felix Schulthess, head of Credit Suisse and one of the three major 'Gnomes of Zurich'. Sales backing from his bank would have carried weight far beyond the Alps. Maudling also wrote to another member of the gnome triumvirate, Edgar Paltzer of the Swiss Bank Corporation, seeking an appointment for Hoffman. Letters extolling REFA went to Herman van den Wall Bake of Amsterdam's Algemene Bank Nederland and Johannes Green of the Danish Privatbanken. Maudling also wrote to Switzerland's equivalent of the Governor of the Bank of England, Edwin Stopper of the Swiss National Bank, whose support could have been influential.

However, Maudling's invitations to sell REFA or meet Hoffman were politely declined by almost every banker to whom he wrote. Similar lack of success accompanied his efforts in West Germany with the Deutsche Bank, Belgium with the Banque de Bruxelles, Sweden with the Skandinaviska Banken, Stockholm's Enskilda Bank and the Svenska Handelsbanken, and Portugal with Banco Pinto & Sotto Mayor. Only in Italy did Hoffman perhaps realize his hopes of using Maudling's reputation and influence to overcome hard faced money managers' caution. In June, 1970 Hoffman launched a locally based Italian fund. This might have been helped by Maudling's friendship with a top official in the Italian central bank, which had lead him the previous year reportedly to express confidence that he could get REFA into Italy.

The failure of so many banks to respond to Maudling's invitation is not entirely surprising. By 1969 the Continental banks, hard hit by the profit sapping drain of clients' funds to IOS and GRAMCO, were more concerned to build up their own competitive funds than sell yet another rival. Also there is no doubt that certain bankers at least, after examining REFA, failed to share its first President's confidence.

So, having failed to win over the banks with Maudling's charm and charisma, Hoffman swiftly joined his offshore competitors in illegal money transfers through undercover salesmen as well as the normal sales campaigns.

Reginald Maudling's confidence that his bizarre business associate had the 'best possible hands' into which the bankers could entrust their clients' cash received a massive jolt on June 22, 1969 when the *Sunday Times* publicized the Lefkowitz injunction banning Hoffman from dealing in shares.

Hoffman's attitude towards Lefkowitz's accusations and the injunction took one of two approaches. Either he ignored them – as in the REFA prospectus or sales literature – or he explained them away as politically motivated and purely technical. 'It was a political manoeuvre to prevent me from building the sports arena in Harlem and cashing in colored votes for the Democrats', he declared on one occasion. By way of further justification the REFA boss was able to point to the fact that IOS in 1967 had consented to a veto by the Securities & Exchange Commission on selling to Americans anywhere. And in June, 1969 Hoffman was still able to make capital out of the fact that he had voluntarily consented to the injunction, not accepted the charges, faced no trial and was the target of no further legal action.

Such ambivalence came second nature to a man who, despite his frequently used motto of 'I say what I mean and mean what I say', often experienced great difficulty in separating fact from fiction and dream from reality.

After the ban became known Maudling, who denied any

prior knowledge, was heard to say he was 'bloody angry with Brentford', no doubt because of the embarrassment caused by such an unfortunate association. For the astonishing truth is that he had made no meaningful check on Hoffman's background before joining REFA. He had relied on Lord Brentford's recommendation and the other 'names' associated with the fund.

However, the alarm bells were now starting to ring about REFA and its promoter and not just in the then Board of Trade and at Scotland Yard, both of whom now began paying a close interest in Hoffman's activities.

On July 3 William Clarke suddenly discovered a conflict of interest between being a Management director and his positions at National & Grindlays Bank and the Bank of London & South America. Clarke told Maudling he was resigning and left without any public announcement. Confidence dwindled further after BBC TV's Money Programme on July 10 revealed more details about the New York mortgage swindle.

The pressure on Maudling to resign from REFA was mounting fast. About this time Kleinwort Benson informed Maudling of what they had discovered about Hoffman from New York. The bank suggested Maudling should break with REFA.

This decision became inescapable when Maudling learned that, for the third time in a month, REFA and Hoffman were to come under attack, this time from *The Times*. Now his image as deputy leader of the Tory Party could not escape damage if he persisted as President. Maudling decided he could no longer afford a connection with Jerome Hoffman. At an interview with the newspaper on July 18 Maudling announced his immediate resignation as President of Management and as director of Sales because 'as the election draws nearer I am finding I need more and more time for my political work.'

The next day *The Times* broke the news of his departure and the previous defections by Spaak and Clarke. In one move Hoffman had lost three of his four European front men, dealing a heavy blow to investor confidence.

However, all was not totally lost. Maudling's resignation statement that 'in my judgement the Real Estate Fund is a good and sound investment' and the ex-President's apparent efforts to ensure he was not seen to be resigning over Hoffman personally, enabled the REFA boss to continue exploiting the connection long afterwards. The wording of the statement was money in the fund and its value can be judged from the £3,800,000 subsequently conjured into REFA. In fact minus two inconvenient paragraphs referring to the injunction, Maudling's resignation statement was helpful enough to be featured in a press release the following month announcing Holmes Brown's succession as President.

Unfortunately only a hint was given in the statement – mention of the need to maintain 'a continuous and detailed check' on the fund's day-to-day operations – that perhaps the first President no longer shared the same absolute confidence in the promoter as he did in the product.

By not voicing the suspicions he hinted at subsequently and by not severing all links with the REFA chief, Reginald Maudling helped Hoffman overcome a near disaster in this stage of the fund's life which could have made selling REFA much more difficult.

Perhaps nowhere outside REFA's London headquarters was news of Maudling's departure more unwelcome than at the Norske Creditbank in Oslo. For this leading Norwegian bank had been Maudling's first and perhaps only sales success.

The ex-President's success was not altogether surprising because, as in so many of the banks he approached on REFA's behalf, inside help was to hand in the shape of managing director Johan Melander. Maudling and the banker were old acquaintances having first met ten years or so before during the negotiations to form the European Free Trade Area.

Thus Melander was agreeably inclined towards

REFA when in April, 1969 he received a letter from his old acquaintance informing him of his link with the property fund and asking the banker to meet Hoffman in order to discuss the Norske Creditbank's possible involvement. In fact, Melander was impressed as much by the association of Maudling, Brentford and Spaak (who had already resigned) with REFA as by the opportunity for what his friend termed an 'interesting' investment. So much so that he replied to Maudling that the bank would indeed consider making an investment. REFA's first big catch was on the hook. Hoffman came to Oslo to complete the sale in May.

The Norske Creditbank made one of the largest investments in REFA, buying £140,000 worth of units in the fund. Another £60,000 in Euro-dollars (US dollars held by foreigners outside the US and traded on European money markets) was held at the bank on the fund's behalf. The Euro-dollars represented the prospectus requirement that 30% of the fund's assets should be in cash. This splitting of its investment was soon to pay an unexpected dividend for the Norwegians.

The reaction of Oslo to the news that Maudling had walked out of REFA was slow to form but decisive. Melander decreed that the bank must withdraw its cash, even if it had to suffer a 10% redemption charge. Accordingly on September 11, the Norske Creditbank wrote to Hoffman asking for its £200,000 back.

This sudden request could not have come at a more inconvenient time for Hoffman. He had just bought REFA's first property, a nine-storey apartment building on Staten Island, New York. The total cost was £887,000 financed mostly on two mortgages. But there was still £135,000 in cash to be found, partly to pay Management's brokerage commission of almost £50,000. REFA was teetering on a knife edge. The sudden loss of the Oslo bank's £200,000 could have been disastrous. Hoffman therefore prevaricated, in order to delay paying back the Norwegians. His initial reaction was to turn on the

Maudling magic. Hoffman telexed the bank that he had discussed its requests with the former President who would be contacting them. (Maudling denies this.) He stressed to the Norwegians that Maudling remained a supporter of REFA despite his resignation. This was proved two weeks later when an elated Hoffman received an open letter reaffirming Maudling's confidence.

Hoffman kept assuring the bank by telex that Maudling would be in contact and so would they mind waiting for their money. But by October Melander's patience had given way to suspicion and concern. Unprepared to trust Hoffman any more he turned to the man who had brought him into REFA in the first place. Maudling had got the bank in; maybe he could get them out.

On October 16 Melander wrote to Maudling asking him to intervene. He complained about misleading information and that Hoffman was refusing to repay their £200,000.

Maudling tried to act as a peacemaker. He suggested to both sides they should meet and talk. Finally on October 28 Hoffman telexed that he would repay the bank's money, but not immediately. Instead they could have the £140,000 back in six months' time. This was to be done by simply paying into a special bank account money from the sales of REFA units during this period. Hoffman's proposal was wholly at variance with the terms of the prospectus. It also contravened every code of conduct for handling public money. But it allowed REFA to stay afloat just for over a year.

The Norske Creditbank could do little but accept Hoffman's offer. However, it still had the comfort of the £60,000 which had never left Oslo. When the six months were up in April, 1970 the Norske Creditbank duly requested its money once more. It was not repaid then or indeed ever.

The unhappy experience of REFA's first major investor indicates that probably as early as October, 1969 and certainly by April, 1970 the fund could not meet its liabilities to investors when they fell due and so was technically insolvent. Yet REFA continued to fraudulently solicit funds from the public around the world until December, 1970 using advertisements which proclaimed 'A client has the right to redeem his investment on demand.'

Some business ventures are born frauds, some gradually become frauds and others have fraud forced upon them by impending disaster. The saga of how the Norske Credit-bank invested £200,000 in Hoffman's Real Estate Fund of America and what happened when it tried to take the money out is crucial in determining which of these descriptions fits REFA.

As the Norwegian episode illustrated, although Hoffman had lost Maudling as President of the management company he was still able to trade on their continuing relationship, which survived through the politician's role as a shareholder in Hoffman's company. Maudling certainly attempted to get Hoffman to exercise the option he held to buy back the management company shares. However, the American declined the offer.

Hoffman was a seller not a buyer of Management shares. He peddled shares from his own holding – cost £2,400 – to directors, salesmen and clients at ever escalating and totally unrealistic prices. According to one estimate he netted £160,000 this way. Hoffman himself admitted to at least half this figure but claimed most of the proceeds went to pay REFA's overheads.

However, the most significant reason for Hoffman refusing to exercise the option and buy Maudling out was the boost to REFA if the first President remained a shareholder.

Hoffman's action or lack of it put Maudling on the spot. But instead of legally renouncing the shares or transferring their ownership he kept his shareholding and did little to sever this bond until the summer of 1970.

Meanwhile Hoffman could and did continue to exploit at any opportunity Maudling's connection with the fund and his declared confidence in it. This was especially useful in countering the 'black' propaganda mounted against REFA by its rivals.

It was in order to combat this type of attack that Maudling wrote the open letter to Hoffman on September 26, 1969 repeating his earlier endorsement that he 'considered the Real Estate Fund of America was a good and sound investment.' So ecstatic was Hoffman that he had 10,000 copies printed and circulated around the world. Attached to the letter was the postscript: 'Should anyone query the authenticity of the above, they are free to write to Mr Reginald Maudling at the above address' (his Belgravia home).

This letter's value to Hoffman is unquantifiable but undeniable. Its wide usage in Latin America and beyond enabled him to exploit Maudling *in absentia*. The letter was, after all, close to an endorsement of REFA by one of Britain's most prominent political figures. It neutralized much of the bad publicity prompted by Maudling's resignation. So too did Maudling's surprise appearance at the 1969 Christmas party Hoffman gave to wind up a sales conference in London for REFA's general managers, salesmen and executives. Hoffman ensured that a photographer was at hand to capture Maudling's presence. The event was celebrated in the next issue of the house magazine, thereby reaching clients and salesmen alike. REFA investors were no doubt suitably impressed, as Hoffman intended they should be.

This way the fund chief was still able to promote the idea that REFA had Maudling's reassuring backing in June, 1970, almost a year after his resignation, when the first President became an even greater publicity asset as Britain's new Home Secretary – following the surprise Conservative victory in the General Election.

'Congratulations Reggie' drooled the Hoffman house journal. Beneath a photograph of the beaming Maudling his 'pleased former colleagues' reiterated his opinion that REFA was 'a good and sound investment'. Hoffman magnanimously concluded: 'Today it can be seen that Mr Maudling's resignation served the highest possible purpose in the affairs of the United Kingdom'. To celebrate, a four-page leaflet was also produced entitled simply 'IIG (International Investors Group, the name adopted the previous December) congratulates its first President'.

Jerome Hoffman had used the twelve months since Maudling quit to good effect. 'Don't worry about me, I'm growing like a weed' was his reassuring boast during this period. And, incredibly, by the end of August, 1970 REFA had indeed multiplied in size from little more than the Norske Creditbank's £200,000 to over £3,000,000. Sales during July and August were running at the rate of almost £5,500,000 a year.

By this time the REFA message had spread to at least 29 countries and some 1200 investors. Banned from officially selling in the US or Britain, REFA, like most offshore funds, concentrated on rich, financially unsophisticated and politically volatile areas such as Latin America, Africa, the Arab world and the Far East. West Germany too was a fertile source of sales.

However, most of the £4,000,000 that ended up in REFA came there illegally. In only three countries did it sell with official approval. Illegally exported money became REFA's life blood. Waiting for official approval would have been futile. Few governments welcomed residents salting cash away abroad. And anyway REFA's rivals were cheerfully bulldozing their way through tax and currency regulations somewhere every day.

For a while such was Hoffman's success that REFA was even able to shrug off the crisis of confidence in offshore funds provoked by the problems inside IOS which surfaced in April, 1970. Redemptions from the fund were very small, a fact that owed much to Hoffman's simple device of refusing to repay except under duress.

Spurred on by the successes of his salesmen Hoffman embarked on an ambitious schedule of buying, if not building, properties. REFA paid £1,700,000 for 214 apartments and houses in Branford, Connecticut; £3,300,000 for the Ambassador Arms West apartments in Flint, Michigan; £6,000,000 for a half-interest in the Wilshire Hyatt Motel, Los Angeles, a dozen apartment houses in Michigan and the Squire Village apartments in New Windsor, New York State.

The American promoter also began to cultivate ideas for further funds. There was some talk of a Newspaper Fund. National funds were planned for Italy and Greece. However, Hoffman excelled even his own huckster talents with the near mythical Fund of the Seven Seas.

FOSS — the 'Foremost Fund of the Soaring Seventies' as its prospectus called it — inspired Hoffman to scale new peaks of hyperbole and misrepresentation. Not content with using promotional material featuring ships and terminals the fund did not own, plus the support of banks who had no intention of becoming involved in such a venture, Hoffman proudly proclaimed that FOSS would 'have one of the largest shipping fleets in the world'. It was 'arranging for $100,000,000 worth of commitments for ship construction within the next three years'. There were even glowing descriptions of jet-propeled FOSS ships using a revolutionary, automated, FOSS container port in Cornwall. None of this ever got beyond the magnificent world of Hoffman's imagination. Long before he could order so much as a lifeboat FOSS sank from lack of public interest.

More seriously pursued, however, was the statement by IIG chairman Robert Wagner that the fund management group intended to buy a part or all of a bank 'every 30 days somewhere in the world'. IIG loaned Hoffman, Wagner, Brown and Zeiberg the £100,000 deposit to buy the Investment Bank in Zurich. However, though bought with IIG money, the bank was seemingly destined to be owned by the four directors who signed promissory notes for the money. Possibly IIG would have also provided the remaining £240,000 — money that it in turn creamed off REFA, via its double commissions — to complete the purchase in October, 1970 had not the well run dry by that time.

Another bank on Hoffman's shopping list was the National Bank of Dubai, but the deal never went through.

All of this naturally ignored the fact that neither the REFA or FOSS prospectus mentioned a word about spending fund money to buy banks.

However, Hoffman's vaulting ambition did not stop at ships and banks. In May, 1970 he stepped into the IOS crisis by flying to Geneva and making a £56,000,000 take-over bid which only got as far as Bernie Cornfeld's secretary and the newspapers – for whom it was mainly designed. The following month he popped up in New York with a £10,000,000 bid for the New York Yankees baseball team. Again he was not taken seriously. But he was not dismayed by such rebuffs. 'We have $150,000,000 a year to invest – not everything can go right,' he remarked.

Then on August 18 Hoffman made REFA's biggest buy – 12 shopping centers stretching across seven states. The cost was almost £18,000,000 including a £1,000,000 fee to Management. With this deal Hoffman calculated the fund had passed the $100,000,000 mark in terms of assets. The auditors disagreed and put the figure at three-quarters of this amount. But even so this was no mean achievement given that, after overheads, commissions and other expenses, the amount of cash REFA had available for investment was less than a tenth of this figure.

However, the August shopping center spree sent the 'gearing' – borrowing against properties still unpaid for – bounding up from a loans to assets ratio of a disturbing 5:1 to a fatal 12:1. Furthermore, REFA now had to find over £2,000,000 in mortgage repayments by the middle of 1971 although interest rates were soaking up most of the income from the properties.

Only by pushing sales ever higher could REFA hope to meet these rapacious demands. This already difficult task was made even more so by a series of quarrels and disaffections within IIG.

Holmes Brown resigned in July over his uneasiness concerning the way Hoffman was running the fund. Other top executives and salesmen followed. Much of the dissension and unease within IIG's Thorn House headquarters sprang from Hoffman's paranoiac suspicions that his colleagues were conspiring to seize control. At least one sales chief received a midnight telephone call announcing that his treason had been discovered and he was fired. Out in the field the sales force became angry and disillusioned by delayed commissions, bouncing checks and compulsory deductions made for the phoney share option scheme. Soon the army of 3,000 REFA salesmen had dwindled to less than 300.

Hoffman created further problems by refusing to pay creditors. Soon the Butterfield bank began bouncing checks when the IIG overdraft topped £80,000. This resulted in a spate of writs. It also lead to complaints which activated a Fraud Squad investigation into IIG in June.

The final demise of the 'good and sound investment' followed the suspension of redemptions by GRAMCO on October 7, 1970 and a subsequent new outbreak of criticism of Hoffman and REFA in the British Press. Both events started a panic among REFA investors who rushed to get their money out. Cash that had flowed in so fast during the summer flooded out even faster as winter approached. Or would have done had Hoffman let it. For now investors found it harder than ever to redeem the savings REFA had so eagerly accepted. The fund was tottering into a bankruptcy that only a sales miracle could prevent and which Hoffman's policies had made all but inevitable.

Jerry Hoffman had said that his answer to a crisis like that GRAMCO had faced would be to 'work hard, sit tight and pray'. These intentions were soon put to the test and, like so many of his promises, were found wanting.

Faced with pressing demands for the Thorn House rent, a steadily growing pile of other unpaid bills and demonstrations outside the offices by ex-employees demanding their pay, he decided to pull out of London and head for

Rome. This decision was followed within days by the appearance in the IIG headquarters, now almost deserted, of two Department of Trade inspectors acting on the recommendations of a Fraud Squad report completed early in October.

Hoffman himself departed for Rome on November 2, leaving behind IIG debts of £260,000. Four days later the management company was given notice of eviction from Bermuda. IIG retrenched to some 30 employees on the ground floor of an apartment house in Rome's Via Nicolo Porpora where Hoffman still cackled irrepressibly as REFA fell in ruins around him. He wrote to former senior vice president Dawn Rice: 'GRAMCO went out of business. PAR Fund went out of business. IIG stayed and fought back. In fact we are the only major company in the world.'

Not for long. REFA was reeling before a blizzard of redemption demands. By the end of November Hoffman estimated it had reached £1,700,000. Sales meanwhile were almost nothing.

On November 16 he faced a crisis meeting of the remaining Management directors in New York. He tried to bluff his way through by stating that the debts were less than suggested and were being paid off. Neither was true. In fact the very next day Diners Club in London obtained a court judgment against the sales company for £35,000. On discovering this, following his return to London, Brentford cabled Lang and Wagner recommending REFA halt sales immediately and be wound up.

Events were accelerating out of Hoffman's control. A firm of London printers petitioned for the winding up of the IIG service company on November 24. The vendors of the Investment Bank took it back when Hoffman and his partners could not make the second payment, so losing not only the bank but also the sales company's £100,000 which they had 'borrowed'. Bailiffs seized the office furniture in Thorn House as part payment for the rent. Brentford and his son tried to follow Lang in diving overboard

from the IIG ship but found Liberian law did not allow
directors to resign unless they nominated substitutes. Not
an easy task at that particular moment.

Harried now also by creditors in Italy – one estimate put
the debts there at £60,000 – Hoffman finally bowed to the
inevitable and suspended sales and redemptions of REFA
on December 3 before disappearing to New York via
Zurich, Belgrade and Athens. The Italian fiscal police
closed the Rome office and seized most of the contents.
However, Hoffman's white Rolls-Royce managed to make
it back to New York only to be impounded by his ex-
attorney Milton Zeiberg in payment for an unpaid bill.

Hoffman was sacked by Wagner and Brentford, the
senior remaining sales directors, who then set about finding
out where the £4,000,000 invested in REFA had gone.

Very quickly Brentford formed the view that at least
half had been dissipated in overhead expenses, advertising
and commissions. Another £100,000 went for the Investment Bank while a similar amount was loaned to the
management company, guaranteed by Hoffman but not
repaid. However, curiously enough, as late as September
one IIG bank account in Zurich contained almost
£1,000,000. By December, however, this had shrunk to
a mere £3,800.

So where had the investors' money gone? Reliable
estimates suggest that some £1,000,000 probably went in
overheads. Another up to £2,500,000 was eaten away in
brokerage charges, lost deposits and payments on
properties. However, that still leaves some £500,000 that
seems to have just disappeared. Only Hoffman probably
knows where that went.

Nineteen hectic months after its birth the Real Estate
Fund of America was dead. It had contained from the
start the seeds of its collapse. Lax Liberian laws gave no
protection to investors against the directors' actions or the
management company's hefty commissions. These same
commissions and Hoffman's other excesses deprived the
fund of its cash reserves without which it could not meet

the guarantee of repayment on demand. For property, unlike shares, cannot always be sold readily without taking heavy losses. There is no such thing as 'liquid property' as GRAMCO and REFA tried to suggest and their investors learned to their cost.

The policy of heavy borrowings for property purchases had saddled REFA by September, 1970 with debts of over £28,000,000 and interest charges of £2,000,000 a year. The management company and Hoffman benefitted from this through the brokerage commissions. But without regular and growing injections of fresh cash REFA would bleed to death from the efforts of its own expansion. Paying for properties alone was becoming impossible, never mind repaying investors too. Meanwhile soaring costs and Hoffman's depredations gobbled up any semblance of growth in the underlying assets.

Chronic illiquidity, super 'gearing' and bloated overheads alone decreed that nothing as ramshackle as REFA could survive once redemptions outpaced sales. But that is to ignore the basic fact that the Real Estate Fund of America was at best misrepresentation, at worst fraud.

But promoters, like bad pennies, rarely disappear forever no matter how big or obvious the fraud. Jerome Hoffman was no exception.

He reappeared in London in February, 1971 declaring 'I am broke' but still offering to pay a third of the £46,000 owed by the service company if his co-directors, Brentford and Joynson-Hicks, would do the same. His 'offer' unaccepted, Hoffman left London in April for Israel. The American was in no hurry to return to the US. For a month later it was announced that a Federal Grand Jury in New York had indicted him on 32 counts of mail fraud over the Institutional Monetary Corporation mortgage swindle. He faced a 5 year jail sentence on each charge.

The Fraud Squad report on REFA was completed in August, 1970 and recommended a prosecution for Fraud against Hoffman. However, the Director of Public Prosecutions favored a prosecution under the Companies or

Prevention of Fraud (Investments) Acts to be brought by the Department of Trade. This meant no prosecution unless Hoffman returned once more to Britain. But the REFA promoter was far too busy to leave Israel. That was until January, 1972, when he suddenly flew to New York to plead guilty to one count of the mortgage swindle indictment.

Hoffman explained his reappearance by saying he wanted to 'face his responsibilities'. But the more probable reason was that he had put together yet another investment proposition and needed to be able to sell it in the US.

The new venture was offering for sale plots of land on the slopes of Mount Canaan. Enticing brochures were dotted with the requisite Jewish historical references amid winning lines such as 'Don't forget us, daddy, when you think about Israel' and 'Come home, Israel is waiting for you.' The huckster from St. Louis had not lost his touch.

In September, 1971 Hoffman had bought 190 acres of land, enough for 750 plots, from the Israeli government for £400,000 he did not have. His Liechtenstein company paid a £32,000 deposit and promised to pay the balance over five years. Hoffman claimed this deposit and the £20,000 he spent on lawyers for the New York fraud case were all the money he had left and had come from his REFA salary plus selling shares in the management company.

For Homesteads Mount Canaan to work Hoffman needed to unlock the biggest and richest Jewish community in the world. But this he could not do if he faced arrest for fraud. That was why he gave himself up. He may also have gambled on getting a light sentence or even a fine in return. If so he was either unlucky or ill-informed. On St Valentine's Day, 1972 the tearful and astounded would-be new master of Mount Canaan was sent to prison for two years.

As prisoner 74972-158 at the Federal penitentiary in Marion, Illinois, spending all but the first 30 days as a cook, Jerome Hoffman presented a powerful argument against any British prosecution over the REFA fraud before 1974, if then. For no prosecution, it was argued, should be mounted without Hoffman and Hoffman could not be charged until he was released – and then only if he came to Britain or could be extradited.

In fact, Hoffman was paroled in December, 1972 and returned to New York to plan his next comeback. For by then he had lost both the land in Israel and his deposit because of his inability to complete the second payment.

Little more was heard of him or REFA for over a year until in February, 1974 an out of court settlement was reached in various civil suits brought against IIG. Wagner, Brown and Lang, while denying liability, agreed to pay £31,000 between them. With the Los Angeles property, the proceeds of selling the Branford apartments and the remaining cash left when REFA crashed, this added up to almost £400,000. After legal costs this was divided out among those investors who could be located. At the end of the day the REFA fund holders had lost 90% of their money.

There is absolutely no suggestion, of course, that any of the British directors were involved in anything improper, but, and this is the reason for including the *cautionary* tale of Jerry Hoffman, public figures need to be extra careful about their associates and above all check how their names are being used. They have a responsibility for as Judge Edmund L. Palinieri of New York said 'nobody worked for nothing. They all had their feet in the gravy pot.'

A few weeks later a warrant finally was issued for Jerry Hoffman's arrest on fraud charges – in the unlikely event he returned to Britain. Three years later Scotland Yard were still waiting to serve it. Meanwhile reports indicate the irrepressible Hoffman is indeed back in business, first in oil exploration and then in fast food franchises.

The most significant factor in explaining the REFA crash was the man who devised, ran and controlled the fund from the beginning. Every part of the operation bears Hoffman's indelible mark. The Real Estate Fund of America was a skyscraper built not so much on sand as his hot air and hope. And when both ran out there was no doubt in Jerry Hoffman's mind as to what he would do. As he informed the remaining survivors in REFA's Rome office a month before the end: 'If things get worse Abboud (his assistant) and me are going to take the money and run, and you guys can look after yourselves.'

And that is exactly what happened.

THE TRUSTING HEIRS OF
SIR FRANCIS DRAKE

Oscar Hartzell used to be a farmer in Iowa, and who knows, it could have been his agricultural background that enabled him to sow the seeds of belief in his bizarre project so deeply, that his victims were his most ardent defenders – when he eventually did come to trial.

In 1921 some of his friends back home were put into a state of some excitement to receive from Oscar a letter. (The letter was sent, *not* mailed, incidentally, for Hartzell knew his law – the main risk of prosecution was attempt to defraud by using Government Mails.) The letter revealed a wondrous discovery. Oscar had *proof* that Sir Francis Drake had had an illegitimate son and the heir of this son was entitled to the full Drake fortune. Oscar had incontrovertible proof of this heir's identity and (wait for it) the estate was now worth $22,000,000. The only problem was that money was needed for the legal costs involved in establishing the claim and restoring the rightful heir.

The heir – who couldn't be named because secret but official pressures would be applied by the British Government – had appointed Oscar Merrill Hartzell to organize the case – stipulating only that campaign contributions should be made by people called Drake or with Drake blood in their veins. 'Keep it in the family' was Oscar's motto and he estimated that once the claim had been established contributors would get a $500 to $1 pay out.

Oscar decided to appoint agents to collect the campaign contributions and the lucky Iowa appointees were Mr and

Mrs (nee Drake) Shepherd. They collected and passed on almost $170,000.

As he appointed more agents the 'Rule' on Drake relatives was relaxed and Hartzell soon had eleven agents in several states. Moreover, Oscar had by now evolved a near perfect wall of protection around this crusade.

First, all encouraging messages of progress, appointments of agents, etc, were sent by telegram and contributions from the faithful – $2,500 per week flowed in – were sent by American Express. Use of the Government Mail was strictly forbidden!

Second, all donators had to sign an undertaking of 'Silence, Secrecy and Non-Disturbance'. Anyone breaking the vow would be blacklisted and miss the pay-out. As a result, communication between Oscar and his followers was through his agents who would convene meetings to recount their leader's progress.

These meetings by all accounts must have had a revivalist air about them. Cables were read out describing how a settlement was near, how Hartzell had found the birth certificate of the illegitimate heir, how the English Government were employing underhand methods to thwart their plans. Small wonder, decided the faithful followers that Perfidious Albion was worried because latest 'proven' assets of the estate – due no doubt to the effects of compound interest – totalled $400,000,000. A report in a New York paper of pressure on the pound was all the proof the investors needed that the issue could bring down the Government and the President's trip to England was taken as evidence of international concern. An Iowa minister, from the pulpit, added the titbit that not only bankruptcy but scandal faced England – because the mother of the illegitimate son was Queen Elizabeth the First!

By now the numbers of the donators had reached almost 70,000 trusting souls and Oscar had taken up permanent residence in England – the better to fight the legal battle. Cabled messages fed the agents new discoveries and pressured for more campaign funds. Such was Oscar's inventiveness and persuasiveness that it was *eleven years* – not until 1932 – before the authorities were able to construct a case of usage of the US Mail for fraudulent purposes – and then only against certain agents. Oscar retaliated by request:ng the donators to write to their Congressman, Attorn y General and to the President complaining of the 'trumped up' case.

This was too cheeky for the State Department who managed to accumulate enough evidence to have Oscar deported from England as an undesirable alien. On arrival in New York, the heroic Hartzell was arrested and indeed jailed in 1933 in Iowa. Proof, complete proof, said Oscar (from his cell) was that the English were rattled – and therefore the case for the legacy *must* be solid! This logic so convinced his followers that they promptly coughed up $15,000 for Oscar's English lawyers, $68,000 for his bond and $50,000 for his personal use.

With Oscar out on bail, the prosecution had a problem – how to convict him without willing witnesses. Not one of Oscar's investors/victims was willing to testify against him. Hadn't they signed the pledge of silence? Besides they didn't want to lose their share in the pay-out now confidently expected on July 1st.

Nevertheless, the authorities were equal to the problem. They brought over copies of Francis Drake's real Will (he did actually make one even though none of the investors had thought to request a copy). They also imported an English barrister who explained that the Statute of Limitations anyway applied to a death over 300 years old and who read out part of a letter written by an Englishwoman and produced as a kind of 'Anti-Character' witness. 'I know Hartzell quite well' – it read – 'He swindled me out of most of my jewellery. It was right after he was made a premier Duke of Buckland in a private investiture by His Majesty'.

Oscar Merril Hartzell got 10 years – but that only further convinced many of his investors that the US and UK Governments were collaborating to prevent the case from wrecking the English economy. Contributions amazingly continued to flow in and rumors abounded. Oscar was not in jail – it was related – but in protection from English Secret Service agents sent to gun him down, a ship was moored off Galveston with the first instalment payment in the form of gold bullion – and so on and so on.

Nonetheless, the light was beginning to dawn and with the jailing of eight of Oscar's agents in 1935 the scheme began finally to crumble. However, there is a fitting postscript to this extraordinary saga. When, at the trial of the above agents, witnesses from among the investors were called their main concern was that their donation 'receipts' taken as evidence should be both examined and stored with extreme care because, they explained patiently, 'They are very valuable'.

SHINWELL –
THE NAME IS THE GAME

by Michael Gillard

Most wheeler-dealers start with the decided disadvantage of having to establish credibility. This they often do by recruiting as associates well known or respected figures – respectability, like guilt, coming by association.

Ernest Shinwell, however, did not suffer from this problem. He was born not with a silver spoon in his mouth but a golden key in his pocket, a key that opened the doors of banks, embassies, govenment offices and eventually prisons around the world.

This key was the fame and respect for his father, Emanuel 'Manny' Shinwell: veteran British Labour MP, former Cabinet Minister, and, from 1970, Peer of the Realm. An MP for over 35 years, 'Manny' Shinwell was one of the best-known Ministers in the Attlee Government of the Forties, rising to become Minister of Defence, and in Opposition a vocal left-wing critic of both the Conservatives and his own party.

The Shinwell name combined with his own convincing charm, gambler's ambition and flair for the extravagant made Ernest Shinwell an ideal con-man. He was, as one who was all but taken in by him put it, 'a clever individual who could have made good in any business he would have inclined to'.

Unfortunately for the gifted and stylish Shinwell, like the heroes of Greek tragedy he seemed to possess within his character the ingredients for his own inevitable failure. Every Shinwell scheme flourished for a short time, long enough for him and his associates to live in the style to which they would like to be accustomed. Then it would falter and fail among the contradictions between his Olympian ideas and Heath Robinson approach.

In the end Shinwell's charm, which along with the name kept him in business even after his first prison sentence, was not enough. Though still planning grand schemes of his own he became little more than the willing tool of those who could exploit the father's name and the son's talent more successfully.

'Manny' Shinwell's youngest son emerged from the Second World War aged 27 and with all the qualifications for a successful career in business or politics or both.

A major in the Black Watch regiment who later trained Belgian resistance fighters, Ernest Shinwell left the Army in 1946 a Lieutenant Colonel. The Minister of Fuel & Power's son soon decided to go into business as a sales and publicity expert. He joined a firm of silk and cotton wear merchants. This led to his own menswear sales company and then the post of publicity director for Swears & Wells, the Oxford Street store. In between, the dapper London-Scottish rugby three-quarters and amateur boxer launched a magazine to raise funds for expanding the Victory Club, used by ex-servicemen.

By 1950, with his father now Minister of Defence, Shinwell was all set for the next and obvious move, politics. He was adopted as the prospective Labour candidate for Hove, a 'no-hope', rock-solid Tory seat but a worthwhile first step on the ladder to Parliament.

Then for the first but by no means the last time Ernest Shinwell blew this chance with an ill-judged venture for which he had insufficient experience and which he tried to salvage by an abuse of his name and his father's position.

Shinwell had developed a keen interest in farming. He purchased two farms in Sussex for £11,000 and, after selling one, early in 1950 bought a third, the run-down 86-acre Stone Farm near Crowborough, Sussex, for £3,500. It was his intention to modernize it.

Because of the inheritance of wartime shortages, building materials were licensed and all building work strictly controlled

Shinwell hired a builder to renovate the farm and licenses were granted for work totalling £2,250. However, when the builder sought approval for another £750 of improvements this was rejected. But by then that work and a whole lot more had already been completed.

Undeterred by such minor hindrances as permits, the Minister's son assured the builder that he had 'fixed up' everything in London and that approval would be obtained. 'That is one advantage of being connected with the Government' the builder said Shinwell told him. 'He assured me that everything was in order and an Englishman's word is his bond. It was promise after promise and nothing came'. That was to become a familiar complaint about Shinwell.

Shinwell certainly sought support in the corridors of power, apparently relying on his father's position to open doors and win influence. He believed in going straight to the top: 'That is where you can get satisfaction'. He went to see a junior Minister at the Ministry of Agriculture and also claimed to have seen a top official at the Ministry of Works.

But it did not succeed. He returned to Stone Farm unsatisfied. By now Shinwell had spent £4,500 on the farm, not only more than he had approval for but also more than he could afford. Building temporarily stopped after a check for £1,000 bounced, the first of many over the next 25 years. Shortly afterwards Shinwell began querying the cost, whereupon the rebuilding stopped altogether amid the crossfire of writ and counter-claim.

By this time too the Ministry of Works was investigating what had been happening down on Stone Farm. As a result, Shinwell was charged with exceeding a building permit, for which the punishment was a £2,000 fine or three months' imprisonment in February 1951. The Socialist Minister's son was told by the chairman of the magistrates: 'You should have known better. The magistrates are quite clear that you knew you were doing wrong. You knew well that in the villages and towns around here there are many families living in appalling conditions. These regulations are designed to see that in these times of shortages there is an equitable and fair distribution for all'.

That ended Ernest Shinwell's hopes of a political career. He did not stand in the General Election later that year which saw the Attlee Government defeated and his father out of office.

The Stone Farm affair also started him down the slippery slope to bankruptcy, fraud and prison. For his characteristic extravagance had brought him to the edge of insolvency. However, like Dickens' Mr. Micawber, Ernest Shinwell was always waiting for something, a rich client or a fat contract, to turn up and save the day.

In the case of Stone Farm the something that saved him was the last-minute payment of the fine by his father.

This was not to be the last time that 'Manny' Shinwell would come to his son's rescue. But even he could not prevent the slow and inevitable drift into bankruptcy that turned Ernest Shinwell's agile and inventive mind to using his name and contact in doubtful schemes that would lead to the good life. 'I've had a setback, but adversity is the real test of ability', Ernest Shinwell said after the court case. And so, undaunted by his narrow escape from prison and his finely stretched finances, he agreed to buy another farm, this time one of the most modern in Scotland, for £57,000.

He had entered into this deal without selling the mortgage-encumbered Stone Farm and, despite assistance from his father, Shinwell was soon in difficulties on his newly acquired Ayrshire farm. Ever the optimist, he had purchased the farm relying on realizing £9,000 from his English farms, raising £35,000 on mortgages and borrowing the rest. Such ramshackle financing needed very little to go wrong for it to collapse. And with a man like Ernest Shinwell that possibility was never far away.

Sure enough, instead of £9,000 he received exactly £170 from the English farms. Repayment of the mortgages took the rest. And his previous financial escapades did not help his creditworthiness as a borrower.

Come January 1953 the roof was ready to fall in at Dalgig Farm. It looked as though the farm stock would have to be sold to meet the creditors who were pressing hard for their money. Additionally the previous owner was about to repossess the farm for non-payment.

A month later Barclays Bank petitioned for his bankruptcy. The total debts were soon declared to be over £50,000.

When he was finally made bankrupt in June, 1953, Shinwell was out of Scotland and on another farm in Worcestershire. 'He seems to be quite indifferent to the fact that he owes nearly £9,000 to Scottish creditors', declared the creditors' solicitor.

However, the MP's son did return – in police custody. In January, 1954 Shinwell told the bankruptcy court that he blamed his failure on 'overoptimism'. He owed £60,000 after losing £10,000 on farms in England. He put his assets at just over £2,600. 'I thought the people I approached with various schemes would be able to carry out their promises. They were not'. Ten years later similar complaints would be heard from those who did business with Shinwell. They would have done well to heed the words of the solicitor for Shinwell's trustee in bankruptcy: 'I would suggest that this fantastic loss can in no way be attributed to innocent loss, but falls into the category of undue and culpable conduct'.

The Scottish debacle finally forced Shinwell to abandon his farming ambitions. Instead he became a marketing consultant. A public relations-cum-business consultancy lasted for four years before going into liquidation in 1961 owing £50,000. This was followed by a travel agency which also crashed owing £17,000.

But most of all the Scottish setback made it necessary for Ernest Shinwell, at 35, to look farther afield for his new business ventures. Shinwell soon fixed his eyes on West Africa as a suitable location for a man with his slightly shop-soiled credentials to make a fresh start.

The 'wind of change' that was blowing through Africa in the late Fifties and early Sixties, creating political independence from the old colonial powers like Britain, brought with it new and eager clients for ambitious and convincing businessmen with grandiose schemes to sell. Each independent country was enthusiastic to celebrate its political maturity with major projects to develop new industries and wide-ranging building projects for new roads, schools and homes.

Men who could show how all this could be done quickly and cheaply or could provide both the ideas and the finance were assured a friendly governmental ear. Furthermore, in the post-independence scramble for power and wealth politicians of the highest rank and repute were not above supporting those schemes that also offered a little something extra in the way of personal reward.

That attitude permeated its way through to the officials whose job it was to influence and execute government decisions and to the local bankers who advised on their financing. As one international banker put it: 'There is no question but that in some developing areas there are those who, it would seem to me, are very quick to lend themselves to this kind of an operation [making dubious loans] always, one, out of innocence or, two, out of knowing what is going on and believing they can get by with it because this kind of thing happens on occasion and it is nothing to be greatly disturbed about'.

Such a milieu was made for a charming and convincing hustler like Ernest Shinwell, who not only dreamed up grand schemes and ways of finding the money to pay for them but had excellent Socialist credentials through the reputation of his father. Rich, new states like Nigeria and Ghana, whose independence had been supported by the Labour Party, were now run by political leaders who would look kindly on the son of 'Manny' Shinwell. He could be assured of a warm welcome in Lagos or Accra. Also he had contacts in the area already, having been involved in a small way in the disastrous ground nuts scheme dreamed up by his father's ministerial colleagues in the final years of the Labour Government.

Shinwell's *modus operandi* was subtly effective. First, he would make contact with officials in London of the African state he wanted to cultivate, using his name to effect an introduction. Once inside the High Commission he would work up that relationship while looking for an appropriately attractive venture to sell. He concentrated in particular on development schemes for new industries that would receive sympathetic treatment from the local government in terms of cash grants, subsidies and guarantees. Shinwell's aim would be to persuade the local government to go ahead with one such scheme on which he would receive consultancy fees and possibly commissions on equipment ordered or products sold.

Once such a scheme was lined up, Shinwell would visit the country, armed now with not just his father's name but also introductions and references from the High Commission in London. This would get him into the right political circles. (He gave Ghana's President Nkrumah a pet dog as a present when seeking a refuse plant contract there.) That accomplished, he would look for a friendly banker as a source of both local finance and external credibility. Again this would be done employing now the combined persuasion of the Shinwell name and his political contacts in the country. Backing from a resident bank would enable him to further develop his activities and finance the necessarily expensive cultivation of politicians and officials on whose help he relied if the government was to be brought in.

His bankruptcy behind him, by 1962 Ernest Shinwell had a variety of deals in both Nigeria and Ghana. These were handled through a new company, International Marketing Consultants, whose chairman was Prince Michael Radziwill, a London businessman who headed one of the once richest Polish families, was a descendant of King James I and the cousin of United States President John F. Kennedy's brother-in-law. The other directors were Shinwell's wife, Peggy, and E. P. Shinwell, his 11-year-old son.

Among the deals Shinwell claimed to be putting together were the refuse plant in Ghana, a scheme for 3,000 houses in Eastern Nigeria, plus a shirt-making plant and a supermarket development elsewhere in that country.

Never one to talk in less than telephone numbers, he mentioned contracts worth from £9,000,000 to £18,000,000, from which large commissions would flow to IMC in London. However, he was as over optimistic in the steam heat of West Africa as he had been on the misty hillsides of Ayrshire.

Although he talked a good deal Shinwell never pulled one off. This meant there was little coming in to finance the outgoings incurred by his regular jaunts to Africa. And, as the bankrupt consultant had no capital to begin with, disaster was never far away.

It finally arrived when, despite his threadbare finances, Shinwell, with a gambler's foolhardiness, agreed to buy the Nigerian interests of Pearl and Dean, the London advertising agents. These were held through Overseas Marketing & Advertising, which owned some valuable building concessions.

In September, 1962, Shinwell and Louis Larholt, an undistinguished London financier, agreed to buy control of OMA from Pearl & Dean for £61,000 by repaying a £20,000 banker overdraft and the £41,000 the Nigerian company owed to its controlling shareholders.

As always with Shinwell's schemes there was a little problem of money. However, he was nothing if not resourceful. Turned down for a £20,000 loan by a minor London bank, English Transcontinental, on the perfectly understandable grounds that he was an undischarged bankrupt, Shinwell came back with a request for the same sum on behalf of Ross Ensign, part of Larholt's Whitefriars Investment Trust, to finance a shipment of optical instruments to Nigeria. English Transcontinental agreed to lend the cash against a formal resolution confirming the loan from the Ross Ensign directors. This was produced by

Larholt as signed by him and the company secretary, together with bills of exchange from Shinwell for the instruments. Armed with the bank's £20,000, Shinwell and Larholt went ahead and bought the shares for two bills of exchange drawn on Whitefriars and a personal check from Shinwell for £20,000.

However, the deal fell apart in double quick time even for Shinwell. In December OMA collapsed and Pearl & Dean were then unable to collect on the two bills of exchange because Whitefriars would not pay out. Larholt by now had left the company, which had made substantial losses. Needless to say, the £20,000 Shinwell check bounced. As for English Transcontinental, they discovered there had never been any optical instruments. The £20,000 had only gone to pay off certain OMA creditors in a bid to keep the company afloat. Not only that, the bankers then discovered that the Ross Ensign directors had never even considered the Nigerian loan. Only Larholt had signed the resolution they held as security for the £20,000. The company secretary's signature was forged.

Once the dust in Nigeria had settled, retribution was swift in seeking out Ernest Shinwell. He was arrested in November, 1963 at his Sussex farmhouse as he was eating breakfast. Three months later Shinwell was made bankrupt in England with debts of over £100,000.

However, he took this, like his arrest, in his suave unperturbed stride. Later Shinwell told his creditors that, far from being insolvent, his assets were three times his debts. This was entirely due to the £300,000 Shinwell claimed he would be paid as commission on the deal for the houses in Nigeria by a company called Legal & Industrial Property. Unfortunately, fact outstripped fantasy and his assets were just £27,000. Shinwell attributed his problems to the travelling and entertaining expenses incurred by the West African projects. Naturally, he was 'optimistic' about the prospects of repayment for his creditors.

In May, 1964, Shinwell and Larholt appeared at the Old Bailey charged with false pretenses, conspiring to cheat and defraud English Transcontinental, and inducing Pearl & Dean to dispose of its OMA shares by misleading, false or deceptive statements. Larholt was fined £750 for false pretenses while Shinwell was acquitted on the conspiracy and false pretenses charges but found guilty of inducing Pearl & Dean to sell. Fining him £50, Judge Aarvold told Shinwell:

'This scheme started as something of a zany one and it seems to have affected your judgment. You are not convicted of dishonesty or fraud but of recklessness which does not seem to have done any serious damage. Nevertheless, people who are persuading others to part with shares in companies must be careful as to what they say and mean'.

Unfortunately, Ernest Shinwell did not take these homilies too much to heart. 'I am down at the moment, but not out', said the seemingly penitent and relieved Shinwell as he walked from the court. 'As my father might say, this business has knocked another chip off the young block. Now let me get back to work and wipe this blot from my character'.

Top of the list in achieving this rehabilitation was the housing scheme in Nigeria. There was also a proposed £12,000,000 plantation and the supermarket. Appearing in the London Bankruptcy Court two months after the Old Bailey trial, Shinwell said that the promised £300,000 would be forthcoming when he returned to Nigeria and completed the housing contract.

He never made the trip and, less surprisingly, his creditors never received their money. For in the middle of August Shinwell was arrested at home for the second time in ten months, this time on three fraud charges involving the issuing of forged share certificates and seeking to obtain £13,000 with forged share certificates.

In May, 1962, Prince Radziwill had introduced Shinwell to William Lowenthal, a 'fringe' banker without too much money. Lowenthal controlled C. H. Perry, which owned farms in Rhodesia that Shinwell decided to buy. The banker also had a former Malayan rubber company, Johore Para, which had assets of £72,000 in cash. Shinwell subsequently agreed to buy Perry for £50,000 and control of Johore Para for £72,000. The rubber company's cash was pencilled in to pay for Perry's farms. There was, however, the usual Shinwell problem. He had no ready cash and certainly not the amount of money required to get Johore Para and so start the ball rolling. He was already struggling to arrange the cash for the OMA deal. There also turned out to be problems in obtaining control of the Malayan company's cash, which was in Lowenthal's effectively insolvent bank.

To keep the deal alive, at the beginning of March, 1963 Shinwell offered Lowenthal 2,000 shares in the U.S. F.W. Woolworth Co., then sitting in the Enugu, Nigeria branch of the African Continental Bank as security for completion. Meantime, in return for Shinwell going ahead, Lowenthal was to pay off his £3,000 overdraft at the Nigerian bank, which was pressing for payment, and lend him another £10,000 through a bank in Britain.

Lowenthal agreed to this unorthodox deal because he was keen to sell. He had been made bankrupt in October, 1962, and it was alleged by Board of Trade inspectors that his Richardson bank faced a similar fate. He was going to get the £13,000 from borrowing against the Woolworth shares, which were 'worth' some £50,000.

However, this financial gavotte overlooked one important factor – the Woolworth shares were counterfeit. Shinwell knew this but also knew Lowenthal would not part with any cash until he had checked them out. Meanwhile, this would keep the banks quiet. But he still had to come up with a scheme that might put real money in his pocket rather than 'dummy' shares.

Such an opportunity fell into his lap a few days after he reached agreement with Lowenthal. He was introduced by an old acquaintance to Michael Walker of the Fraser Walker Aircraft Corporation in New York. Walker wanted finance for a jet autogyro project. Shinwell immediately offered to provide $1,300,000 (£500,000) in return for control of the company. The cash was to be used for a Nigerian factory to build the autogyro – a rival to the helicopter.

How was the impoverished Shinwell to find such an amount? Simplicity itself. He would supply 20,000 Woolworth shares as security for a loan.

Of course, Shinwell did not have 20,000 Woolworth shares. He only had 2,000 and these were already pledged to Lowenthal. And they were worthless anyway because they were forged.

Even Shinwell quickly realized he could not pull such a switch. But one forged share is very much like another. So he simply exchanged 20,000 counterfeit Woolworth shares for 14,000 equally counterfeit shares in another American company, Quaker Oats Co., supposedly worth $1,400,000.

Walker was somewhat amazed when Shinwell refused a receipt for the shares, as the certificates were in 'bearer' form and so could be sold by anyone. When the American pointed out that he could just walk away with them, Shinwell replied: 'You could, but you would have your head shrunk'. This remark was perhaps a hint as to the source of the forgeries and the sinister circles in which the MP's son was now moving as he sought new ways of making that elusive fortune.

Not that anxious for money, the suspicious Walker sent the certificates to Quaker Oats for verification. The company quickly confirmed Walker's suspicions. The news that the shares were forged was conveyed to Shinwell, along with the extra titbit that the certificates had been handed over to the Fraud Squad.

Shinwell expressed surprise and said the shares had been left at his office by an unknown caller while he was out. He promised to 'chase round' so as to clear up the matter and put it right.

He was still chasing in November, 1963 when, the day he was arrested with Larholt, he received a visit from Detective Inspector Arthur Slater of Scotland Yard's Fraud

Squad, who was interested not only in Quaker Oats but also the Woolworth shares in Nigeria.

Shinwell brazened it out. He said he could not say anything about the Woolworth shares as Nigerian government ministers were involved and it could jeopardize the housing contract which was about to be signed. If the Inspector would come back in a month's time he would tell him all about it. A flagrant name-dropper, Shinwell lost no opportunity of seeking to impress by referring to his father and the other MPs or influential people he knew. 'He did like to use the names of important people', Slater recalls.

Unimpressed, Slater did come back and was told that the Woolworth shares had been put in the bank by a South African who had approached Shinwell regarding opening a shirt factory in Nigeria. The shares had been deposited in the bank as a bribe to a Nigerian minister in return for approving the project. Then, said Shinwell, the South African had tried to cheat him. However, Shinwell was very vague about the origin of these and the other forgeries. Later all he would say was that 'they came from America'. As for the Quaker Oats shares, Shinwell said these he received from a Lebanese, one of a quartet of international businessmen who had duped him. The others included a notorious British arms dealer who once sold tanks supposedly converted into tractors to the Egyptians, and a French count who had been involved four years before in a £2,000,000 Costa Rican coffee swindle. Exotic company!

After Shinwell was fined on the OMA charge, Slater saw him again. What, asked the Fraud Squad detective, was he doing with the forged Woolworth shares? 'I am just the middle man', replied Shinwell, 'Mr. Fixit they call me'.

Shinwell was then asked why, when he discovered the Quaker Oats shares were forged, he had not become suspicious of the Woolworth shares too? 'After I heard the Quaker Oats shares were, I guessed they might be', he replied.

In that case, asked Slater, why did he still go ahead and try to obtain £13,000 from Lowenthal with the shares? 'He is a shrewd man and would not have parted with any money until he had verified the shares'. Seeing the prison doors swinging open before him, the MP's son shrugged his shoulders and added knowingly: 'Well, if you are going to arrest me, give me a bit of warning, won't you?'

Slater did not oblige. Two months later, knowing that the Woolworth shares were indeed counterfeit, the Inspector called again. This time he disturbed if not surprised the urbane 'Mr. Fixit' by arresting him at his Sussex home.

Despite stories of bribes, conspiracies and being 'an entirely honest man who, in looking for capital for his projects, came upon a nest of rogues' Shinwell was found guilty of fraud in February, 1965. Judge Aarvold, no doubt recalling his previous ignored advice, told Shinwell:

'You became involved in schemes which appealed to your vanity but, alas, were beyond your abilities. I have little doubt that you genuinely believe in the prospects of the ventures in which you were concerned. Thereafter you felt that whatever deceitful steps you took were justified. I take no adverse view of your character. I take account of the fact that in this case no money was actually lost as a result of your activities. You were clearly aiming for high rewards. You were playing for high stakes and knew that those stakes were false'.

He sent Shinwell to prison for three years.

The night before he was sentenced he told a journalist: 'But for my arrest on another matter I would have put through two big construction deals in West Africa which would not only have wiped out my debts but would have made me a millionaire'. Instead, Shinwell admitted, he was now penniless. His parting words were to recall what his father had once said when introducing him to Sir Winston Churchill: 'You two should get on well together, you are both adventurers'.

Like adventurers, fraudsmen rarely give up. Released on parole after a year of so in prison, Shinwell was soon back in Africa in the same line of business. With Nigeria in the grip of civil war, he now concentrated on Ghana, where the family name still opened doors. Nkrumah had been deposed but Shinwell soon made contact with the leaders of the new regime. The son-in-law of one prominent Minister was rapidly recruited for Shinwell's latest and most ambitious venture, Agricultural & Industrial Development (AID).

This time the project was a massive cattle breeding scheme. Shinwell joined forces with a consulting engineer and two English farmers, who put up most of the 'front' money for the Ghana project through Overseas Land Development (OLD).

Shinwell, not surprisingly, stayed behind the scenes. But OLD soon acquired an impressive 'front man' – the Earl of Ypres. The grandson of Sir John French, the First World War military commander, he had the sort of title which added prestige to a letterhead. However, like Shinwell, he was rather short of cash.

Using £65,000 put up by OLD, Shinwell negotiated an agreement with the Ghanaian government in December, 1967 to set up the cattle breeding project. The government was to take a 45% interest and to lease the land. Finance was to come from the U.S. through a Swiss banking contact of Shinwell's who was to provide $4,000,000. Armed with that contract, Shinwell spent 1968 persuading assorted British contractors and suppliers to come in on the scheme. Several agreed to do so and paid commissions for the privilege to Shinwell, unbeknown to most of the OLD directors.

However, in Ghana there was opposition to the scheme within the government as a result of which the necessary government guarantees were delayed. So too was the promised American finance.

This was perhaps not altogether surprising as the money was coming from a mysterious American lawyer named 'W. Adler'. Now the mysterious thing about 'Adler' was that no one other than Shinwell ever met or corresponded with him. Perhaps the explanation for his elusiveness and a clue to his possible real identity lies in the experience of one Shinwell associate who answered the door at Shinwell's London home to be greeted by a TV repairman who had arrived to fix 'Mr. Adler's' TV set. Shinwell explained that the invisible lawyer generously had rented the TV, then left. 'Adler' was to appear again later in the AID story.

Undaunted, Shinwell and others continued to spend their way through OLD's money and the commissions. Shinwell rented a £1,400-a-year, 11-room house in St. John's Wood, which he talked of buying.

During the summer of 1969 the OLD well finally ran dry and it became clear that no U.S. finance would be forthcoming. The convenient explanation for 'Mr. Adler's' reluctance was the American government's ban on overseas investment plus the absence of any guarantees from the Ghanaian government. With OLD not prepared to put in more money, the whole project collapsed, the backers lost their investment and as a result a year later the Earl of Ypres was made bankrupt.

But already Ernest Shinwell was actively planning even grander schemes in previously untouched territories with new and powerful partners.

Agricultural & Industrial Development, a Panamanian company, and its British registered twin, Agricultural & Industrial Marketing, were ostensibly set up by Shinwell and others to extract, as in Ghana, fees and commissions by offering to finance and manage ambitious schemes overseas or to provide buyers for overseas companies. The fees would come from those individuals, companies, or governments that could be persuaded to join Shinwell as partners, or from those credulous or desperate enough to believe he could raise money for them. The commissions were to come from bringing in contractors and negotiating equipment purchased for the orgy of high-sounding schemes Shinwell now launched himself into, not just in Africa but in Britain, Latin America and the Far East too.

Shinwell had also raised his sights in another way. After the failures of the early Sixties with small-time con-men and 'job lots' of forged shares, he was now running in much faster company – the Mafia.

Either before or after he obtained the Woolworth shares 'from America', through, he says, the ever-present if imperceptible Adler, Shinwell had met Dominic Mantell. A member of the Mafia 'family' in Buffalo, New York headed by Stefano Magaddino, Mantell was the Florida representative of not only Magaddino but also the Angelo Bruno 'family' of Philadelphia and the Carlo Gambino organization in New York. This connection resulted in a 1970 meeting in London between Ernest Shinwell, the Labour peer's son and the Mafia chieftain Angelo Bruno. The game Shinwell and Mantell sat down to play following this meeting was unloading counterfeit and stolen securities, one of organized crime's newest and fastest-growing rackets.

This was done by using the shares or bonds as collateral for bank loans. These loans were either straight frauds or the more sophisticated variety, whereby the loans were used to acquire real assets which could then be sold quickly and cheaply to realize something for nothing. The front men who negotiated the loans usually received 25% of the proceeds. The rest of what was taken in went to the Mafia suppliers.

Ernest Shinwell was just the partner for Mantell and his bosses in the stolen securities racket. With his family background, likeable manner and considerable ability, he was an ideal 'front' and 'scam man', manipulating a 'friendly' banker or loan-hungry businessman. He had the credentials to talk his way into unloading 'hot' stocks on unsophisticated or unsuspecting foreign bankers. And he also knew how to deal with those who were neither, just corrupt and greedy. Equally he was at home negotiating the real or illusory deals for which such loans were to be used.

On the Englishman's side, stolen securities gave him

what he had always lacked – the ability to raise large amounts of cash. Shinwell claimed later that at his peak he could have raised worldwide no less than $200,000,000. It may only have been 'funny money', but it came in such amounts as to make all things possible. Shinwell, backed by Mantell's ready source of stolen or forged shares, proved the power of the Italian saying that 'money makes the blind see and the lame walk'.

His new partners enabled Shinwell to collect advance fees and commissions as well as play the international 'Mr. Fixit' role he so coveted. But such achievements came at a high price. Philip M. Wilson, an American specialist in international bank frauds, later described how high:

'If a person in the organized criminal activity of white-collar fraud chooses to be involved extensively in the stolen securities business to meet his ends, the end result is being taken over by the more traditional concept of organized crime people. The end result is that the white collar fraud individual ends up being dominated and owned by the Mafia-type criminal. This necessarily happens because the normal white-collar fraud criminal, in essence, is a non-violent type of person. Another point is that the white-collar fraud individual becomes dependent on the organized crime people to supply him with the securities to keep going further'.

Louis Mastriana, a minor racketeer turned stolen securities 'mover' brought in to help unload some of the Shinwell 'paper', saw it the same way: 'Angelo Bruno had cultivated Shinwell and they turned the operation over to Mantell'.

Shinwell and the other Mantell 'paper hangers' went to work in the following fashion. A world-wide network of 'dummy' companies was set up with names like Intercopa, Cornucopia, Juglar and, most important of all, Zurich International Investment Corporation. These would issue worthless letters of credit – often with the innocent involvement of reputable banks like Credit Suisse, Union Bank of Switzerland, Bank of America and Chase Manhattan – and bills of exchange which could be cashed or pledged at banks for fraudulent loans. Another play was to deposit this worthless paper or stolen or forged securities in a reputable bank, like Credit Suisse, in the name of one of the 'shell' companies and then use confirmation by that bank of their existence (the bank having no reason to check as it was not lending against them) to deceive other reputable banks, like Chase Manhattan, into providing letters of credit, loans or credibility. The dummy companies could also be used to acquire businesses – which could then be sold for cash – either in return for stolen, forged or worthless securities or on the back of money borrowed against stolen or counterfeit securities. That was where Dom Mantell came in. The Mafia 'families' would steal or forge the securities that the 'paper hangers' would move via Shinwell's paper empire. Unprepared to pay the rent on his London home, Shinwell set up Agricultural & Industrial Marketing in a £45,000 mansion, once the British headquarters of General Motors, outside Derby. He never paid more than a 10% deposit.

From here during 1969 and 1970, AIM was used for several bread-and-butter advance-fee operations (commissions paid in advance for loans that never materialize) on British businessmen. Every move was orchestrated by Shinwell, who wrote out for his less gifted associates an AIM manual, called the 'red bible', which instructed them what to do in any eventuality. (Usually that meant 'Call Ernie'). The associates were in that way as much part of the con-man's classic front as the bought-but-not-paid-for mansion and Rolls-Royce.

The Bruno meeting soon propelled Shinwell into much bigger things, across the Atlantic in Panama.

By August, 1970, Shinwell had apparently charmed the president of Panama's Banco Exterior and was negotiating a series of ambitious acquisitions. He wanted to buy a local bank plus timber, ranching and resort properties. The total involved was some $5,500,000 (£2,000,000).

Initially this was to be paid in cash, but naturally this

soon altered to two letters of credit drawn on the Zurich International Investment Corporation. But Shinwell had primed the pump well. So high a premium had he agreed to pay that the vendors did not want to wreck such an opportunity by opposing the switch. Registered in the Bahamas, Zurich International Investment featured as one of its directors and signatories the elusive 'W. Adler'. Later, when Scotland Yard detectives wanted to speak to him about the company's activities, Shinwell explained that, unfortunately, the never-present lawyer had recently died!

To help run the Panamanian keystone of his burgeoning global empire, Shinwell approached an American banker, David W. Slater. A cautious and well-connected man, Slater made inquiries about Shinwell and learned of his bankruptcy. When he was indelicate enough to raise this during a visit to the Derby mansion, Shinwell, unabashed, explained away not only this but also his jail sentence by saying he had been framed by corrupt politicians in Ghana.

The Shinwell entourage turned up in Panama during August, 1970, to receive the red carpet treatment. Even for an ex-convict and a bankrupt, the Shinwell name still worked wonders.

The small Central American republic was soon agog with word of Shinwell's plans. In addition to the earlier deals he also negotiated for two cattle ranches and persuaded the government to pass a special law giving his group title to a nearby island which was to become a $80,000,000 (£30,000,000) tourist resort operation. But then Shinwell was supposedly raising $200,000,000 for Panama itself.

His credibility being (temporarily) established, Shinwell sailed in and socked it to the locals with a simple strategy. Slater later described how it worked:

'He went in; he bought properties at inflated prices. He gained the attention of the sellers. They were most careful to see that the deal went through. They were willing to wait with delays'.

Unfortunately, even now, on the verge of pulling off his biggest coup ever, Shinwell was still handicapped by his old inability to raise the finance required to turn his deals into reality. 'One of his representatives there had ambitions greater than those of Shinwell and committed him beyond what Shinwell was able to come up with at the time and threw the timetable off', explained David Slater. 'Shinwell was, I think, put into a position of having to operate without having all his strings tied. The problem was that they just couldn't make their securities work for them, the kind of securities they wanted to work for them'.

Even the Mafia seemingly could not beat the Shinwell luck. First of all, the $5,500,000 in cash did not turn up. Then the $6,000,000 (£2,200,000) in Zurich International letters of credit to Intercopa drew a blank when, much to Shinwell's chagrin, Slater had them presented at Credit Suisse, which purportedly held the Bahamas company's account, in Zurich. Some $800,000 (£280,000) in securities was supposed to be in an Intercopa account at Credit Suisse in Zurich, too. These proved stolen and useless for cash-raising purposes. Then Shinwell said $10,000,000 (£3,700,000) in securities was being cashed by a U.S. broker in Switzerland. These were followed by $10,000,000 in First Liberty Fund certificates and $2,000,000 in equally worthless Bank of Sark cashier's drafts obtained from Phil Wilson. These had to be used to replace $5,000,000 worth of securities brought to Panama in December, 1970, by Mantell personally. However, when Slater had one of these presented, it turned out to be forged. At this point the American bailed out and informed the U.S. authorities.

In Phil Wilson's view: 'To complicate matters when you commit a fraud is one of the prerequisites'. That was one thing Ernest Shinwell could always be relied on to do, and do well.

Meanwhile, the 'paper hangers' had geared up ever more exotic and fast-moving schemes.

Worthless bills of exchange drawn on the Panamanian companies flooded into banks in the U.S. and were exchanged for cash. Chase Manhattan and First National City Bank of New York were approached with proposals for loans of almost $2,000,000 against the security of cattle on ranches in Panama that Shinwell did not own.

He looked into buying two banks in Florida and also purchasing a fleet of aircraft. While in Panama in December, 1970, Shinwell met Herbert E. Creekmore, an American aircraft broker. He persuaded Creekmore to fly to Los Angeles with an associate in order to buy an executive plane with a loan secured on securities he would provide. Shinwell told Creekmore he intended to buy several bigger aircraft. However, the proposition fell apart when his companion became drunk and told Creekmore that the securities were counterfeit.

Despite this setback, Shinwell contacted the American again the following month. He said he had come up with some different securities which Creekmore could check. When, not surprisingly, Creekmore remained dubious, he later told how Shinwell 'reassured me that he, being the son of a member of the House of Lords, would not be involved in such a shady deal'.

Partly persuaded by Shinwell's protestations of honesty and the offer to verify the securities, Creekmore went to Los Angeles again. In a hotel room there, Shinwell showed the aircraft broker a suitcase and a briefcase crammed with securities worth $70,000,000 (£26,000,000).

He took the cases to an associate, who chose some securities and went to arrange the loan. A few hours later Creekmore received a telephone call telling him that the securities were stolen. Creekmore eventually retrieved the securities and returned the suitcase to Shinwell, who expressed surprise at his reluctance to go ahead. He told the American that his group had obtained loans with stolen securities in Europe which had not been traced because they had later been replaced with counterfeits. However, this time Creekmore was not convinced by Shinwell and left.

Other proposals involved utilizing $15,000,000 (£5,000,000) worth of Kingdom of Greece credit notes and $17,000,000 (£6,000,000) in assorted South American currencies.

Then there was a cement project in Mexico and a cattle breeding scheme in nearby Nicaragua. This involved Shinwell agreeing to buy £50,000 worth of prize bull semen from Britain. This fell through when, while negotiating the deal (six times larger than the previous largest export order) in London under the name of Daly, one of the participants discovered his real identity.

Bills of exchange were to be issued by the Panamanian companies for expensive farm machinery to be bought in Europe. Shinwell proposed that on arrival in Panama the equipment should be transferred across the Isthmus to the Pacific coast and then shipped to the Far East where it could be sold for half price in cash. This ingenious caper never came off either.

The Philippines was marked down for Panama-style build up. Elsewhere in the Far East, Shinwell conducted negotiations to buy control of a prestigious hotel group in Singapore. This was to be the cornerstone of the Shinwell empire's expansion into South-east Asia. The chairman of the hotel group was sufficiently impressed by Shinwell's price and plans to advance him a fee of £50,000. Like all the others this deal never came off.

Through all of this Shinwell continued to string along the sellers in Panama, its Banco Exterior and the government. He managed to do so until the spring of 1971 by when the Shinwell promises finally had lost their attraction.

But time and luck for Ernest Shinwell ran out, not in Panama, but in Luxembourg, where in June, 1971, he was arrested inside the Investors Bank and charged with borrowing £62,000 on stolen or forged securities. This was part of a scheme to move £20,000,000 worth of paper through Investors Bank and Bank of America in order to purportedly put £7,000,000 into the long-suffering Banco Exterior, provide £13,000,000 in the Luxembourg bank for AID and, along the way, pick up some much-devalued but still possibly usable Nigerian currency plus perhaps 300,000 tons of butter. The securities used were part of £3,200,000 worth stolen, instead of shredded, in Los Angeles earlier that year.

In February, 1972, while still in custody, Shinwell was indicted in Los Angeles on charges of conspiracy and theft for his part in this caper. However, he was never tried on the charges; instead he was jailed for four years by a Luxembourg court just before Christmas, 1972.

While still in the Luxembourg prison he was indicted once more, in July, 1973, this time in New York on charges of conspiracy to distribute during 1970 $18,000,000 (£6,500,000) worth of counterfeit and stolen securities. Among those also indicted was Dominic Mantell. He later pleaded guilty and was jailed for three years.

However, Shinwell avoided trial on this charge, too. Although wanted by the U.S. authorities he was released from prison in 1974, on grounds of ill health, and simply deported from Luxembourg supposedly to London.

He never arrived. Aware that he faced possible charges over AIM plus probable extradition to the U.S. and another prison term there, Shinwell headed for his old African haunts.

He turned up in Zambia, where he set to work on yet another ranching scheme. Not, however, for long. After a tip-off to the Zambian authorities, Shinwell left in something of a hurry for London, apparently preferring a British court to an African jail.

Waiting for him at London airport was Detective Sergeant Brendan Gibb-Gray of the Fraud Squad.

Ironically, Shinwell was arrested in March, 1975, not for any of his multi-million-pound projects in Latin America, Africa or the Far East, but for, while a bankrupt, buying £70 worth of clothes on credit four years before. However, he soon faced charges over AIM. Not, though, over any of those extravagant AIM schemes but for defrauding a Welsh farmer – whose cattle slaughtering business Shinwell could have bought very cheaply had his intentions been genuine – of £21,000 and an entertainment company in the north of England of £5,000 by offering to buy or finance their businesses; and for running a business while bankrupt.

In June, 1976, Ernest Shinwell received a three-year jail sentence for what Judge Lawson called 'a mean and nasty fraud'. Sentencing him at the Old Bailey, the judge told Shinwell:

'You have brought dishonor and disgrace upon an honored and cherished name. Your case is a tragedy of wasted talent'.

The Shinwell saga does indeed read as a chronicle of 'wasted talent'. However, it is unlikely that the world of international high finance has yet heard the last of Ernest Shinwell.

THE CASE OF THE BANDAGED TOFF

He was a playboy, handsome and apparently wealthy. He also had a penchant for disguise which suited his particular form of crime.

Like all good con-men he used a variety of names. Wearing his monocle he was Colonel Carruthers; in his well-cut sober suit he was John Smithson, a financier with offices in London and Paris. In other outfits he was Stern, Griffiths and Compton.

The real man behind the masks of disguise was Julian Woods, ex-public schoolboy, who was well-known to the smart set of West London.

Julian Woods was quite the most stylish of that genus of con-men called the 'long firm fraud' specialists. Their method of operation is to set up a company and build up a list of suppliers, all the while paying invoices promptly. In this way the fraudulent company gains a good 'credit rating' and suppliers become more willing to give a larger amount of credit for goods purchased.

At a pre-planned date orders are simultaneously placed by the swindlers, the goods are delivered and immediately sold below cost for fast cash. If there are enough suppliers a 'long firm fraud company' (the legal term) can easily snatch £100,000 or more and literally disappear overnight, leaving all the latest invoices unpaid, of course.

For Julian Woods the slow build-up of most long firm frauds was, well, too long and too slow. Moreover the fraudsters normally have to disappear overseas as their identity is known. Woods developed a characteristically swashbuckling short-cut.

He picked on a solicitor and made an appointment. When he arrived the solicitor was a little discomfited to find his client's face swathed in bandages, with only his eyes and mouth showing. He explained he had had a bad car accident.

Woods then arranged the formation of a £30,000 nominal value company and provided evidence (forged) of his ownership of £10,000 worth of stock of goods. He was then able subsequently to refer prospective suppliers to the solicitor for a reference in order to obtain goods on credit.

Each day for a couple of months afterwards, Julian Woods would leave his luxury West End flat and drive off towards his office in his limousine. Each day he would stop in a quiet square, put on a false moustache, dark glasses and a homburg hat and continue on his way.

Thus attired he would arrive at his small office as Mr Stern where he was popular with the staff. They knew him as the manager for the mysterious owner who had only appeared once – hidden in bandages. Mr Stern made few demands on them and used the telephone for just a few hours a day, ordering large quantities of goods, which he promptly sold at cut prices. He could afford to as he had no intention of paying for them.

When things grew too hot he merely moved offices, reached for his bandages and visited another solicitor.

When the police did arrive to investigate, the evidence was, to put it mildly, confusing. No-one was sure who the owner was and certainly no-one could describe him – after all his face had been completely hidden in bandages!

The 'bandaged toff' as he became known, continued to cut a larcenous and mysterious path through the textile industry of England and then France. When retribution and the Fraud Squad finally caught up, his brief case contained five different passports and a well worn set of bandages!

THE MILLION DOLLAR
COMPUTER CONS

The arrival of the electronic and automatic accounting age
has potentially opened up the biggest opportunity yet for
the sophisticated con-man. The scale of the successful fraud
in this area can be mind boggling. The subject is a book in
itself* and we are, therefore, only giving the briefest account
of some typical rip-offs – but enough to indicate that the
strongest security is needed.

A Double Helping of Diners

The credit card companies are very security minded but
even their arrangements can be pierced – and they were in
1967 by a small time criminal called Alfonse Confessore.
And rather easily. Alfonse was carrying out repair work for
the plastics company that stamped out the coded Diners'
Club of America credit cards. He secretly contrived to learn
how the machinery worked and to be alone during the lunch
hour breaks. He then quite simply duplicated credit cards.

At first he duplicated only a few, then as the potential
scale of his fraud dawned on him he made contact with the
only organization big enough to exploit his (unofficial)
license to print (plastic) money – the Mafia.

It was his undoing. For the 'Mob' knew that it was only a
matter of time before the real owners of the duplicated cards
began to scream. Therefore, the name of the game was
speed. Hit the streets with as many phoney cards as fast as

* An excellent account does exist in 'Computer Crime' by Gerald
  McKnight.

possible. An 'army' of counterfeit card users was recruited, buying everything from airline tickets to furs to liquor.

The Mafia leaders had made a deal with Confessore to deliver 1,500 embossed cards for a $40,000 advance. Because the source was fairly obvious the Fraud Squad were breathing down his neck and attempting to obtain hard evidence to confirm their suspicions of him. Alfonse was, therefore, trapped in an unenviable no-man's land. He had not yet duplicated the promised total of credit cards, thereby incurring the syndicate's displeasure but to complete his undertaking risked arrest.

In the end, despite handing over cards with which the Mafia took down Diners' for a reported $621,000 – Confessore reaped the worst of both worlds. He was arrested and found guilty on 20 counts. As he walked out on bail, late on the night of November 24, 1969, two cars pulled alongside him and three figures got out. Inside sixty seconds Alfonse Confessore lay dead with three bullets in the back.

The first of the new generation of computer con-men had been killed in the line of 'duty.'

The Z to Z of Computer Fraud

The trouble with computers is that they unquestioningly obey instructions however bizarre or fraudulent.

In fact they will as happily obey a self-destruct instruction as an order to prepare a ledger adjustment. Witness:

In January, 1968 a young French computer programmer was caught using his company's computer to calculate his mistress's husband's accounts (!?). He was dismissed but worked out his notice and when he finally left no one suspected the legacy he had left behind. Indeed it was not until January 1st, 1970 that anything went wrong. New Year's Day was the time when an automatic updating program of all records was carried out. However, to that year's program the long departed programmer had added one final instruction – DESTROY ALL RECORDS. As the program spun relentlessly on inside the computer, every trace of information was totally wiped off!

Two years later in America another computer con-man was caught out because he was unfamiliar with the Polish telephone directory. The programmer was employed by a well-known and large bank and had access to its program controlling the crediting and debiting of customers' accounts. To the master program he added his own modest refinement – it was the instruction 'Deduct the odd cents below 10 cents from every current account in the ledger at the month end and credit the total to the last account in the Bank's records.' Thus an average of almost 5 cents was deducted from every one of several hundred thousand customer accounts each month and credited to the last account.

The electronic fraudster then opened up an account in the name of MR ZYGLIT. Dreams of becoming a millionaire however were rudely dashed when only six months later a Polish immigrant opened an account with the bank. His name was Zyzov. He was pleased but puzzled at the sudden and dramatic improvement in his finances and unfortunately for Mr Zyglit, Mr Zyzov's query precipitated an investigation by the men in blue.

The relevant question is – how many more computer con tricks are in progress *right now* where no coincidence has alerted the authorities?

ED MARKUS –
A VERY ACCOMPLISHED DRUMMER

By Michael Gillard

'No man need despair of gaining converts to the most extravagant hypothesis who has art enough to represent it in favourable colours,' remarked David Hume, the eighteenth century Scottish philosopher.

This acute observation on human behavior was never more justified than 200 years later amid the murky waters of the world of offshore funds. For it seemed, in the heady days of the late Sixties, that no proposition, no matter how bizarre, was unsaleable to investors somewhere in the world. All that was necessary were the magic offshore ingredients: tax free capital gains made in Swiss bank secrecy and payable in US dollars.

Shares and property were followed by oil, ships and paintings, then by even more exotic offshore offerings. Whisky, films, casinos, even brothels, were dressed up in fine sounding financial language as bait for the teeming shoals of the inflation scared, tax conscious or politically nervous on whom the offshore promoters preyed.

In this climate the concept of investing in food was almost mundane. But it was that very common-place quality that made the Agri-Fund a winner. Especially in the hands of a high powered and slick promoter like Edward Jules Markus, sometime bar owner and former orange grove salesman. As prosecuting counsel William Forbes Q.C. remarked at his trial: 'Agri-Fund was probably a very cracked and empty drum (but) Mr Markus was a very accomplished drummer.'

'Today the need for food is greater than ever before,'

intoned the opening words of the appropriately green and gold colored Agri-Fund prospectus. 'Throughout the world the long-term impact of uncontrolled population growth is daily becoming more apparent. Demand for food is steadily increasing while land itself is in fixed supply . . . it becomes rather obvious that the demand for food far exceeds the supply.'

Thomas Malthus, that pessimistic prophet of the population explosion inspired world famine, could not have put it better. Agri-Fund surely was 'an investment that is sensible, because it depends on man's prime necessity of life, not only sometimes but for ever and ever.'

By July, 1969, when the fund was launched, the tide of offshore money was starting to recede. But there was still enough action to make Markus' F.O.O.D. Plan attractive. Incomes, especially in happy offshore hunting grounds like West Germany, were still rising, creating surplus savings looking for a home. Elsewhere in Europe, Latin America, Africa and the Middle East political uncertainties, currency upheavals and inflation still made offshore funds a desirable fund hole.

For fund promoters by then, however, the play was 'The Switch Sale'. That meant persuading salesmen, the mercenary army of front line shock troops who dictated who got what from the offshore money pot, to transfer their allegiance and their clients' money from IOS, GRAMCO and other first generation funds to their newer rivals. Early entrants, jaded by the now less dynamic growth of IOS or GRAMCO, and newer recruits, hoping to make up for missing the initial big profits, made sure that if the level of money in the offshore pool was no longer rising so fast it sure was circulating a lot quicker.

Ed Markus served up his tasty Agri-Fund dish through a network of companies, stretching from Luxembourg through London to Miami and Panama, in such a way as to make it irresistible to some 3,000 investors, most of them in West Germany. In little more than 18 months he pulled in almost $6,000,000 (£2,500,000). But when the F.O.O.D. Plan fell apart in 1971 those who had accepted the invitation to dine at Markus' table were very angry investors indeed. For they lost every penny. Balding, burly and brash Ed Markus cut an almost Runyonesque figure. Loud, flashily dressed, big cigars between bejewelled fingers, he combined the manners and style of a successful second-hand car salesman with the presence and appearance of a night club bouncer.

Markus came to offshore funds with a minor police record, one or two not so successful promotions and a series of financial problems behind him. Born in Toronto in 1933, the son of local lawyer Jacob Markus, he first came to the attention of the police when he was 20. He was sentenced in Las Vegas to 15 days imprisonment on a charge of vagrancy. That was the inside of the last prison Ed Markus was to see for 20 years. But that is not to say during this time he was pursuing the paths of righteousness. Far from it. He was serving a con-man's apprenticeship and making some interesting connections.

By 1964 he had already graduated to the investment business. He was also in Nassau, Bahamas running International Citrus & Commodity Corporation. This offered orange groves in nearby British Honduras to American investors who could be persuaded there was money as well as juice in oranges. Markus approached a Florida concern with an offer to buy certain land that it owned in Britain's Central American colony. When they rejected his offer Markus, undeterred, went ahead and sold plots of their land anyway.

As a result of these unorthodox activities complaints were made by irate investors to the Bahamas police who in turn filed a complaint with the Board of Trade in Toronto where ICC was registered. In June, 1964 the Canadians made a cease and desist order against ICC and Markus issuing any further sales literature. A few days later he was deported from the Bahamas to his home in Miami.

Perhaps because of this official interest Markus switched to selling oranges as drinks rather than in groves. For the next two years he ran the Red Lion Bar & Grill in Coral Gables, a Miami suburb. However, this was clearly not such a success. For in 1966 he and his wife Zena lost their home when the mortgage was foreclosed. By 1969 Markus was back among the citrus groves, this time working for American Agronomics. Markus was sent to Europe to size up the sales potential there. He was so impressed that instead of selling for the Miami company he decided to set up his own scheme, Agri-Fund.

But if Ed Markus had an interesting background even more so did some of the contacts and associations he had made on his journey from Toronto through Las Vegas, Nassau and Miami to the Agri-Fund. And these raise a still unanswered question about the Agri-Fund swindle – to what extent was Ed Markus the pawn or partner of other more sinister figures and purposes in his offshore operations?

On the evening of July 5, 1971 two Americans landed at Tel Aviv's Lod Airport from Geneva having travelled from Miami via London. As they stepped from the aircraft they were immediately met by waiting Israeli immigration officials and taken into custody. Just after dawn the next day they were put on board a London-bound flight. Five days previously another traveller from London had similarly been refused entry into Israel. The reason? 'Israel has no intention of becoming a center for the activities of undesirables,' explained an official of the Interior Ministry. The Israelis had been tipped off by Interpol who had secretly monitored the movements of the Americans since they left Miami.

The two Americans who were turned back at Lod Airport were Benjamin B. Sigelbaum and Bernard Rose. The third man refused entry earlier was Ed Markus.

The Americans returned to Miami, their mission unaccomplished. That mission was to confer with Meyer Lansky, one of the most powerful figures in American organized crime, who had been living in Israel for a year in order to avoid Federal indictments in New York, Las Vegas and Miami.

Meyer Lansky had been the financial mastermind behind

many of the moves by organized crime into gambling, banking and legitimate enterprises as a means of 'laundering' the 'dirty money' earned from narcotics, vice, extortion, illegal betting and racketeering. In the Prohibition Era he and Bugsy Siegel had run the Bugs and Meyer Mob of contract killers which predated Murder Inc. After the Second World War 'The Little Man', as he was known, from his headquarters on Miami Beach organized the moves by the crime syndicate into casinos in the Bahamas, Cuba and other Caribbean islands as well as Europe and further afield. He engineered the control of banks in the US, the Bahamas and Switzerland in order, as one associate once put it, to ensure syndicate money could be 'washed clean in the snows of the Alps.'

Benny Sigelbaum was a long standing business associate of Lansky. He had been variously described as a 'bag man', i.e. money courier, for him, the man in charge of his property interests and a money mover, a major source of money from Las Vegas'.

His travelling companion, Bernard Rose, another known associate of Lansky, ran a chain of Miami cinemas showing pornographic films.

If the business conference that never was had been the only link between the friends of Meyer Lansky and Ed Markus' Agri-Fund it might just be put down to coincidence. However, the events at Lod Airport were the final chapter in a series of similar coincidences.

One of the few genuine, if not too successful, businesses bought by Agri-Fund was American Fruit Purveyors, a Miami concern run by Harry Sturm. The fund bought a 50% stake in December, 1969 for $1,000,000 (£420,000), to be completed within a year. At the time of the deal Sturm was reportedly glad to sell. He was said to owe a large amount to casinos in Las Vegas. Two months before, on October 3, Sturm and his wife took a third mortgage for $100,000 (£42,000) on the company's Miami Beach offices. This was to be repaid in November, 1970. The money came from Sigelbaum and Rose. Then along came Markus to pay more than the business was worth for Agri-Fund's half share. That year American Fruit Purveyors made a small profit and the following year a loss. Out of the $710,000 down payment made by the fund $205,000 went to Harry Sturm as an unsecured loan. All of which makes a very convenient coincidence.

Sigelbaum and Rose had been accompanied on the London leg of their flight from Miami by another name often linked with Lansky, banker and property man Benjamin C. Wheeler. He too appeared in the Agri-Fund swindle, as treasurer of the Fund's management company.

With Sigelbaum and others Ben Wheeler had been involved since 1963 in control of the small Exchange & Investment Bank in Geneva. This bank and the Miami National Bank were the route whereby undeclared or 'skimmed' profits from gambling tables in Las Vegas found their way to the Swiss bank accounts of Lansky and his partners. It was mainly as a result of Federal indictments in Miami and Las Vegas for 'skimming' a total of $36,000,000 (£15,000,000) from the Flamingo casino that Lansky was keen to stay in Israel.

Also known to 'The Little Man' was another Agri-Fund official, Reuben Miller. His investment company shared offices in Miami with Sam Jaffe, a director of the fund management company. Asked about Sigelbaum, Wheeler, Miller and Lansky, a leading US Justice Department expert on organized crime stated: 'They are all personally known to each other.'

Another resident in the fund's offices was Jan D. Engstrom, a colorful character if not an investment expert. Tough looking and heavily built Engstrom accompanied Markus most of the time but on occasions stayed behind to 'mind the shop' when the Agri boss was on one of his many trips to Florida or Switzerland. Engstrom's position in the Agri set up was ambiguous. A one-time insurance salesman he was said to be in charge of its 'insurance' side, which was non-existant in any conventional sense. He was also described as Markus' golfing companion.

However, possibly the real reason why he was there may lie in a story told by a former Agri-Fund salesman.

Engstrom was given a wide berth by almost every one inside the London office. He had his own office there in which the top drawer of his desk was always locked, even when he was in the building. On one occasion Engstrom was asked by the salesman what was in the drawer that he was so security-minded about it. 'Do you really want to know?', Engstrom asked. The salesman persisted so Engstrom unlocked the drawer and pulled it open so that he could see the contents. Inside were two hand guns. 'They are for Ed and me. We keep them for protection,' Engstrom told the startled salesman, closing the drawer again.

Given this background it is perhaps not altogether surprising that Agri-Fund turned out a swindle from day one.

The companies involved in the swindle were Agricultural Investment Corporation S.A., the management company, and First National Investment Corporation S.A., which was to handle the selling. The fraud began right here.

Agricultural Investment Corporation, like most of Markus' companies, was registered (in April, 1969) in Panama – conveniently close to Miami and where company law requirements are as minimal as the tax. Markus claimed it was a $10,000,000 (£4,200,000) company. This claim was a total fiction. AIC was only a $10,000,000 company as far as its authorized share capital was concerned. But that was meaningless. It meant no more than that this was the maximum number of shares that could be issued. The more important paid up capital was just $2 – one share each, taken up by Markus' lawyer Teodoro Franco and a secretary in the lawyer's office.

First National Investment Corporation was incorporated in Luxembourg in June, 1969, a few weeks before the first Agri-Fund prospectus was published. Markus put up most of the $20,000 (£8,300) capital.

It was not by accident that Markus should chose a confidence boosting name like First National Investment or a company logo showing the world at the hub of a four pointed star. Both bore a remarkable resemblance to the title and logo of the prestigious First National City Bank of New York. This was the classic con-man's trick of 'passing off' at work, i.e., obtaining credibility by using a name that is so similar to that of a reputable organization that even the sophisticated may be taken in long enough to be swindled.

Unfortunately for Markus the resemblance was so remarkable that First National City Bank felt obliged to act quickly to prevent such an embarassing confusion. The New York bank not only filed a complaint with the Luxembourg authorities and began legal proceedings in the Grand Duchy but published a disclaimer in the Paris-printed *International Herald Tribune*.

As a consequence FNIC was refused a license to trade in Luxembourg and was driven out to London where in May, 1970 Markus set up headquarters in Mayfair's Green Street, not far from Park Lane. But for this attempt to pass FNIC off as associated with First National City Bank Markus would probably never have moved the fund's operations to London and by so doing brought himself within the jurisdiction of Scotland Yard's Fraud Squad and the Prevention of Fraud (Investments) Act.

Another result of this enforced migration was that Markus replaced FNIC as the sales company in August, 1970 with another Panamanian corporation, Agri International.

The move to London also marked the start of the main sales drive by Agri-Fund, for which Ed Markus had coined three main selling plusses. 'Agri-Fund does not invest in the stock markets or commodity markets which tend to fluctuate, but only invests in income producing assets, such as cattle ranches, farming, citrus groves, sugar mills, fisheries, etc. and in the production of finished marketable food products.'

Not for Agri partners therefore the fate of being at the mercy of share prices that slumped when a political leader sneezed. No. Instead, Agri-Fund promised investors 'Security, Growth, Income'. How? By investing only in established but not public companies. Companies which had shown profits rising at a mystical 15% a year plus the ownership of prized property assets. That's how. As the fund did not intend to pay any dividends but re-invest its burgeoning profits, where the income came in is unclear. But then there never was any growth or security either.

The second titbit which Markus used as bait was 'leverage', the financial principle he colorfully likened in the prospectus to 'the cave dweller of old who used a small stick to move a large rock.' In reality 'leverage' is nothing more complex or original than the method most people use to buy their homes, putting down a 10% deposit and borrowing the rest from a building society. The effect of 'leverage' is that if the house goes up in value, say from £10,000 to £20,000, then the £10,000 'profit' has been made for an outlay of just £1,000. However, out of that must be deducted the not insignificant cost of borrowing the other £9,000.

Somehow Markus forgot to detail the cost of the investors' interest payments when revealing the mystical properties of 'leverage' to potential Agri partners. In fact on the investment plan pushed hardest by the prospectus Agri-Fund had to show growth of at least 42% over 10 years just for the investor to get his money back. Not that this bothered Ed Markus who, like any good promoter, took the line that in the long term we are all dead. Unfortunately for Agri-Fund investors that long term was to come sooner rather than later.

But if potential investors doubted Markus' mathematics or even if they were not totally convinced that food was a cannot-miss-investment they could surely rely on the third Agri-Fund attraction, the promise that they could take their money out immediately. The prospectus left no doubt about that. With Agri-Fund it was repayment on demand. 'Your money is available when you need it! Immediate liquidity . . . means that the investor simply signs the back of the program certificate and mails it to First National Investment Corporation, and his money is sent to him immediately on receipt of the program certificate.' To back up this promise 20% of the fund's assets were to remain in cash.

Later many Agri investors would ruefully admit that it was this unconditional guarantee that persuaded them to part with their money. Ironically it also helped convict Ed Markus of fraud.

However, this was but one, if the most crucial, of the prospectus promises broken to investors.

It was stated that the fund's holdings would be made only after consultation between the directors and an 'Advisory Board' made up of 'knowledgeable and capable personnel in all fields of agricultural endeavour (who had) a vast wealth of knowledge in Agricultural Financing, Distribution, Development, Warehousing, Shipping, Appraising, Acquiring, Marketing and Management.'

American Jack Meily, who was a director of the fund management company, later declared that not only did this board never meet to his knowledge but he did not know the identity of any of the 'astute and knowledgeable persons in their respective fields' who were members.

Every acquisition to be made by the fund also first had to pass through the eye of a rigorous four stage investigation. Independent auditors were to evaluate potential earning power. Suitable management and product marketability were also investigated. Finally, the acquisition was 'fully examined in the area of cost and financing in order to give Agri-Fund the maximum future return.' Just how fictional all this financial mumbo-jumbo was is demonstrated by the purchases that the fund actually made. None would have passed even the first hurdle of an independent audit – had it ever existed.

Like most offshore funds Agri promised to produce at weekly intervals a statement of its net asset value per share. However, that presented no little problem because of the very advantage Markus claimed for the fund, that its holdings were not quoted on any stock market and valuations were therefore notional – very!

For one thing, private companies at best produce monthly

profit statements and mostly only quarterly or half-yearly balance sheets.

So how did Markus manage to produce weekly net asset value figures for the fund, figures which showed the net assets to be ever rising?

This was a question that fascinated Meily and certain sales managers in Germany because of Markus' unwillingness or inability to produce audited accounts for any of the secure and growing companies in which the fund had invested. Eventually in November, 1970, under pressure from Meily, Al Landin – who kept the books for Markus – came up with an incredibly complex valuation formula derived from accounting practices for retail chain stores!

Not surprisingly no evidence was ever found of such complex calculations being made. But then, according to his former employers American Agronomics, Landin was sacked because he was 'inept, incompetent and not capable of handling detailed or extensive accounting work.' Hardly the type to perform the miracles of mathematical skill Agri-Fund required each week.

When the fund suspended operations in January, 1971 its net asset value was advertised as $4.70 per share. Sixty-five weeks before in October, 1969 it had stood at $4 – a rise of 1.07 cents a week equalling by coincidence the magic 15% a year growth that was promised. As Meily, guessing the truth, wrote on reading Landin's memo: 'Al and Ed automatically increased the Net Asset Value each week by 1 cent.' But you could hardly put that in a prospectus!

Agri-Fund also promised periodic and annual reports plus audited financial statements. Only one periodic report was ever produced, in June, 1970. It was the work of Aragon & Asociados, whose staff the prospectus said was 'comprised of the finest accounting experts in Panama.' The truth about Señor Aragon was about as convincing as his figures.

Attempts to contact Panama's 'finest accountants' were fraught with difficulties once Agri-Fund closed its doors. When Detective Sergeant Eric Lilley of the Fraud Squad visited Panama he was unable even to locate the firm at its supposed address. However, he did discover that the address was also in the same building as Markus' local lawyers Franco & Franco, AIC and another Markus company, Fiduciaire Guaranty. Four different street names were obtained for all these by the simple device of using the streets or alleys on each side of the building.

Leonidas Aragon Junior was not even a qualified accountant. He was entitled to call himself a registered accountant, but not a chartered public accountant as he was titled in the prospectus, by virtue of seven years experience as a book-keeper. He was not even a full time accountant being employed mainly as a Government official. A former deputy Finance Minister, Aragon was described by a local businessman in highly uncomplimentary terms as 'a fixer who drinks like a fish and has friends in all the right places.' He simply accepted without question what Markus said was the position concerning where the Agri millions had gone. But then accountancy skills were not really necessary as far as preparing the Agri prospectus was concerned. For in describing AIC's financial position all figures were simply dispensed with by Markus.

Eventually Sergeant Lilley tracked down the elusive Aragon. But on learning that Scotland Yard wanted to discuss his book-keeping activities with him the former minister left Panama 'at short notice'.

Another protection that was not all that it seemed was the 'independent' custodian who was to hold the fund's assets. Fiduciaire Guaranty International had been formed only just before Agri-Fund itself by Franco & Franco. It operated in name only from their offices and apart from one of the lawyers its officials included one of Markus' partners in the swindle, "Judge" Edward Walterman. A sometime professor of law at the University of Miami, Walterman was either respected or feared among those who knew or did business with him.

Like other offshore sales literature the Agri-Fund prospectus was full of holes to anyone whose eyes were undimmed by greed. But for doubters Markus had in reserve the international swindler's elixir, the backing of well known and respectable figures to lend credence to the promotion and its promoter. Unfortunately for Markus, by the time Agri-Fund arrived the rosters of available American and European out-of-office politicians, retired diplomats, government officials, generals and aristocrats had been plundered by earlier offshore press gangs.

All Markus could pick up was a Cuban crumb, Dr Marcos A. Kohly, a former diplomat who had once been a national director of the Organization of American States. But that had been some time ago. By 1969 he was reduced to the less imposing status of a public relations man for the city of Miami. Not that that bothered Markus. He was good figurehead material on his past if not his present. Markus offered Kohly £10,000 a year to act as chairman of the management company. Needless to say the Cuban did not need too much convincing to accept. While polite to Kohly in public Markus treated the chairman like an office boy in private. When asked if the chairman should be consulted about some decision he would say: 'Absolutely unnecessary, nothing to do with Kohly. I will deal with it.' Later Markus did recruit a former West German Economics Minister but just missed out on an English earl.

This then was the product and the people that Agri salesmen, motivated by high commissions of $2\frac{1}{2}\%$ to $4\frac{1}{2}\%$ of the face value of each Beneficial Payment Plan, set out to sell.

Execution of the Agri-Fund swindle, whereby Ed Markus made $5,800,000 vanish, was delightfully simple. He merely did what he said the fund would do – invest in food companies. The difference was that where Agri-Fund bought anything at all they were shares in either dummy companies, companies worth far less than they cost or companies that simply did not exist at all. Furthermore, the fund only bought these bargains, or claimed to have bought them, from Markus or his associates like Edward Walterman or Harry Sturm.

A leading supplier of meat to hotels and restaurants in Miami Beach , Sturm was a friend of Markus. He employed his eldest son after Agri-Fund crashed. But that was perhaps a small return for the estimated $205,000 (£85,000) Markus had put in his pocket. A fellow gambler, Sturm shared Markus' interest in gambling sufficiently to equip his office with a full size pool table.

American Fruit Purveyors was the first but not the only Agri-Fund winner in which Sturm featured. There was also Critchley Florida which it was said would 'have the potential to expand as one of the major suppliers to cruise ships in the world.' Critchley never traded after its formation in 1968. It was dissolved in 1971 and there is no evidence the fund ever owned any shares.

Ronden Trucking – 'engaged in the leasing of vehicles and equipment' – was another Sturm company. Ronden also never traded from incorporation in 1968 to its dissolution in May, 1970, the very month its attractions were lauded in the prospectus.

Some $100,000 (£42,000) went into International Beef Processing whose only remarkable feature was to have as a director lawyer Blanche Tonic. This company, the prospectus said, was supposedly 'engaged in the importation of frozen meat from South America.' It was also busy supplying wholesalers with meat using the 'CRY-o-VAC process which creates a vacuum around the meat (which) reduces shrinkage and waste to the point of insignificance.' The Agri investment could have done with similar protection. Formed after Agri-Fund itself there is no evidence this company ever traded.

These company histories may explain at least partly what Markus meant when, in answer to a question from Jack Meily about up-to-date financial statements from the fund's investments, he said to Landin: 'Can you imagine Harry Sturm allowing an audit at this time?'

The other prolific provider of business opportunities was Markus' Miami attorney and partner, "Judge" Edward Walterman.

There was Marlee Fruit Growers 'engaged in the development, production and shipping of citrus, principally limes, avocados, papayas and other tropical, semi-tropical fruits.' Marlee was formed only three months before the prospectus including its name was printed in May, 1970. It was owned by the Walterman family. The company was dissolved in 1972 without the concern ever having traded.

Then there was Prize Herd Ranch formed with Walterman's help on the same day as Marlee. This was said to be 'raising', feeding and supplying a herd of at least 2,000 head of the highest grade cattle.' That was in May, 1970. The company did not obtain an interest in so much as a horn or a hoof until February, 1971, by which time Agri-Fund had passed into history. Ultimately, some $155,000 (£64,000) of fund money went to finance two cattle schemes, one in Texas, from which Agri partners at least never received any benefit.

Walterman was also involved in the formation of Visa Gourmet International in February, 1970. This was said to own 'retail stores in prime locations throughout South Eastern Florida.' It never owned anything. Intended as a move into delicatessens the company never traded and was dissolved in 1972.

But to be fair, the Agri-Fund did not only invest in non-trading companies. Some of the money was actually invested in the acquisition of shareholdings in 'going' concerns. The only trouble was that the investments appeared to be jinxed with exceptionally bad luck.

Control of Everready Foods, for example, was acquired in March, 1970 for $36,000 (£15,000) plus loans that were to total $145,000 (£60,000). In 1971, the original owner bought it back. Unfortunately the first payment was directed not to the fund holders but to Walterman.

Further investments in two private companies, Overnight Food Express and Fro-Sun Food Transportation, linked with Arthur Schlossman who was a director of the management company, cost the Agri-Fund at least $50,000 in 6 months.

But Ed Markus' ambitions for Agri-Fund were not only confined to Florida and Panama, where he formed Agri-

Beef Products for the fund to invest in. In time he was also to be found investing the fund's money in equally curious propositions in Europe.

Alimentaria Sud was claimed to be under construction in Lecce, Italy. It was a $25,000,000 (£10,000,000) project for the 'importing of poultry and cattle, raising, slaughtering, packing and shipping of meat products.' Italian lawyer Roberto Memmo sold Markus the idea and an interest for $80,000 (£33,000). The plan was to launch an Italian Agri-Fund which would help finance the project.

Marcos Kohly was to be engineered into an audience with the Pope, through a relative of Memmo who worked in the Vatican, in order to provide publicity pictures which could be used to convey the idea that the project had the Papal blessing. However, even £10,000 a year was apparently not enough to make the Cuban risk the Pope's undoubted displeasure had this trick been pulled on His Holiness. Fortunately for Kohly he avoided having to choose between Markus' anger and excommunication because of a row between the promoter and Memmo. The less than cultured Canadian fell out with Memmo when the Italian, who treated Markus as his equal in business but not socially, would not invite him to a party at his Rome palazzo. This quarrel resulted in Agri-Fund pulling out of Alimentaria Sud which never got off the ground. Markus also bought a slice of a Bavarian liver sausage maker whose products had been criticized on medical grounds.

But perhaps the prize for the most amazing investment of all made by Agri-Fund must go to Marco S.A., yet another Panamanian company but this time one with a difference. According to the prospectus 'Marco S.A. is engaged in the maritime shipping industry, principally the leasing of ships to corporations in need of facilities to transport raw materials in the processing of food products. The company currently has contracted with some of the larger food manufacturers in North America.' An earlier draft prospectus had said that the fund was to pay some $500,000 (£200,000) for Marco and had already made a 50% deposit.

Marco certainly existed. The company that is. It was formed in 1968 when it was said to own the 22,000 ton *S.S. Marco* which it had acquired for just $4,000 (£1,700). This was quite a bargain. The break up value of a ship that size would be $180,000 (£75,000). However, if its owner could be located, the good ship *Marco* itself was as much a maritime mystery as the *Marie Celeste*. No trace of it could be found at either Lloyd's of London, the premier center for shipping insurance, or in the maritime records of Panama or the US. According to Markus the *Marco* was an ocean going barge anchored at Fort Lauderdale, Florida. However, Walterman thought it was at Jacksonville and besides was a freighter. In fact he claimed that the company owned two ships and had been shown pictures of them. But then neither Markus nor his lawyer knew much about the sea.

Just how much money was really swallowed up by Agri-Fund's supposed investments is still a matter of doubt. For what it is worth the March, 1970 'balance sheet' produced by the elusive Leonidas Aragon said that over $2,000,000 had been paid in deposits. But then he also said this mixture of dummy, dormant and decrepit companies earned profits of a similar amount!

What is certain is that well over $1,000,000 (£420,000) of the $5,800,000 put up by investors disappeared into companies sold to the fund by Markus or his associates. Other large sums went the same route but even more directly.

Ed Markus and his friends might have continued to find 'shell' companies and non-existent ships for Agri-Fund to buy if a tidal wave had not ripped through the offshore sea in summer, 1970. This was caused first by a cash crisis inside IOS which led to its founder Bernie Cornfeld being deposed in May. Then a similar shortage of liquidity caused GRAMCO to suspend redemptions in October. As the two giants of the business began to totter, every offshore fund was suddenly besieged by frantic investors wanting their money back. Greed was being replaced by its twin market mover-fear. And fear banished confidence. Money was soon haemorrhaging from the funds faster, much faster, than it had ever come in as investors continued to panic.

With little new money now being invested and large amounts of what was already in either looted, lost in bad investments or locked in unsaleable ones, few funds could hope to survive such a crisis. Agri-Fund was no exception. In theory the fund held 20% of its assets in cash to meet the promise of instant repayment. And as late as December 1st, Markus, through Meily, reassured his sales managers in West Germany that the fund held $8,000,000 (£3,300,000) in the bank, $1,000,000 of it in Germany. Another amazing piece of astute money management. The fund never attracted that amount altogether.

Meily was forced to provide this fictional assurance not only because of the difficulty German investors had experienced since October in getting their money out but also because of the tell-tale non-payment of sales commissions. This became so bad that two determined German salesmen came to London and confronted Landin saying they would not leave without their money. Landin only had a cash check signed by Markus which he reluctantly gave to them. He had been hoping to keep it for himself. When Markus discovered this he bawled out Landin for being so rash as to give the Germans anything.

By December, as the flood of redemption demands continued to mount, threatening to wash Agri-Fund away, Markus privately instructed the London office: 'No more repayments.'

Faced with neither the ability nor the wish to repay the $5,800,000 but not wanting to admit either Markus came up with a new ploy that was as simple as it was audacious. He would tell all the fund holders that, naturally in their best interests but without their having any say, their money had been switched into a new company which had acquired the Agri assets and they would have to wait 5 years to be repaid. This also had the advantage of avoiding the looming necessity to produce a first year's audited financial statement in order to quell the suspicions of the sales force.

The decision to take this step was made at a meeting of

Markus, Walterman and their other close associates in Miami over Christmas. It was announced to the stunned investors and salesmen in a letter from Kohly dated January 18, 1971. The new company the Agri partners had now involuntarily become investors in was Investors Financial Management Corporation, 'an international holding and operating company with assets throughout the world', which claimed an authorized capital of no less than $50,000,000 (£21,000,000). IFM's assets were 'broadly diversified into real estate, consumer orientated corporations, securities, government obligations and bank deposits.' In reality IFM was a 'shell' company with no assets of its own that had been incorporated once again by the ever present Teodoro Franco just six months before. Its authorized capital was not $50,000,000 but $1,000 of which only two shares had been issued.

When Jack Meily, who though a director was not at the Miami meeting, was told of the plan by Markus on January 3 he saw through it immediately. 'It's a flimflam (fraud)', he told Markus. 'The investors will never go for it.' Markus was unperturbed. 'If you romance something enough they will buy it,' he replied confidently.

Knowing the suspicions of the Press and the sales managers in West Germany, Meily was not convinced. This made Markus very angry. It would be 'immoral' said the ex-convict and swindler to liquidate the fund just to repay the investors, adding significantly, 'Look, it's my money and I am not going to give it up.'

Following another angry slanging match over the trans-Atlantic telephone Meily was fired after being accused of plotting a 'palace revolt.'

The wavering Al Landin, who clearly knew a lot more than anyone else in London about where the money had gone, was escorted to a Miami-bound flight by Engstrom. Before he left Landin discreetly let it be known that he had deposited certain papers in a safe deposit box which were to be his 'insurance policy' if anything went wrong. However, when later asked about this by an investigator Landin refused to say what was in the box. 'Why don't you tell them' his wife pleaded. 'Shut up', the agitated book-keeper shouted.

So Kohly's bombshell letter went out to inform the 3000 investors that, in order to prevent a 'distress sale of its assets (due to) the irresponsible actions of a small minority' (whose crime was to want the fund to honor its instant repayment pledge) Agri's assets had been sold to IFM. No price was given. However, the investors were assured this had been done 'in keeping with management's responsibility to provide the Agri investor with security, growth and income.' Furthermore, this had only been done after 'top level discussions have taken place with leading international financial organizations throughout the world.' No doubt a reference to the Christmas meeting in Miami. Some romancing!

Markus, as president of IFM, summoned a board meeting in Miami on January 25 at which he and the other two directors turned themselves into an executive committee leaving Teodoro Franco and his brother as directors together with former professional golfer Tommy Warren. Warren, real name Thomas Warren Smythe, had been running a steak restaurant in Miami which Agri-Fund was to buy. In November he had flown to London to be told by Markus that he was to open an office in Panama. Some several weeks later he was summoned back to Miami to be told about IFM and that he was to be president. 'T. Warren Smythe has a nice ring about it,' explained Markus. It also avoided the Markus name appearing on any IFM documentation – something which might not have 'romanced' anyone for very long.

Another part of the 'romancing' was that Agri-Fund investors appeared to receive their new IFM certificates from Panama where the 'international holding and operating company' (a slight contradiction in terms but never mind), had its headquarters in a first floor apartment in a wealthy suburb of Panama City. The certificates were supposedly being processed and despatched by the Registrar & Transfer Corporation, a 'recognized financial institution' formed by Markus' busy Panamanian lawyers. In fact the certificates came from London. They were merely sent to Miami where the mail was either collected by Smythe or forwarded to him in Panama. He then merely stuck on some Panamanian stamps in order to lend credibility to the sham.

However, the time for 'romancing' had long disappeared at Agri-Fund. By March protests were flooding into the fund's offices in London, Miami and Panama from angry Agri partners.

But Markus had shut the door. There would be no more money paid back. For there was nothing to pay them with. The Agri drum had finally split to reveal that it was, as it had always been, empty. The Department of Trade later estimated that all that was left in the Agri/IFM cupboard was at best a highly doubtful $1,000,000 (£420,000) and probably nothing.

So where had nearly $6,000,000 gone?

Something like $1,000,000 (£420,000) went into companies connected with Harry Sturm and another up to $500,000 (£210,000) into those involving Markus, Walterman and their other associates. Up to $500,000 disappeared (after Agri-Fund closed) into a proposed film fund with which Markus intended to rise from the Agri ashes. This money went to help finance a projected new spectacular epic film titled 'Isabella and Ferdinand,' starring Glenda Jackson. The film was to cost as much as $15,000,000 (£6,250,000) which was mostly, so Markus was told by a veteran Hollywood producer, to be put up by the Spanish government. Markus agreed to put up $3,000,000 (£1,250,000) as 'front money' to be 'secured' on a one-third interest in the film. He also paid the premium on insuring the producer's life. He should have taken out some insurance for himself. The film never even went into production and was abandoned before any serious filming had begun, in December, 1971. However, not before during the first six months of that year at least $250,000

(£100,000) of Agri money had been used to set it up.

Still, Markus had enough money to console himself and his pride. For he had pocketed at least $1,100,000 (£450,000) of the fund's money himself. He took just over half of this money in the three months between November, 1970 and January, 1971 from the management and sales companies' bank accounts where he was the only signatory.

The rest he took more discreetly. That summer Agri had staged a sales drive in Frankfurt and as an exhibition gimmick Markus sought to borrow gold worth $500,000. Not surprisingly no bank was prepared to trust him to that extent. So he agreed to buy the gold on the understanding that it could be sold back at cost. The management company paid for the gold but when it was resold the proceeds went not to AIC but to Markus personally.

Other very large sums, some estimates put the figure as high as $1,000,000, are said to have been flown to Miami in suitcases. Who this was for and whether that is included in the previously mentioned amounts is still a mystery.

Large amounts were also accounted for by the high cost of the Agri sales operation. Here Markus did not stint. Salesmen were told to spend whatever was required to make the sale. Towards the end sales commissions were being paid out of the same bank account into which the investors were making their payments. The house in Green Street cost $145,000 (£60,000) while there was also the cost of the plush offices in Miami and the not inconsiderable cost of commuting between the two. Just how expensive that was can be seen from the fact that two years after the fund crashed Markus was bankrupted in London by TWA to whom he owed $58,000 (£24,000) in air fares.

On top of all this there was also the cost of Markus' own free spending life style which was somewhat extravagant for a man without personal wealth whose home had been foreclosed on just four years before. Just how much of this was financed by the fund holders' money is unknown.

Markus was supporting two homes for most of the time he was running Agri-Fund. One in Miami for his wife and five children and another in London for his mistress and her son. But the most costly item was his gambling. Soon after his arrival in London, Markus was renowned in casino circles as a high roller, playing dice regularly anyplace that ran big money games. His particular favorite was the Pair of Shoes in Mayfair. Control of the Pair of Shoes had been acquired the previous year by Noel Souter and Derrick Daggers.

The Pair of Shoes ran some of the biggest dice games in London. Playing regularly Markus was reputed to have won or lost up to $120,000 (£50,000) on several occasions. However, his regular appearances at the casino began to attract comment regarding his exact relationship with Souter and Daggers. It was gossiped that he was the money behind them. All this was denied by Souter who merely said of Markus: 'He has been a very good gambler. He has lost a lot of money here. We look after him well.' However, these links with the Pair of Shoes also interested those at Scotland Yard concerned to prevent infiltration by American organized crime elements back into British casinos. In early 1967 veteran film 'gangster' George Raft and several other Americans connected with the Colony Club casino had been banned from re-entering Britain. This action was taken after the Home Office were reportedly tipped off by the FBI that Raft had been associated with Lansky and two prominent Mafia figures, Angelo Bruno of Philadelphia and Charley 'The Blade' Tourine from New York, who had visited London the year before.

The presence of Miller and Wheeler with Markus at the Pair of Shoes was therefore of more than passing interest. Especially so when it was whispered that Lansky himself had visited the casino travelling from Dublin under the name 'Harris'. The police acted when it was learned that 'junkets' of American gamblers were being flown into London to play at the Pair of Shoes. The men behind the trips all had previous connections with organized crime-run gambling operations in Cuba, Florida and Las Vegas. The police opposed a renewal of the casino's license saying: 'The junket organizers are more or less front men, the people behind them are the organized crime syndicates.' The licensing authorities were also told: 'to some extent (Souter and Daggers) are in contact with and being controlled by influences from America which, to put it at its lowest are very highly undesirable. 'The Pair of Shoes' lost its license in May, 1971 and closed.

Now Ed Markus had to find new places to roll the dice. One was Kinshasa, capital of the former Belgian Congo (now Zaire), where Souter moved to take over the running of a casino. Markus visited Kinshasa several times. After his arrest his mistress flew there to collect some money he was owed. But the payment was made in counterfeit dollars.

Daggers by this time had switched from gambling to drug smuggling. After being arrested once in Beirut he was caught at London Airport in 1973 trying to smuggle heroin worth £150,000 into the US and was jailed for 7 years. He received another 2 year sentence later that year for masterminding, while in jail, another scheme to bring £500,000 worth of cannabis into Britain.

But Ed Markus did not spend or gamble away all his or Agri-Fund's money. He still had enough cash and confidence to start 'romancing' another swindle even before the uproar from the first had died away.

On June 25, 1971 both Markus and Engstrom notified Kohly they had severed all connections with the now defunct Agri-Fund and its successor IFM. But, despite the fact that for some time both the Fraud Squad and the Department of Trade had been actively investigating Agri's affairs, Markus did not leave London. Instead the confident Canadian started looking for new offices from which to launch the latest of the 'absolutely unique investment vehicles' he had promised the former Agri-Fund sales force.

On August 9 in Panama the faithful Teodoro Franco formed yet another company, Vanguard Investment & Portfolios, for his client and meanwhile in Curacao, Netherlands Antilles, Intergrowth Securities Corporation was taken down off the shelf, where it had laid since July, 1970, and dusted. By November the stage was set for a new exercise in flimflammery.

This took the form of a $10,000,000 (£4,200,000) offering of shares in Intergrowth Securities. The prospectus declared: 'The purpose and objective of the company are to achieve capital appreciation for its shareholders by means of timely investments in international securities.' Intergrowth Securities shares were to be readily saleable and could be converted into cash at any time through any bank or stockbroker. Instead of the part-time Señor Aragon, this time the auditors were to be the at least impressive sounding Societe Anonyme de Revision et d'Expertise Fiscale. There was a custodian bank too, the Banque de Titres of Geneva, once owned by GRAMCO. Markus also hired James Roosevelt, an old IOS stalwart, as public relations advisor.

All of this could have sounded very familiar to any Agri-Fund investor who might happen on an Intergrowth prospectus. However, he would not have made any connection. For one name that did not appear anywhere was Edward J. Markus. Clearly that no longer had any value for 'romancing' purposes of a financial nature. After all, memories are not all that short. Especially where $6,000,000 (£2,500,000) is concerned. Instead, ISC boasted yet another impressive and multinational board, including an Italian aristocrat and an English Knight. One name, however, is particularly interesting – Richard C. Pistell.

'Pistol Dick' Pistell had been helpful to Robert Vesco, who had taken over IOS from Cornfeld and was busy looting its funds. Pistell introduced Vesco to the people that mattered in the Bahamas, Costa Rica and elsewhere. He also brought various deals to Vesco. In return Pistell companies received $4,000,000 (£1,700,000) of IOS money and Pistell himself $170,000 (£70,000) for acting as a contact man. Meanwhile Pistell's attempts in 1969 to take over the Armour meat packaging group were under-going investigation by the Securities & Exchange Commission who the next year accused 'Pistol Dick' of fraud. (Vesco was also charged with fraud by the SEC in 1972 and accused of stealing over $200,000,000 of IOS money.)

A sales drive in over 20 countries throughout Europe, Africa and Latin America was planned plus a first off stock market quotation for ISC in Beirut. But Markus' ambitions for his new vehicle received a rude jolt when, protesting 'I am being harassed', he was arrested on fraud charges arising out of the Agri-Fund swindle upon arrival at London Airport for Miami on December 4, 1971.

For a while he kept Intergrowth Securities alive. Spurred by his arrest and a visit from the Department of Trade, Markus moved the headqarters to Switzerland. Attempts to promote sales of ISC were still going on in March, 1972. But by then there was little left in the offshore fund pool and Son of Agri-Fund never really got started.

Ed Markus appeared at the Old Bailey in October, 1973 facing 42 counts of defrauding the Agri-Fund investors. Walterman and Landin were named as co-conspirators but as the charges were brought under the Prevention of Fraud (Investments) Act neither could be extradited from the US. To those who wondered why he had stayed in London when he would have been safe in Miami Markus boasted in typical fashion that he would get off. He was wrong. A month later he was convicted on 12 charges and jailed for 7 years. 'I am only sorry the law does not allow me to give you a longer sentence,' declared Mr Justice Lawson. This was the first time an offshore fund promoter had been jailed by a British court. Those of Markus' rivals who used London as a base either avoided arrest by remaining out of Britain, such as Jerome Hoffman, or were clever enough not to provide any legal basis for a British court to claim jurisdiction.

Markus managed to get his sentence cut to 5 years on appeal and was released from prison in late 1976, having lost remission through being less than a model prisoner.

The key witness at the trial was Jack Meily, brought from a secret address in the US under police protection to testify against Markus. These precautions were said to be necessary because Meily feared 'unnamed parties in Miami.' Ironically some felt Ed Markus too shared a similar fear, though for a different reason. 'I think he double-crossed them' was how one Agri-Fund executive explained Markus' curious refusal to stay in Miami.

The identity of these unnamed individuals, their role in the Agri-Fund swindle and the extent to which they shared the vanished $6,000,000 is a matter for conjecture. However, in examining the story of the Agri-Fund it is worth recalling the words of a witness before a 1971 US Senate committee investigating how organized crime operates elsewhere in the financial world with the stolen securities racket:

'Where one person shows it is because he is involved in representing another person. In other words, they act in concert. There are groups that act together. If one person from one group shows, then generally speaking the rest of the group is there at the same time, although perhaps not on the surface. The object is to insulate the major people at all cost. That is the total purpose of it.'

THE DAWNING OF 'SEPTEMBER MORN'

The public likes to believe that all Public Relations consultants are con-men. Who knows – it depends on the definition. Certainly PR men have one thing in common with the other characters in this book – they earn their living by presenting the best possible image – and sometimes that image needs a bit of 'adjusting'.

Harry Reichenbach was no con-man – he was indeed one of the highest paid publicity experts in America. But his techniques – as he himself admitted – sometimes owed more to hoaxing than a straight recounting of the facts.

One of his earliest clients was a smallish art shop in New York. In conversation one day the owner mentioned that he was stuck with ridiculously high stocks of a lithograph picture of a nude girl contemplating a placid pool of water. He had 2,000 copies, but even at ten cents each no-one was buying.

Reichenbach arranged a window display of the print – then he and some confederates rang the office of the Anti-Vice Society to protest at the 'outrage to public decency'. A few days later, after no action was forthcoming, he made a personal visit to the President of the worthy Society to claim that the picture was corrupting the youth of the City and 'an affront to its morals'.

The President was persuaded to visit the scene of this disgraceful exhibition and to his concern was met with the sight of a group of New York's innocent youth who were leering at the picture and gleefully uttering ribald commentaries.

The President demanded the prints should be removed – and when the art shop owner refused he appealed to the Courts. Overnight, the neglected lithograph became a national talking point; denounced, praised, joked over but above all noticed.

Seven million copies were sold at $1 each. The name of the picture – 'September Morn'.

OLD MASTER, DON'T TOUCH – THE PAINT MAY NOT BE DRY!

by Maggie Ward

One art forger conned Goering out of £160,000, one persuaded Picasso himself to authenticate a fake as his own work, another painted seven Picassos before breakfast and yet another filed criminal charges against himself to *prove* he was the author of celebrated 'medieval frescoes'.

As Rip-off Artists, art forgers are generally in a class of their own. As often as not, the individual faker's motive is more to obtain recognition than money – or to obtain revenge on the seemingly artificial world of the art experts. A picture from an unknown artist may be valued at £50 but it could overnight be worth £250,000 if erroneously attributed to a 'master' painter by the experts. Yet it is the *same* painting – nothing has changed. Such a five-thousand-fold increase is not just theory. It has happened. Moreover, once the picture has been accepted as a genuine 'old master', the art forger has the critics' pride working for him. No-one likes to look foolish by admitting that he has authenticated a fake – and equally the purchaser will not willingly accept that his prize exhibit has suffered an overnight loss in value of perhaps £100,000 plus. It is an unwelcome blow to the bank balance.

The history of art faking is long and almost respectable – Michaelangelo and Goya were not above a bit of passing off and many an art gallery has its tributes to man's gullibility (or greed).

Han van Meegeren was one of the better class forgers. He was painstaking to a degree. The son of a stern moralistic schoolmaster who disapproved of his career as an artist, he had a fairly successful early career – winning a gold medal for art in his native Holland. Unfortunately, his early promise was not maintained and the critics failed to award him the recognition he felt he deserved. (One did offer to give him a good review for a painting but only if bribed.)

By 1932, at the age of 43 and thoroughly disillusioned, van Meegeren decided he would paint a work in the style of an acknowledged master and have it authenticated. He would then reveal his authorship, return the check and generally take his revenge on the art snobs and experts. He was finally decided in his intention when his friend, Theo Wijngaarden, suffered at the hands of the top expert, a Dr Abraham Bredius.

Theo had genuinely believed he had discovered a Frans Hals painting and indeed had it authenticated by art expert De Groot. The self-important Dr Bredius, Holland's most revered expert, however, disdainfully dismissed the 'discovery' and dashed their hopes.

Wijngaarden had immediate revenge. He painted a 'Rembrandt' within four months of his disappointment and presented it to Dr Bredius for his opinion. The good Doctor enthused over the quality and pronounced it unquestionably a Rembrandt. Whereupon Wijngaarden took his palette knife and before the horrified gaze of Dr Bredius slashed the painting from top to bottom.

Having also decided to 'expose' the illogicalities of the art world, van Meegeren embarked upon his plan with tremendous thoroughness. He resolved to produce a master-piece to pass as the work of Vermeer (who had also lived in his home town Delft and had the same initials). Vermeer was a 17th Century painter and van Meegeren took four years to perfect his methods and subjects before attempting the fake. Through his previous studies, he had a sound know-ledge of the way a 17th Century painter would mix paints.

Vermeer painted in oils and van Meegeren found that he could reproduce the crackles (tiny cracks caused by the drying over years, or in this case centuries) by stripping a low value, genuinely 300 year old oil painting down to the last layer of paint or 'ground'. (Oil paintings can of course have many layers of paint.) The last thin laycr itself had the authentic crackles and van Meegeren found that as he painted the new picture over the old one, the original crackles came through and gave the new paint the old look.

The faker had chosen a religious subject – ultimately entitled 'Christ at Emmaus' because only one allegedly true Vermeer with a religious subject existed for comparison. He bought articles – pots, chairs, etc. – of the 17th Century period, so that the objects should be authentic. This thoroughness could not extend to models, of course, and his model for Jesus was a passing Italian tramp. Later, with the pomposity born of hindsight, experts were to say that the painting could not be genuine 1600's as the faces had the unmistakable signs of modern neuroticism. (Rather more subtly, other after-the-exposure-critics pointed out that no 17th Century painter would have painted a Disciple with his hand resting on Jesus, due to the untouchable divine nature of the principal subject.)

Van Meegeren's canvas (and frame), of course, was exactly the right age and he was equally meticulous with his materials. Vermeer was famous for his ultramarine blue which had been made from powdered lapis lazuli. One main source of supply existed, Winsor & Newton in London, and van Meegeren bought up their stocks. The only alternative was a paint with a different chemical composition which had not been invented until 1802 – 127 years after Vermeer had died. Many of the other base colors he ground between stones to ensure the minute color particles were of authentically uneven texture. He then mixed the colors with lilac oil and phenol resin to give the paints the correct viscosity and quick drying properties. He knew that although an oil painting might look dry, it could take over 50 years to be convincingly dry and hard.

To give his finished painting the necessary hardness, van Meegeren baked it in an electric oven at 105° centigrade for about two hours. Not yet content, he applied a light coat of varnish and then – when the crackles had broken through – brushed the whole painting over with indian ink. When this in turn was wiped off there was a residue of ink in the crackles which reproduced the dirt of three centuries. He then applied a last coat of brownish varnish – to simulate the yellowing, ageing appearance – and when this was quite dry he rolled the canvas to encourage a few more crackles. The finishing touch was to deliberately damage a small area and then 'restore' it.

The meticulous attention to detail paid off – perfectly. Van Meegeren now had his masterpiece but needed a certificate of authenticity. He visited a member of the Dutch Parliament and explained he had discovered a genuine Vermeer in Paris. The owners were a Dutch family living in Italy who wished to be anonymous; could the Member of Parliament obtain the opinion of an expert – perhaps, suggested van Meegeren, the famous expert Dr Bredius would oblige?

Oblige the Doctor did. He checked the painting from close quarters (he was getting near-sighted as he got older) and every clue checked out, including the signature. The certificate of authenticity was willingly issued and the picture was snapped up by the prestigious Boymans Museum in Rotterdam (for £58,000) and went on exhibition in 1937, to excited newspaper headlines. 'The Art Find of the Century' was one of the more restrained.

Dr. Bredius basked in the glory of 'his' find and considering all the other experts were equally convinced was not the least put out when van Meegeren appeared and sniffed that the picture 'looks like a fake to me'. The opinion of the by then unpopular artist was dismissed as trifling. The supreme irony and retribution.

But . . . the temptation was too much for van Meegeren He had triumphantly achieved his (privately expressed) ambition. The critics were well and truly hoaxed but he could not bring himself to return the money, and he indulged himself in an extravagant life style. More forgeries followed. Two forged de Hooghs sold for £46,000 and five more forged Vermeers were sold varying from £47,000 to £160,000 each. The total money paid for van Meegeren's forgeries between 1937 and 1943 was £730,000 – worth almost £2,000,000 at today's values.

Few could resist such a golden cascade and van Meegeren produced a passable imitation of the playboy of the Western world. A succession of ladies appeared who did not confine their services to modelling, he bought fifty properties and became such a habitué of nightclubs that he bought one.

But the cover story he had used was wearing a little thin (he said he had won the state lottery – three times!). Rumors that he might be a collaborator with the Germans began to circulate and when, immediately after the Second World War, the 'Christ and the Adulteress' painting he had sold – through an agent – to Goering in 1942 was found, the police traced it back to him.

Van Meegeren was arrested for collaboration. He was interned and interrogated for three solid weeks, facing the death penalty if found guilty.

His position was a bitter irony. The only way he could clear himself was to confess to forging the Goering painting, thereby proving he had fooled the Germans, rather than collaborated. He admitted to 14 forgeries, including 'Christ at Emmaus'. The sensation rocked the art world and threatened to destroy Dr Bredius' reputation.

The authorities' natural reaction was to first denounce and then challenge van Meegeren to prove he was the forger. A real reversal of roles.

Van Meegeren's bizarre solution was to announce he would paint one last Vermeer. He did – while in custody. His painting 'Young Christ' was incontrovertible proof of his technique and the charges of collaboration were dropped.

Now, however, in addition to the bankruptcy petition against him, van Meegeren faced a charge of forging signatures. The courtroom of the one-day trial in 1947 looked like an art gallery. He was pronounced guilty and sentenced to one year in prison. The value of his nine infamous forgeries was now given as £500 and served only to highlight the artificiality of the system. Before he could even start his sentence however, van Meegeren suffered a heart attack and within six weeks was dead.

He had indeed proved his point but hardly in the way he had originally planned.

Nevertheless, when the full story of his 'deal' with Goering was finally revealed, van Meegeren received the public acclaim he had sought for so long. It turned out that he had struck a very tough bargain indeed with Goering – comrade of former house-painter, Hitler. Van Meegeren had demanded the return of no less than 200 works of art looted from Holland by the Germans in exchange for the fake Vermeer. To his surprise his terms were agreed to, thereby putting him automatically on the Nazi death list had his audacious deal been discovered.

It was an act of considerable and selfless courage. So much so that detractors of van Meegeren, not anxious to show him up in such a favorable light started the amusing but untrue rumor that Goering had paid van Meegeren in cash with banknotes that had been forged!*

Not all forgers, however, are or apparently need to be, as meticulous as van Meegeren. Faking modern painting naturally does not call for the elaborate reproduction of old materials and the specifically simplistic style of some modern masters makes forgery that much easier.

---

* Note: This rumor was fuelled by the discovery after the war of a grandiose Gestapo plan, code-named 'operation Bernhard' – after Bernhard Kruger, who directed it under the guidance of Himmler. The aim of the plan was to break Britain's economy by flooding Allied countries with colossal quantities of counterfeit notes.

Engravers and printers were recruited from concentration camps and they produced forged notes from a center near Berlin. Agents in neutral countries began successfully to pass the notes.

When the Allied victory seemed certain the operation was moved to the Alps and switched to forging false papers for escaping Nazis. When the new center was discovered thousands of notes were found floating down the River Enns in Austria (the first floating pound?) together with £21,000,000 in one single vehicle. Estimates by the Bank of England of Kruger's total exceeded £140 million – not all of it recovered.

In addition, many genuine artists will produce, three, four, five or more versions of the final painting that is ultimately sold and acclaimed. This, too, makes detection of fakes more difficult. Indeed, one forger currently operating in London is using an epidiascope, a machine which illuminates the original and projects the illustration onto a drawing board. With this simple equipment he is taking illustrations of Picasso sketches out of a book and producing 'limited editions'. The editions, in practice, are limited only to the number of tourists prepared to pay £100+ each for copies he makes in ten minutes. Moreover, his legal position is probably quite safe as, in common with most sellers of such fakes he never claims outright to be selling a genuine Picasso – merely that 'it seems to be' but 'he is not quite sure'. In the subtle pyschology of the deal the buyer persuades himself he has stumbled onto a bargain and is eager to pay up.

Given real talent, however, such crude forgery is quite unnecessary. A Frenchman, Jean-Pierre Schecroun arrested in 1962 and described by French police as a 'virtuoso of art forgery' could produce a water color or sketch by Miro, Chagall or Leger, with whom he had studied, in an hour. Reportedly two pictures alone netted £70,000. It also seems that Schecroun was involved with a well organized art fraud gang and certainly today a major art forgery business exists centered in Brussels. This center co-ordinates European craftsmen with a wide range of talents, and boasts of a card index system, thousands of reference books and a research laboratory for faking techniques. An order for a particular work of art is placed with the Brussels' Head Office by an unscrupulous art dealer; the Belgian function is to locate the man with the talent to produce the work and provide him with the correct materials, references, etc. Belgium then undertakes to monitor progress, provide the Quality Control function and finally the certificate of authenticity. The art dealer receives the finished antique or old master and, presto, another satisfied client.

Such organized business, however, is rare in the world

of art fraud. Artistic conmanship essentially attracts individualists and one of the most swashbuckling and talented of these is self-confessed, but now reformed, faker, David Stein.

It is claimed of David that he could paint 'Three Picassos Before Breakfast'. Well, that was not strictly accurate. The actual incident referred to was when David's career was zinging along nicely in the US and he found himself one evening with an appointment, scheduled for the next day, with an art dealer to whom he had promised to deliver a set of seven Picassos he had 'discovered'. The only problem was that they had yet to be painted!

Feeling tired, David Stein went to bed but conscientiously put his alarm on for a six o'clock start. Waking next morning he was able – reports his wife Anne-Marie – to dash off the whole seven sketches of the master before grabbing a quick breakfast at 8 o'clock. The appointment was kept and the sale consummated.

David Stein has immense talent but he was not especially motivated by revenge, in fact he more or less *started* as a forger. Born near Paris on January 25th, 1935, on Mozart's birthday, he came from a cultured family, interested in most of the arts. His father, delighted with the coincidence of birth, bought a grand piano to celebrate.

David himself never took a painting lesson in his life and in fact concentrated in college on literature – supplemented by sessions as a jazz musician in Paris night clubs. He served part of his National Service in Algeria, where he experimented with painting frescoes. Rather depressed on his return to Paris, he was encouraged in his painting by a friend and the first picture of David's that was sold was a 'Cocteau'. It made $100 and an auspicious and encouraging start.

Over the next four years – until the early 1960's – David painted enthusiastically and with a catholic choice of styles; he turned out *hundreds* of fakes – Chagall, Picasso, Dufy, Modigliani, Van Gogh, Cezanne, Renoir, Van Dongen and Marie Laurencin. While his versatility is staggering he claims only to be able to paint convincingly in the style of a master once he has got into the 'mood' of the artist whose style he is copying.

He invariably stuck to crayons, water colors or gouache as oils were generally more time consuming and had the distinct disadvantage of being catalogued and, therefore, easier to authenticate by checking the records. He would take a theme and improvise upon it exactly as the original artist would have done. He deliberately never copied although he would use an original as a guide line.

When an ageing process was needed he found he could 'mellow' his paper with cold tea (Lipton was the preferred brand) and dry his water colors with a sun lamp. However, David showed a sound knowledge of the laws of demand and supply as well as the tricks of the trade and his forgeries of this period were by no means produced on a whim. He would move from city to city in Europe, gauging from art shop visits what painters were in vogue and would then retire to his hotel room to satisfy that demand, never selling more than 2 or 3 per town. Significantly only 110 out of 400 Stein forgeries have subsequently been recovered and in 1974 he was able to claim that 'I can open an art catalogue anywhere in the world and recognize my stuff.'

In 1965 the lure of America grew irresistible and Stein set off for the States intending to make enough money to 'go straight'.

His arrival in America was only 6 years after another giant of the forgery world had left. His name was Elmyr de Hory and he had a highly successful 'mail order' business in forgeries for two years. De Hory's postal technique had been to write to leading galleries and museums asking if they would be interested in his 'small collection' of modern artists. The reply was nearly always 'Yes' and he would send them a photograph of whichever picture they were interested in and when a price was agreed the painting was mailed to them – custom painted.

In fact de Hory's Picasso technique was so good that the elegant con-man once had the nerve to ask Picasso himself to authenticate one of his fakes, a nude. Picasso replied 'I remember painting her. It did take rather a long time to complete though as I could not resist making love to her.' Picasso signed and the Hungarian walked away with an authentication.

Even de Hory could not, however, fool all the people all the time and after nearly 10 years in the US, during which time he had sprinkled the country with a liberal supply of modern Masters, the art world was alerted to 'watch out for a suave 50-year-old Hungarian with a monocle in his eye and a Matisse under his arm.'

Yet despite the suspicions aroused by de Hory, David Stein made a storming start in his very first week in America. No doubt finding energy from the vitality of New York he dashed off 40 Cocteaus in four hours selling them at $100 each and celebrated with a Chagall gouache, very appropriately titled 'Quelle Vie, Quel Plaisir' (What a Life, What Fun) which fetched $4,000. $8,000 for two days' work was rather encouraging.

His wife, in her book 'Three Picassos Before Breakfast', gives a breakdown on the profitability of the forger's trade which would make any good Wall Street Investment Analyst salivate.

Cost of Painting Two 'Chagalls'	
Tea	$0.02
Paper	$3.00
Colors	$8.00
Framing	$30.00
Total	$41.02
Sold for	$10,000
Profit	$9,958.98
A profit of 99%	

It is difficult to be precise about Stein's earnings but the Manchester Guardian article reported them at £350,000 over an 18 month period during his US heyday and the Daily Mail in 1973 estimated his total income at £1 million.

Certainly David was sufficiently prosperous to be able to 'forge' ahead in 1965 with the opening of his new Gallery

Trianon which had a bold mixture of genuine and fake exhibits. Ironically, the nearest he came to disaster at this time was when a bronze head he had been innocently looking after for a client was examined and found to be faked. The police sniffed around but never thought to investigate the pictures.

The Gallery did well at the start and traded successfully in many genuine pictures. Stein has the distinction too of being the first dealer ever to introduce original works of art to a discount store. Korvettes, the well-known American hypermarket chain, opened an art gallery alongside its cut price clothes in Queens and did very well from its experiment.

All may have been well but for Stein's inclination to the extravagant life of the *bon viveur* which induced him to take risks.

The game came to a sudden end one day in 1966 when a dealer, Irving Yamet, requested Certificates of Authenticity for two Chagalls. Stein said he would obtain them by writing to Paris. Yamet's suspicions were instantly aroused when David appeared within 3 days with the documents. Not believing US and French mails were capable of miracles he reasoned that the Certificates could hardly have arrived from France in that time and Yamet voiced his suspicions to the police.

David Stein realized his mistake and, being a man of fast action, packed up at his home all evidence of his forgery. When the police did arrive it was to find a flat with 110 genuine paintings on its walls but no Stein. The master faker had made his escape down the service stairs clutching a glass of champagne.

Stein and his wife ultimately arrived in San Francisco hoping to reach Mexico, and Anne-Marie gave birth in a San Francisco hospital to their second child. During this interlude, and despite a promise to his wife, David painted and sold three Cocteaus. They were low on funds by now and needed money for medical bills and baby clothes. It was, however, a very unfortunate lapse as by unlucky coincidence

Yamet was in town on business and, seeing yet another set of the long-suffering Cocteaus, enquired as to their origin. The description of the seller was enough to alert the San Francisco Police Department and the chase was on again.

On January 20th, 1967 in Los Angeles some painstaking detective work involving checking limousine car hire records brought the dreaded sound of a heavy knock on the door at the home where the Steins were then living.

David was taken back to New York and deposited in the Tombs in Manhattan with bail set at $50,000. Their life style had taken its toll and not until bail was reduced to $6,500 some eight months later was he able to raise the cash for his release.

Undaunted, while still on bail, Stein continued to paint. Now, however, he signed his pictures with his own name and with the words 'In the style of . . .' He even continued to paint during interrogation in the District Attorney's office!

Due to publicity sales were good but now at the more modest price of $100 (£60) per picture. In one exhibition at the Wright-Hepburn Gallery in London 70 Stein pictures were sold in 16 minutes for $11,000.

Eventually he was charged on 97 counts, pleaded guilty to some and was sentenced in January, 1969 to three years in Sing Sing Prison. When he was released in February, 1970 he had spent a total of 18 months in jail, but was then deported to France to be charged in Pairs, Cannes and Toulouse. Picasso though refused to testify against him saying that if he did so he would have to do to most of his other friends! He spent a further two years in jail being finally released in March, 1972.

Prison must have provided David Stein with some thinking time, for within 15 months he was launching on the world an exciting scheme that legitimately exploited his wide ranging copying talents. From a single three hour sitting he painted Brigitte Bardot in 25 different styles, each in the manner of a different master, Picasso, Klee, Manet,

Renoir, Van Gogh, Matisse, etc. The concept was to produce a limited edition of 400 lithographs selling at £560 each (£224,000 worth of lithographs!) As one critic put it, enough to 'see off Tretchikoff's Chinese Girl once and for all.' Stein's half serious fear is that 'someone might try to forge a genuine Stein picture.'

Today, only in his 40's, David Stein is a noted painter whose activities include lecturing – the subject matter?

'How To Spot a Fake'!

In practice spotting fakes is not so difficult, particularly with carbon-dating equipment and X-ray machines, which show up the brush stroke patterns used to produce the finished result. Since those patterns can be almost as distinctive as fingerprints, it is difficult not to believe that art dealers sometimes choose to ignore the evidence of their eyes and pass on work they know to be suspect.

Sometimes, however, *everyone* is fooled and only the faker's own desire for recognition reveals the forgery. Such was the case of the Lübeck forged frescoes.

In 1951 the West German Chancellor Adenaur himself was escorted around the newly restored frescoes of the Church of St Mary by Dietrich Fey, head of a firm of art restorers. Art lovers marvelled at the medieval masterpieces and the event was celebrated by the issue of two million commemorative stamps.

When the next year an unknown artist, called Malskat, suddenly announced that the frescoes were entirely created by him, no-one believed him. Malskat's credibility dropped even lower when he explained that he had used photographs of Marlene Dietrich and his sister-in-law as models, plus pictures of Rasputin and Genghis Khan (although these latter worthies were not sporting haloes).

Malskat grew so annoyed at the lack of seriousness shown at his claim that he actually instructed his lawyer to file charges against himself (and Fey).

Gradually the truth dawned on the scornful experts and the figures were re-examined. To their collective horror, the resemblance of some of the disciples to certain violent historical gentlemen slowly became apparent and one of the angels did, on second perusal, have rather a film star quality. . . .

Once again the only way the faker could achieve the attention of the critics was by revealing his own forgery.

The story of the last and latest of our fabulous fakers raises question marks over the role of the dealers. For while there cannot be forgeries without fakers neither can there be a motive without a ready market for those fakes.

Not that Tom Keating seems motivated by financial reward. An amusing and engaging character with ruddy cheeks and a white beard he seems more like a genial Father Christmas or Santa Claus than the one-man art factory he claims to have been.

Tom Keating's spur was apparently not even fame. In 1976 he stated 'My aim was to get back at unscrupulous galleries and dealers. Five or six times dealers approached me to do copies and I did them. I was conned. Once a gentleman offered £65 to do two pictures after the style of Krieghoff. He gave me £7.50 for them and hours later they were in a Bond St. Gallery offered for £1,500.'

In his splendid anecdotal style of conversation Keating goes on to claim that certain dealers had false signatures put on the paintings he had faked; 'They have a man like Jim the Penman who goes round the galleries once a month.'

Who *they* are he has not (yet) said, partly because 'I don't want my throat cut', partly because his biography is shortly scheduled to be published. It should be racy reading.

Since he was catapulted into the limelight in the summer of 1976 through some very sharp detective work by Geraldine Norman, Sale Room Correspondent of the *London Times*, Tom Keating has been gradually opening a fascinating window on the art world. The revelations are mostly serious but even these are leavened by titbits such as the fact that 'the frescoes in the Sistine Chapel were done with paint watered down with pee – it was easier to come by than water' and the story of how the luminaries of the art world sat hushed at the inauguration of Turner as Professor of

Perspective at the Royal Academy, waiting for some Eternal Truths from the Great Man's lips. Turner stood glass in hand, gazed at them and declared sagely, 'Painting's a rum do!'

Cockney-born Tom Keating began his Sexton Blakes (his rhyming slang for fakes) after years of struggling to be recognized in his own right – the old impetus. He feels, like van Meegeren before him, a resentment against the system and undoubtedly the extreme poverty of his early childhood has stimulated his sense of grievance. For a man with sufficient talent to 'knock off' a Renoir in a couple of hours, the disappointment of being refused a final diploma from Goldsmiths College must have been a last straw.

At any rate Tom Keating claims to have 'imitated well over 100 artists in the last 20 years' – from about 1950-1971 – 'They must amount to more than 2,000 pictures.' It is quite possible as his speed is staggering. In a TV documentary Keating produced a 'Samuel Palmer' in the space of an evening and in front of the cameras. He started his Sexton Blakes, he claims, as a joke and a protest and 'built in' the joke to his works.

First all his fakes are apparently coated with gelatine so that if any solvent is used to clean them, the paint will come off too. More subtly, if his fakes are subjected to X-ray examination the expert is liable to find the word 'Keating' or 'Fake' or even a rude word written in white lead paint on the canvas *before* he started work. This would be clearly visible under X-ray.

Tom Keating is totally absorbed in painting – indeed Geraldine Norman, who claims to have learned 'more in two weeks interviewing Tom than in seven years as the *Times* Sale Room correspondent' confirms that the spirit of the artist whose style Tom is imitating actually seems to possess him while he is working. The TV film also showed him to be emotionally possessed while painting.

Certainly Tom Keating has enormous respect for his 'old boys' and equally certainly whatever money may have come to him from his 'Sexton's' did not last long. Most of his paintings he says he has lost or given away (one to a tramp, one to a harassed mother of six he met in Woolworth's).

This casual approach explains why it took so long for him to be discovered. For the recipients of this largesse would probably have sold his gift to junk shops and it would often take years before the painting surfaced to more conventional art outlets.

The Tom Keating story will be worth following, when it is fully unfolded, for its full ramifications. Meanwhile, in a recent interview he threw an interesting slant on even those oil paintings whose authenticity is unchallenged. As he pointed out, after a work has received the attention of generations of restorers 'how authentic is it? If the old boys walked the earth again they would not recognize their own work!'

Painting *is* a 'Rum Do'.

THE HATTON GARDEN
DOUBLE BLUFF

This confidence trick took place in Hatton Garden, London, in late 1975. It is an extremely ingenious variation and shows the lengths of pre-planning to which even a fairly small scale con-man will go.

Around 11 o'clock one Saturday morning a well-dressed man entered a small Hatton Garden jewellers. After looking around the store for some time he expressed interest in a watch priced at just under £50. Explaining that he had not sufficient cash with him, he offered a check in payment. The jeweller decided to accept the check and the man left the shop with the watch. Some forty yards away in the first side street after the jeweller's, is a barber's shop and the gentleman who purchased the watch went straight there. During the course of conversation with the barber he brought out the watch and asked if the barber would like to purchase it. The barber explained that, working in the center of Hatton Garden, he was not short of opportunities to buy cut-price jewellery and was really not interested. The gentleman, however, was insistent and reduced his offer by stages to £15. The barber could see that the watch was worth considerably more but was naturally disturbed at the man's attitude. His customer, however, insisted that the watch was a good bargain and finally persuaded him to have it valued at the jeweller's around the corner. The barber was sufficiently intrigued to do so.

The result was predictable. The jeweller was quite convinced that the check must have been a forgery, why else would his customer want to sell a watch for £15 that he had purchased for just under £50 half an hour ago? The police were called and the jeweller, the barber and the policeman arrived at the barber's shop to accuse the well-dressed gentleman of a transparent fraud. The gentleman put on a show of great indignation and explained that the reason he had attempted to sell the watch was that he had discovered, after the purchase, that he had insufficient cash to complete a planned journey at the weekend and also pay for a hotel. To prove it he pulled out his rail ticket and a hotel reservation. He explained that having cash for the weekend was worth more to him than the loss on the watch. However, he continued, 'I have changed my mind. I have decided to keep the watch after all'. Whereupon he grabbed the watch from the jeweller and started to leave the shop. Both the jeweller and the policeman acted on impulse and the man was promptly arrested. At the jeweller's insistence the man was accused of passing a bad check. The gentleman's attitude and actions during the encounter only convinced the onlookers of his guilt and as a result he spent the rest of the day in a police cell. It was only late that evening that he was able to reach his lawyer and arrange bail.

The remainder of the story unfolded simply. On the Monday morning when the bank opened the check was met without any problem and it was found that the gentleman had always maintained a credit balance in this account and of course he was fully entitled to retain the watch. The matter did not end there. A few days later the jeweller received notification of a lawsuit against him for false arrest and defamation of character. The white-collar con-man was able to prove that he had missed a very important appointment that weekend through the jeweller's action and when the case did come to court the jeweller's defense was inevitably flimsy and the trickster won a substantial amount of money in damages.

THE CASINO HUSTLES

If there were such a competition, the prize for the world's most consistently ripped off institution would not be awarded to the U.K. or United States Social Security Services but to the Las Vegas casinos.

In many ways, the Nevada casinos are quite the most unlikely set of 'marks'. Their elaborate security systems are among the best in the world. Not only are the casino con-men up against squadrons of armed detectives, under-cover detectives and the ubiquitous 'eye in the sky' video cameras (which even extend into the toilets) but the casinos collectively employ the world's most sophisticated filing system on known casino hustlers. Weekly meetings are held by the major casinos at which they swap information on known rip-off artists and the latest developments in the ceaseless war between the casinos and the hustlers.

Yet despite this, the Gambling Control Board estimates that *each* casino is ripped off for more than 2 million dollars a year and the total take is probably well over 30 million dollars annually. New variations on old themes are put together regularly but the one activity that all the casinos fear is collusion between the players and the staff.

Probably the biggest ever scam occurred in 1972 when close to 5 million dollars was taken from the major casinos in a period of five weeks. Well over 50 casino employees were inside the operation which was essentially simple. Crooked players would make even-money bets on the dice table, betting with three ten-dollar chips. They would be paid off with an aluminium cylinder which was perfectly moulded to look like a small stack of three ten-dollar chips. Inside the false stack the dealer would insert two real chips of varying denomination. The player would then pocket the cylinder, release the real chips and take a convenient opportunity to return the cylinder to the crooked dealer.

When the con-trick came to light some months after it started, the Sands Hotel calculated that using the false stack system a team of five con men could relieve a craps table of more than $5,000 an hour.

Sometimes the scam is no more complicated than a newcomer passing off counterfeit chips. In fact, if he does so in moderate quantities, there is realistically very little chance of him being caught – providing the quality of the counterfeit is good.

Not all the casino hustles have, of course, to do with counterfeit or stolen chips. Even today there are plenty of 'dice mechanics' who can take a casino for a sizeable sum of money in a short period of time. It is popularly thought that now the casinos universally use transparent dice, the old practice of 'loading' the dice has disappeared. Not so. There are at least two regularly used variations on this theme. Neither can be used for a long period of time because the tables switch dice regularly but it is possible for the skilled 'mechanic' to introduce crooked dice at exactly the right moment. The state of the art has concentrated now on two major techniques. The first involves substitution of pre-loaded dice. The spots on one side of a regular transparent casino die are drilled out to a fraction of an inch and platinum, the heaviest of all metals, is poured into the minute hole. The spots are then re-painted over the top and the die then looks normal. In fact, the only sure test of a loaded die is to place it in a glass of water whereupon the die will turn over with the loaded side to the bottom. Such a test however is not likely to be carried out during actual play! The dice mechanic holds the loaded dice in his right hand with the fair casino dice being picked up with the left hand. Under pretext of passing the dice from left to right hand he palms the good dice (in his left hand) and swiftly throws the loaded dice which he knows have a well above average chance of falling with the required numbers uppermost. It is a risky business but it happens every week. A recent innovation is the development of a type of solvent which has a low melting point and which when pressed on to the casino's own dice in a hot palm for a period of as little as three or four seconds can 'load' the dice to a sufficient degree to give the player the edge.

If all this sounds relatively primitive, it is – compared with the single biggest rip-off in Las Vegas history. This happened in 1975 on, of all places, the roulette table. For obvious reasons, the roulette tables are extremely difficult to fix – from the player's point of view. They are guarded day and night and the casino's legitimate odds are so high in their favor that the management's objective at all times is a totally fair game. Mostly it is – or was – until a group of three Australian technicians hit town. Extraordinary though the story is this is exactly what happened.

The Australians had been playing for three nights in a row and were approximately 2 million dollars ahead, having had a run of luck across three individual casino establishments that was statistically impossible. In fact as against the normal 35 to 1 odds they were regularly collecting on every tenth bet. The casinos knew it was a trick but they could not figure out how it was done. On the fourth evening the Australians were at a center table and were taking one of the major casinos for what was heading to be their biggest single beating of all time. The crowd was ten deep around the table and not only were the Australians winning but the vast majority of the crowd was betting with them. As opposed to the normally fairly discreet background hum of conversation, the noise was deafening as time and time again the wheel spun and the ball dropped into one of three numbers on which the trio were betting. Their winnings for that evening alone were already over 150,000 dollars. The management was looking grim. The croupier was looking bewildered. The wheel spun – and then it happened. There was a noise like a pistol shot and the roulette ball exploded!

The casino was in turmoil. Five 'pit bosses' and four guards descended on the trio and hustled them into a back room. Fragments of the roulette ball were collected and presented to the now sheepish looking Aussies. Bit by bit the story was pieced together. It transpired that the Australians were electronic engineers and had developed a micro device which when inserted in a roulette ball and operated by remote control could slow the ball down and direct it into the roulette cups with a degree of accuracy that could pinpoint to within each tenth of the roulette wheel. The Australians had practiced for countless hours to perfect the system and the control technique. They had then bribed ten casino croupiers to use normal looking but electronic roulette wheel balls. The only thing they did not allow for was that the inner circuitry could overheat, which was what happened and why the ball blew up.

All of which is why, to the surprise of most people, it is hardly the casino players who need protection in Las Vegas but rather the management. The art, or rather science, of ripping-off the casinos has now reached such a pitch that there are actually schools operating where the rather better known of the scam artists, who have long since been banned from playing, are now teaching their skills to new apprentices for either a fixed sum or a percentage of their winnings.

Index

308